PRUSSIA'S GLORY

Rossbach and Leuthen 1757

Christopher Duffy

Helion & Company

Helion & Company Limited
Unit 8 Amherst Business Centre
Budbrooke Road
Warwick
CV34 5WE
England
Tel. 01926 499619
Email: info@helion.co.uk
Website: www.helion.co.uk
Twitter: @helionbooks
Visit our blog at http://blog.helion.co.uk/

Published by Helion & Company 2022
Designed and typeset by Mach 3 Solutions Ltd (www.mach3solutions.co.uk)
Cover designed by Paul Hewitt, Battlefield Design (www.battlefield-design.co.uk)

Originally published by The Emperor's Press, 2003
Text © Christopher Duffy 2003
Cover: The advance of the Itzenplitz regiment at Leuthen, 5 December 1757, by Peter Dennis © Helion &
Company 2022
Photographs © Christopher Duffy 2003
Other artwork public domain
Maps by Paul Dangel © The Emperor's Press, 2003

ISBN 978-1-911628-91-0

British Library Cataloguing-in-Publication Data.
A catalogue record for this book is available from the British Library.

For details of other military history titles published by Helion & Company Limited, contact the above address,
or visit our website: http://www.helion.co.uk

We always welcome receiving book proposals from prospective authors.

Contents

Introduction

To anyone who has more than a passing interest in military history, the campaigning of Frederick of Prussia towards the end of 1757 stands out as the highest achievement of warfare in the Europe of the *ancien regime*. It certainly qualifies him to hold his place among the great captains, among some pretty tough competition.

On 5 November of that year Frederick defeated a greatly superior force of the French and their German allies, in the battle of Rossbach. The French were admittedly at a military nadir, and the associated *Reichstruppen* came together among scenes of comic disorder; one of the commanders (Hildburghausen) was an extreme eccentric, while the other (Soubise) owed his promotion to the mistress of the French king. It would be tempting to dismiss the episode as a farce, but for the fact that so many men were killed or mutilated. The battle of Leuthen was staged just one month later, on 5 December 1757, but it was an entirely different proposition. Here Frederick was dealing with the much improved Austrian army, which had been enjoying an unbroken run of successes, and the Austrians fought hard until the Prussians drove them into the snowy darkness.

These stories have been related many times over the centuries, but a great deal remains to be explained. What, after all, made Frederick and his Prussians so redoubtable? The perspective of his enemies also needs to be taken into account. They were not passive targets, and we have to ask how far they contributed to their own defeats. Without such a context the talk of 'military genius' conveys nothing, just as 'inconceivable blunders' will remain inconceivable. For these reasons the present book abandons the constraints of the conventional narratives, and bases itself chiefly on original manuscripts, most of which are here explored for the first time.

As things turned out, the twin battles of Rossbach and Leuthen were in one way or another disastrous for Frederick's enemies, and exerted their baleful influence until the end of the Seven Years War. The story does not end there.

For the shocked and humiliated French, Rossbach came to stand for a particular kind of political and military failure, and the reaction gave the impetus to martial reform and burgeoning nationalism. Conversely, Rossbach and Leuthen elevated Frederick to the status of a pan-German hero, and put his kingdom on the path to the leadership of the German people. Frederick was scarcely aware of what was going on, and he would have been appalled by some of the later manifestations of Prusso-German nationalism, but he had set in train a cycle of conflict that was resolved only at the end of twentieth century.

All the same, the talk of grand strategies and great historical themes brings with it the danger of pomposity and remoteness. I am therefore at some pains to bring us down to earth with reminders of what it was like to live at those times and in those places. *Prussia's Glory* is therefore also a human narrative, touching, for example, on those cooks who sought to please the successive grandees who arrived at Schloss Friedenstein, on those Austrian officers who staggered about half-drunk on the day of Leuthen, or, when it was over, on that orphaned girl who was found wandering the streets of Troppau.

For their support of this enterprise I owe a great deal to Dr. Rainer Egger and Dr. Peter Broucek of the Austrian War Archives, Dr. Leopold Auer and Dr. Christina Thomas of the Austrian State Archives, Major General Dr. Ervin Liptai of the Hungarian Military Institute, *Conservateur* Samuel Gibiat of the Historical Services of the French Land Forces, Dr. Jürgen Kloosterhuis of the

Secret Prussian State Archives, Dr. Fuchs of the Bavarian War Archives, and the director and staff of the Württemberg Provincial *(Land)* Library in Stuttgart.

I am particularly grateful to Paul Dangel, whose technical skills and historical sympathies have come together to provide the maps for the present book.

The Frederick of legend, as portrayed by Otto Gebuhr in German films of the 1930s.

UNIT KEY & INDENTIFIERS

Austrian and Prussian unit identifiers follow the standardized numbering system adopted after the Seven Years War. Only those units that participated in the 1757 campaign are listed. Non-Austro-Prussian units are assigned arbitrary identifiers for the purpose of this publication only.

Units present at Rossbach, Breslau or Leuthen have the letter (R,B,L) after their name below.

AUSTRIAN & ALLIED

1 battalion	
2 battalions	Austrian Artillery
Austrian Infantry	Cavalry

Bavarian Infantry — Württemberger Infantry — Saxon Chevauleger

Reichsarmee Cavalry — French & Reichsarmee Infantry

PRUSSIAN

1 battalion	
2 battalions	Cavalry Artillery
Infantry	

AUSTRIAN & ALLIED

Fusilier Regiments
1 Kaiser (B,L)
2 Erzherzog Karl (B,L)
3 Lothringen (B,L)
4 Deutschmeister (B,L)
7 Neipperg (B,L)
8 Hildburghausen (B,L)
9 Los Rios (B,L)
10 L. Wolfenbrüttel (B,L)
11 Wallis (B,L)
12 Botta (B,L)
13 Moltke (B,L)
15 Pallavicini (B,L)
16 Königsegg (B,L)
17 Kollowrat (B,L)
19 Leopold Pálffy (B,L)
20 Alt-Colloredo (B)
21 Arenberg (B,L)
22 Sprecher (B)
23 Baden-Baden (B,L)
25 Thürheim (B,L)
26 Puebla (B,L)
27 Baden-Durlach (B,L)
28 Wied (B)
29 Alt-Wolfenbrüttel (B,L)
30 Sachsen-Gotha (B,L)
31 Haller (B,L)
32 Forgách (B,L)
33 Nicholas Esterházy (B,L)
34 A. Batthyány (B,L)
35 Waldeck (B,L)
36 Browne (B,L)
37 Joseph Esterházy (B,L)
38 Ligne (B,L)
39 Joseph Pálffy (B,L)
42 Gaisruck (B,L)
44 Clerici (B,L)
45 H. Daun (B,L)
46 Macquire (B,L)
47 Harrach (B,L)
48 Luzan (B,L)
49 Kheul (B,L)
50 Harsch (B,L)
52 Bethlen (B,L)
55 D'Arberg (B,L)
56 Mercy (B,L)
57 Andlau (B,L)
59 Leopold Daun (B,L)

Auxiliary Infantry
MZ Mainz (B)
RW Red Würzburg (B,L)

Württemberg
1 Truchsess
2 Roeder
3 Spitznas
4 Prinz Louis
5 Leibgarde
6 Georgi
7 Pless
8 Klettenberg

Bavaria
1 Kurprinz Preysing
2 Erzherzog Clemens
3 Leibgarde
4 Minucci
5 Morawitzky

Cuirassier Regiments
C3 Erzherzog Leopold (B,L)
C4 Erzherzog Ferdinand (B,L)
C10 Stampach (L)
C12 Serbelloni (L)
C14 O'Donnell (B,L)
C20 Schmerzing (B,L)
C21 Trautmannsdorff (R)
C22 Kalckreuth (B,L)
C23 Birkenfeld (B,L)
C25 Anhalt-Zerbst (L)
C27 Löwenstein (L)
C29 Bretlach (R)
C33 Anspach (B,L)
Ci Gelhay (B,L)
Cii Lucchesi (B,L)

Dragoon Regiments
D1 Erzherzog Joesph (B,L)
D7 Batthyány (B,L)
D13 Jung-Modena (B,L)
D19 Hessen-Darmstadt (B,L)
D28 Sachsen-Gotha (B,L)
D31 Benedict Daun (L)
D37 Kollowrat (B,L)
D38 Württemberg (L)
D39 Zweibrücken (B,L)

Hussar Regiments
H11 Nádasdy (L)
H32 Széchenyi (R)
H34 Dessewffy (L)

Saxon Chevauleger
1 Prinz Karl (B,L)
2 Prinz Albert (B,L)
3 Graf Brühl (B,L)

French Infantry
1 Piedmont (R)
2 Poitou (R)
3 Mailly (R)
4 St. Chamond (R)
5 Provence (R)
6 La Marck (R)
7 Brissac (R)
8 Rohan-Montbazon (R)
9 Royal Pologne (R)
10 St. Germain (R)
11 Deux-Ponts (R)
12 Beauvoisis (R)
13 Royal Roussillon (R)
14 Salis (R)
15 Reding (R)
16 Wittemer (R)
17 Planta (R)
18 Diesbach (R)
19 Castillas (R)

Reichsarmee Infantry
20 Trier (R)
21 Kronegk (R)
22 Blue Würzburg (R)
23 Hesse-Darmstadt (R)
24 Varrell (R)
25 Ferntheil (R)

Reichsarmee Cavalry
C1 Hohenzollern (R)
C2 Palatinate (R)
C3 Bayreuth (R)
D1 Württemberg (R)
D2 Ansbach (R)

PRUSSIAN

Musketeer Regiments
1 Winterfeld (R,L)
5 Alt-Braunschweig (R,L)
6 Retzow (R,L)
8 Amstell (B,L)
9 Jung-Kleist (R)
10 Knobloch (B,L)
13 Itzenplitz (R,L)
15 Leibgarde (R,L)
18 Prinz v. Preussen (B,L)
19 Markgraf Karl (R,L)
20 Bornstedt (B,L)
21 Hülsen (R)
23 Forcade (R,L)
24 Goltz (R)
25 Kalckstein (B,L)
26 Mayerinck (R)
27 Asseburg (B,L)
29 Schultze (B)
30 Kannacher (B,L)
31 Lestwitz (B)
34 Prinz Ferdinand (B,L)
35 Prinz Heinrich (L)
36 Münchow (B,L)
37 Kurssell (L)
38 Brandes (B)
39 Jung-Braunschweig (B,L)
43 Kalckreuth (B)
46 Bülow (B,L)

Grenadier Battalions
1/23 Wedell (R,L)
3/06 Hacke (B,L)
4/16 Kleist (R,L)
5/20 Jung-Billerbeck (R)
7/30 Lubath (R)
13/26 Finck (R)
17/22 Kremzow (R,L)
19/25 Heyden (R,L)
21/27 Diringshofen (L)
29/31 Ostenreich (B,L)
35/36 Schenckendorff (B,L)
37/40 Manteuffel (B,L)
38/43 Burgsdorff (B)
45/48 Unruh (B,L)

Standing Grenadier Battalions
SG1 Kahlden (B,L)
SG6 Plötz (B,L)

Freibattalions
FB1 Le Noble (B,L)
FB3 Kalben (B,L)
FB4 Angelelli (B,L)

Fuss Jäger (B,L)

Cuirassier Regiments
C1 Krockow (B,L)
C2 Prinz v. Preussen (B)
C3 Leibregiment (R)
C4 Gessler (B)
C5 Prinz Friedrich (B,L)
C6 Baron v. Schonaich (B,L)
C7 Driesen (R,L)
C8 Seydlitz (R,L)
C9 Pr. v. Schonaich (B,L)
C10 Gensd'armes (R)
C11 Leib-Karabiniers (B,L)
C12 Kyau (B,L)
C13 Garde du Corps (R,L)

Dragoon Regiments
D1 Normann (B,L)
D2 Krockow (B,L)
D3 Meinicke (R,L)
D4 Czettritz (R,L)
D5 Bayreuth (B,L)
D11 Stechow (B,L)
D12 Pr. Württemberg (B,L)

Hussar Regiments
H1 Székely (R,L)
H2 Zieten (B,L)
H3 Warnery (L)
H4 Puttkamer (B,L)
H6 Werner (B,L)
H7 Seydlitz (B,L)

I

The Rossbach Armies

The Prussian Army

At places like Ortrand, north of Dresden, you meet the historic boundary between the former electorate of Saxony and the core of the old kingdom of Brandenburg-Prussia. Even now the contrast between the two landscapes is striking. To the south the eye is drawn from the productive farmlands by way of agreeably wooded eminences to the range of hills on the horizon, where Saxony marches with Bohemia in the modern Czech Republic. If your affairs take you to the north, you find yourself almost at once in a forest of conifers which somehow manage to find grip and nourishment in the sandy soil at their feet. Varied by bogs, meres and clearings, this landscape predominates most of the way to the Baltic.

The Brandenburg-Prussian heartland was one of the least naturally productive areas of Germany. It was also one of the least German, for the racial stock was not Teutonic, but that of the Slavonic Wends, which had been overlain but not displaced by centuries of Germanic settlement; Wendish was still spoken among the common soldiers of a number of the Prussian regiments in the eighteenth century, including some of those from Berlin, and the common place names ending in '*ow*,' '*itz*,' '*in*,' or '*a*' all hint at Slavonic origins.

It would be wrong to assail the reader with an exhaustive history of the Prussian monarchy and its institutions, but we still have to explain how Brandenburg-Prussia was able to set Europe by its ears in the middle of the eighteenth century, and finally succeeded in casting the whole of Germany in a recognisably Prussian mould when the region was unified under Prussian leadership in 1871.

If the rise of Brandenburg-Prussia is to be identified with any individual, it must be with Frederick William of Hohenzollern, 'The Great Elector,' who ruled from 1640 to 1688. The Peace of Westphalia put an end to the horrors of the Thirty Years War in 1648, but a sequence of Baltic wars lasted until 1721, which underlined the fact that Brandenburg and its capital Berlin stood within close reach of Swedish forces whenever they erupted from western Pomerania, which was a sizeable bridgehead which the Swedes still owned on the southern side of the Baltic. Frederick William had extensive lands elsewhere—East Prussia further up the Baltic coast, and a constellation of holdings (Minden, Ravensberg, Mark and Cleves) in western Germany. The trouble was that all of these possessions were separated from the central core by other states, and that no immediate help could be rendered to or from them in time of need.

The Great Elector concluded that only by building up independent military power could he spare his states from outright conquest, or, possibly more humiliating still, the experience of seeing foreign forces tramping through them when they were on their way to some further destination. The history of the Brandenburg army as a permanent standing force dates from 1644, though more than three decades passed before it won its first significant victory on its own account, when it beat the Swedes at Fehrbellin on 17 June 1675. This long span of years suggests that the growth of Brandenburg military power was cumulative and evolutionary.

The Great Elector's successor, the elector Frederick (later King Frederick I), loved pomp and luxury, and in that way at least he identified himself less with the emerging style of Brandenburg-Prussian rulers than with that of the petty German princes who modelled themselves on the ways of the court of Louis XIV. In fact some of Frederick's most valuable work was of a peaceful nature. He drove forward the work of internal colonisation, assisted by the Huguenot refugees whom he welcomed into his states, and in January 1701 he secured for himself the title of King of (or technically 'in') Prussia, which derived from his *de facto* sovereignty of the duchy of East Prussia, which was not considered a legal part of Germany.

French fashions were one thing, French expansionism something else. Frederick in his new kingly guise was still unwilling to break with the nexus of anti-French partners which had formed around Austria, Britain and the United Provinces of Holland, and in the War of the Spanish Succession (1701-14) he proceeded to hire out contingents of Prussian troops to the allies—and as paid auxiliaries rather than full belligerents in their own right. Prussian compliance was taken for granted, and in 1711 a force of Saxons and Dutchmen actually barged through Prussian territory in the old style in order to get at the Swedes, regardless of the affront to sovereignty.

The build-up of the Prussian army nevertheless continued without check. The force was far from negligible in numerical terms, rising to 40,000 troops by the time King Frederick died in 1713. More significantly, the early 1700s saw the Prussian infantry begin to march with more precision and shoot faster than any other foot soldiers in continental Europe. This was the work of the brutal but creative Prince Leopold of Anhalt-Dessau (the 'Old Dessauer'), whose formative influence extended into the 1740s.

Frederick William I (ruled 1713-40) became known as the 'Soldier King,' less on account of his active warlike experience (of which he had very little) than the way he re-shaped society according to his notion of military values. Here he was building on the foundations that had been laid by the Great Elector, who in 1653 had made a deal with the noble-dominated provincial assemblies *(Stände)* of Brandenburg and Prussian Pomerania, whereby the landowners gained the freedom to run their estates (and the serfs who dwelt thereon) as they wished, in return for yielding control of taxation to the Elector. He and his successors (unlike the extravagant Habsburgs) were also careful to keep a grip on their family estates, and this double assurance—guaranteed taxation, and the income from the family domains—enabled the Hohenzollerns to plan for the long term, and was going to give Frederick the Great a valuable advantage in this respect over Maria Theresa of Austria and Louis XV.

Nothing could have prepared the nobles for what befell them soon after Frederick William I came to the throne in 1713, when he demanded that they must give up their disposable sons for military service. For many of the young men the process began with a harsh schooling in the new cadet academies, and promotion for all of them depended on their acquiring a mastery of the military trade. These measures were resented acutely at the time, and they would have proved intolerable if Frederick William had not also given the serving nobles a high place in a specifically Prussian military culture.

The moral foundation of the new order was Pietism, a puritanical form of Lutheranism which had developed in the course of the seventeenth century, and established its intellectual stronghold in the University of Halle. Pietism promoted not so much charitable works and holy contemplation (as its name might suggest), but rather a disciplined upbringing, and a selfless dedication to service in an assigned station in adult life. The cult of Pietism was therefore well suited to promote an ideal of state service, and Frederick William appropriated this spiritual force for his own ends in 1718, when he brought Lambertus Gedicke from Halle to direct the new body of army chaplains *(Feldprediger)*.

In the same decisive year of 1718 the king accomplished what has become known as the *Stilbruch*, which was a deliberated distancing of Prussian fashions and manners from the light-hearted ways of the rococo culture, which prevailed at Versailles under the *Régence,* and which were spreading fast in the courts of Catholic Germany. In a matter of months the Prussian officers became almost unrecognisable creatures, for they abandoned their piled-up and flowing wigs for the military pig-tail, and their embroidered coats and waistcoats for plain versions in a dark indigo blue. Frederick William himself lived, died and was buried in his uniform, and his officers came to value the sobriety of the 'King's Coat' as a sign of distinction, and not, as would have been the case in France, as a means of relegating the officer to the status of a hired servant. Likewise the honour of the French officer was expressed through individual bravado, and a willingness to take offence, while honour *(Ehre)* in the Prussian service came to be identified with an application to duty, however humdrum that duty might be. The vanity of the Prussian officer corps was collective, for the king had made commissioned service the preserve of the nobility. This last restriction was not as inhibiting as it might seem, for the Prussian nobility embraced the large and ill-defined Junker squierarchy, and, regardless of wealth, its officer-sons enjoyed a status that was denied to their nearest French equivalent, the *hobereaux*—the poor country nobles who were becoming increasingly marginalised in the French service

Under these influences a number of families were willing to identify themselves wholeheartedly with the dynasty, and the quantity of the officers they ultimately contributed to the military service of Prussia and united Germany probably reaches into the thousands. Amongst others we may cite the clans of Below, Borcke, Bredow, Bülow, Dohna, Kalckstein, Kameke, Katte, Kleist, Krockow, Lettow, Manstein, Manteuffel, Massow, Oppen, Pirch, Prittwitz and Gaffron, Rochow, Saldern, Schwerin, Seydlitz, Tresckow, Wedell, Winterfeldt and Zastrow.

Curiously enough the products of the conditioning process were not reduced to mindless automata, for the officers in the classic Prussian mould could show a respectable complement of poets and philosophers as well as fighting men, and the best of them retained a remarkable capacity for independent action. 'Tell the king' (the cavalry leader Seydlitz is reported to have said at Zorndorf in 1758) 'that my head is at his disposal after the battle, but meanwhile let him allow me to use it in his service.'[1] In 1756 an ensign of the Garde, Friedrich Moritz v. Rohr, made so bold to publish an edition of a French military classic under Frederick's nose at Potsdam. In the introduction Rohr maintained that the foundations for effective senior command must be laid at the outset of a military career, and that even at the most junior level

> the officer must be regarded as something more than a machine, which functions only when it is driven. He must often act without orders. There are occasions when an officer will have to wheel or move a single platoon, or give it particular instructions; sometimes the orders that come to him will be inadequate, or he might find himself in new and unforeseen circumstances. In all of these cases the officer will be able to find his bearings more readily if he has a grasp of the manoeuvre as a whole, of its object, and of his own part in its execution.[2]

Such a mentality was as much of a battle-winner as were the cannon shot and iron ramrods, and much later this way of thinking was to be encapsulated in the command philosophy of united Germany as *Auftragstaktik,* whereby commanders at every level impressed their subordinates with the purpose of such and such an operation, but left those subordinates with freedom of action as to how the end was to be accomplished.

It is not easy to establish how the unique combination could have arisen in the first place. Perhaps it had to do with a reasonable standard of education, or (as in the case of Seydlitz himself) at least a respect for learning. Perhaps, paradoxically, it was a consequence of the militarisation of the Prussian aristocracy, for the nobles were under a kind of military conscription, and the officer corps contained people who in other kingdoms would never have contemplated taking up a military career.

In the course of his reign Frederick William had more than doubled the size of his army to 81,000 troops. By the standards of the time this number was far more than could be readily sustained from Prussia's population of 1,200,000 souls, and the trick was made possible by the fact that the troops were made up of two disparate elements. The one was a standing presence of foreigners who were bribed, inveigled or forced into the Prussian service. Few of these men had any positive motivation, but they filled out the ranks, and as long as they were kept under tight supervision they did good and useful service until they died or ran away.

Staying-power was provided by the other element, the native part-time soldiers who were raised by the 'Cantonal' system of conscription, which Frederick William organised between 1727 and 1735. In peacetime the Cantonists were under an obligation to train for only a few weeks a year, but they remained under military discipline throughout, and in wartime they were recalled to the colours for indefinite service. By the time of the Seven Years War the Cantonists were thoroughly imbued with *l'esprit militaire,* thanks to the army's achievements in the Silesian Wars, the example of their hard-working officers, and the indoctrination imparted by the *Feldprediger* and the local pastors. Freedom of thought did not reach down to their level, and in September 1757 a townsman of Gotha noted that an officer of the Prussian Meinicke Dragoons had placed one of their troopers on guard at the ducal *Schloss,* and forgotten all about him when the army retreated. 'He therefore remained at his post, and, when the townspeople told him what was going on, he answered that he could not abandon his station without being relieved.' He retired into a neighbouring house and awaited his fate, 'but none of the Austrians or French noticed him, and, after the Prussians finally returned and occupied the place, he reported to his officer that he had been standing long enough, and said he would like someone to take over from him!'[3]

Frederick, the eldest son of the soldier-king, encapsulated in himself the recent experience of Prussian society. He was born on 24 January 1712. He was not drawn to the military life by inclination—and indeed he would have been a much less interesting person if he had been a natural soldier. As a young crown prince Frederick cultivated a frenchified way of life that enraged the king, and the confrontation between father and son culminated in a notorious episode in August 1730, when Frederick failed in an attempt to escape from Prussian territory, and was consigned to the fortress of Cüstrin under armed escort. He was forced to look on when his fellow-conspirator Lieutenant Katte was beheaded in a yard in the fortress, and after a further spell of incarceration the Crown Prince was set to work in the civil administration of the Neumark, a primitive and undeveloped province to the east of the Oder.

Frederick's defiance was broken, if not his will and energy, and from March 1732 he devoted himself to running a regiment of infantry as colonel proprietor *(Chef).* Three years later the king promoted Frederick to major general, 'having observed with particular pleasure how our beloved Crown Prince has directed his foremost care and effort to bringing the regiment under his command to a complete and exemplary state.'[4] Everything we know about the king tells us that praise of this kind was not bestowed readily.

Prussia had been gathering strength in the shadow of the dynasty of the Austrian Habsburgs, who were sovereign rulers of extensive territories in central and eastern Europe, and of sizeable outposts in the Low Countries and Italy, and who for centuries had exercised a degree of legal and moral authority over the states of Germany as a whole, which were known under their collective name of The Holy Roman Empire of the German Nation, or the *Reich* for short. The Habsburgs had not so much relied on the support of the Brandenburg-Prussian rulers as taken that support entirely for granted. Frederick William I resented the state of affairs mightily, but his residual loyalty and his sense of caution held him back from open defiance.

The old king died on 31 May 1739, having left to his son the commission to exact Prussia's revenge. The newly-minted King Frederick II scarcely needed the bidding, for his reading and his experiences had convinced him that international affairs were run on the principle of 'dog eats dog.' Emperor Charles VI died on 26 October 1740, and six weeks later Frederick launched the Prussian army into decisive action.

Frederick's target was the Austrian province of Silesia (almost all lying in present-day Poland), which he invaded in December 1740. The young Austrian sovereign Maria Theresa and her small band of loyal advisers contrived to put together an army to reclaim Silesia for her dynasty, and in the snowy April of 1741 the Austrian field marshal Neipperg succeeded in catching the Prussian army off guard. The rival forces clashed at Mollwitz on the 10th. Frederick left the field embarrassingly early, but the Prussians gained a close-run victory while he was running away, and in October he was able to capitalise on this first success by forcing the Austrians to sign away Lower Silesia. Hostilities were renewed in 1742, and after a further defeat at Chotusitz (11 June) the Austrians had to agree to give up the whole of Silesia.

As far as they had concerned Prussia and Austria, the intermittent hostilities between 1740 and 1742 became known as the 'First Silesian War,' while a second bout between August 1744 and December 1745 was termed the 'Second Silesian War.' The treaty of peace at the close of 1745 gained little for Frederick that he had not already enjoyed at the settlement in 1742, but in this second sequence of campaigns a run of Prussian victories in 1745 at Hohenfriedberg (4 June), Soor (30 September) and Kesselsdorf (15 December) completed the apprenticeship of the Prussian army.

As a jackal-like opportunist Frederick had not thought deeply about the consequences of invading Silesia in the first place; rather he was intent on snatching the nearest available prize from the seemingly-disintegrating Habsburg monarchy before it was toppled by the combined efforts of France, Bavaria, Saxony and Piedmont-Sardinia. However by conquering Silesia and the adjacent county of Glatz Frederick had increased the population of the Prussian state by more than one-third, and he appointed expert administrators who developed the agriculture, textile industries and mining, all of which had been neglected under the Habsburgs. In strategic terms the new territories sat comfortably next to the Brandenburg heartland of the Hohenzollern monarchy, and they provided the Prussians with excellent bases from which to campaign in the Habsburg provinces of Bohemia and Moravia.

The loss to the Habsburg monarchy was correspondingly great. Maria Theresa, now Empress, had done well by any reckoning to rally enough of her loyal subjects to ensure the survival of her state in its reduced form. She was not content. In 1748 her minister Friedrich Wilhelm v. Haugwitz brought some stability to the financial affairs, and with the help of Field Marshal Leopold v. Daun the Empress began the work of rebuilding her army on the best modem lines. Another gifted adviser, Count Wenzel Anton v. Kaunitz, was made foreign minister *(Staatscanzler)* in 1753, with the self-appointed brief to form an alliance that would not only help the Austrians to recover Silesia, but reduce Prussia once more to the standing of a minor state. Kaunitz was assured in advance of the active help of Russia, but he made no progress in the much more difficult task of winning over Bourbon France, which was an hereditary enemy of the Habsburgs.

At this juncture Frederick greatly over-estimated the progress the Austrians had made in assembling their alliance. He put out feelers towards Britain, which antagonised the French, and in late August 1756 he initiated hostilities by a pre-emptive strike, intending to throw his would-be enemies into confusion before they could consolidate themselves against him. He proceeded to overrun the innocent electorate of Saxony, and he captured the little Saxon army of 18,600 troops at Pirna, but he failed to achieve anything of consequence against the Austrians. His invasion of Bohemia amounted to scarcely more than a reconnaissance in force, and although Frederick won a little battle at Lobositz (1 October 1756), the combat showed him that the Austrian army had improved greatly since he had last seen it in action eleven years before.

Against all likelihood Frederick was able to achieve surprise a second time, when he launched a full-blooded invasion of Bohemia in the late spring of 1757. He caught the Austrian army (which had been making ready to attack *him)* unprepared, and went on to rout it at the bloody

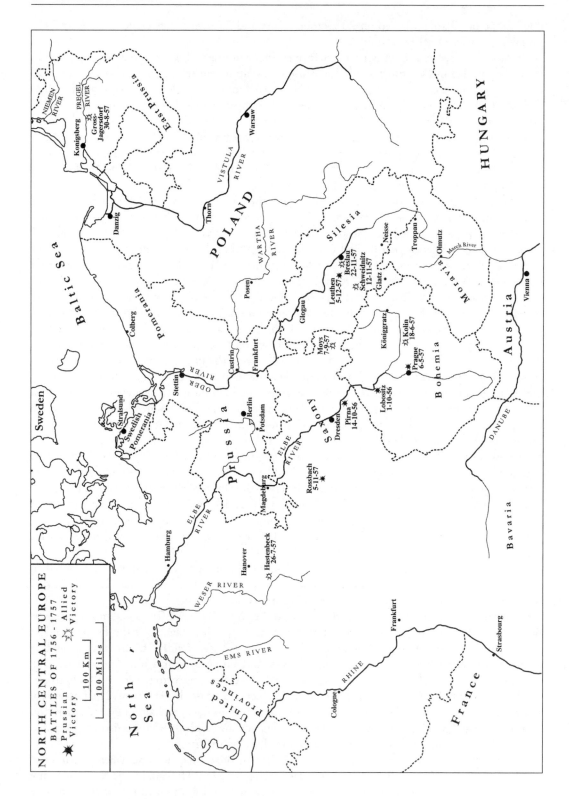

NORTH CENTRAL EUROPE
BATTLES OF 1756 - 1757
★ Prussian Victory   ☆ Allied Victory

100 Km
100 Miles

battle of Prague (6 May), and besiege 48,000 of the survivors in the city of Prague, together with their commander Prince Charles of Lorraine, who was the brother-in-law of Maria Theresa. To all appearances Frederick now had it in his power to dismember or even destroy the Austrian monarchy. Maria Theresa was saved only by Field Marshal Daun, who formed a new army out of runaways and uncommitted forces, and beat Frederick in a pitched battle at Kolin (18 June 1757). Daun rescued Prince Charles and his beleaguered army, and over the following weeks the Prussians trailed out of Bohemia in a state of shock.

Now that Frederick had broken the public peace of Europe, it was much easier for Kaunitz to convert his understandings with sympathetic powers into a continental-scale offensive coalition, dedicated to restoring Silesia to Maria Theresa, and dismembering Prussia in the way she desired. Prussian territories now came under threat not just by the Austrians, but by Russians from the east, Swedes from the north, and from the west by a large if ill-assorted army of French and the troops of the *Reichsarmee,* raised from Frederick's enemies among the states of Germany.

We shall take up the story of Frederick and his army in the late summer of 1757, on the eve of the Rossbach-Leuthen campaign, which was to be the most celebrated episode of their joint history. However it takes a little effort to discover what made the king and his troops so formidable at that time. Foreign tourists and military officers by the thousand came to Prussia in the period between the close of the Seven Years War and the king's death in 1786, and carried back the impression of a Frederick who had hardened and soured into Old Fritz, and of an over-disciplined army which could put on a splendid show, but was beginning to fall behind the times. Observations of the king and his troops as they existed at their prime in 1757 are much rarer, and all the more valuable on that account, and probably the best was penned by the Austrian lieutenant colonel Rebain, who was captured by the Prussians in the campaign of Leuthen, and contrived to send his analysis to Vienna in March 1758.[5] We shall refer to his evidence on a number of occasions.

In his *Testament Politique* of 1752 Frederick had written that kings of Prussia must be their own commanders-in-chief. He certainly lived up to his own prescription in the course of the Seven Years War. He returned from his headquarters to Berlin only once during that struggle (from 4 to 13 January 1757), and his capital did not see him again until 30 March 1763:

> Louis XV devoted himself to exploring refinements of pleasure, and we can figure him as he progressed gently from Versailles to Choisi, and back again, and passed from the embraces of one woman to those of another. At such a time Frederick would be inspecting his regiments—and in just five minutes a cavalry regiment would have to be on horseback and ready to undergo his scrutiny. Neither he nor the princes his brothers wasted their time in the hunt. He had just eighty horses in his stables, and the reports of the stables of the French monarch he dismissed as fairy tales.[6]

Day by day about three hundred items of correspondence were processed by Frederick in person or under his authority, and in times of crisis the king was able to decide what was needed to be done on the spur of the moment, thus getting inside the 'decision cycle' of enemy commanders who were paralysed by the need to consult their fellow generals or refer to a distant capital. Shortly before the battle of Leuthen a French attaché with the Austrians wrote that 'the king of Prussia is devoid of principles, which gives him greater freedom of action than someone who is encumbered by them. He equates right with might, and chooses whatever tends to his advantage. He is active, he commands his armies in person, and he is devoted to his glory and self-interest. His confidence, his style and his enterprising spirit are fed by the success which has almost always crowned his enterprises.'[7]

The Prussian infantry was organised on a uniform basis of battalions of elite grenadiers, and two-battalion regiments of musketeers or fusiliers. Frederick kept up the work which the Old

Perhaps what Frederick looked like in 1757.

Dessauer had put into this arm of the service, and the heavy losses which the Prussians had sustained recently in the battle of Prague (6 May 1757) reminded the king that in modern warfare the infantry must rely on firepower rather than attempting to close with the bayonet. Rebain noted that every Prussian infantryman now had an immediate allowance of eighty cartridges, and that four supernumerary soldiers in each company were told off to bring replenishments from the regimental reserve.

The cavalry had been much neglected in the last reign, and the formidable body of horse which took to the field in the Seven Years War represented a great deal of work on the part of Frederick and some of his generals. Experience taught Frederick that the cavalry of all kinds did much better to charge home with cold steel instead of relying on fire, which was the converse of the case with the infantry. The cuirassiers with their iron breastplates and their jerkins of stout fabric were the battlefield arm par excellence. The dragoons, or medium cavalry, were capable both of taking a place in the line of battle, and carrying out sweeps, raids, ambushes and other operations where there was a call for greater agility.

The hussars were more lightly mounted still, but the Prussian kind were even more versatile than the dragoons, and in the present war they had already gained the upper hand over their Austrian counterparts, who were recruited in the classic hussar country of Hungary, but now proved much inferior both in 'little war' and pitched battle alike. 'The Prussian hussars follow the drill of the dragoons, and are capable of manoeuvering in closed ranks by squadrons, companies or troops as circumstances indicate. As they advance and retire in the style of dragoons, they have battalions with field pieces very often assigned to work with them. For that reason the Austrian hussars are unable to get the better of them, even when they are superior in number, for in such a case the Prussian hussars fall back on their infantry, then come on again in a combined advance, never leaving the flank of the infantry.'[8] It was common for Prussian officers, like the great Seydlitz himself, to transfer from one branch of the cavalry to the other, which made the co-operation between them instinctive.

For the whole of the Seven Years War the Prussian artillery never performed so well as in the final weeks of 1757. Frederick understood little about military technology, and normally plagued the gunners with his ill-considered interventions, but now for once he gave a free hand to Colonel Karl Friedrich v. Moller, who had a peculiar gift for moving heavy pieces at great speed to the sites from where they could wreak the greatest destruction.

Frederick was celebrated, or notorious, for keeping his officers up to the mark. Whereas the French or Austrian major generals might disappear from view in comfortable quarters for days at a time, their Prussian counterparts had to encamp with their troops, on pain of being cashiered, and they had to carry out a rigorous inspection of their brigades from nine to ten in the morning on every day that the army was not on the march. 'In addition the lieutenant general and his brigadier inspect the troops on a given day every week. They go through the ranks… inspect the muskets (which have their bayonets permanently fixed on every occasion of duty), look into the cartridge pouches to make sure that the men have their proper complements of cartridges and flints, and in short they make certain that the infantry and cavalry have everything that is needed for combat.'[9]

Although it was necessary to keep a close watch on the foreign troops, to prevent them from deserting, the discipline as it affected the private soldiers of the Prussian army as a whole was eminently reasonable. Whereas the almost universal modern philosophy of training nowadays is to break down the recruits by a process of collective intimidation, and then refashion the fragments into the desired shape, the classic Prussian style was to deliver the new soldier to the care of a patient corporal, who would take all the time that was needed to instruct the young man in the care of his person, clothing and equipment, and all the motions of the drill, which for wartime service were reduced to the straightforward essentials. Only when the recruit was proficient and confident did he join the other soldiers on the drill square. The punishments in the Prussian army were notoriously severe, but nearly always visited on trained soldiers who should have known better, and thus a good man could put in a lifetime of service without sustaining a blow.

Rebain remarked on the care that went into training the individual cavalry troopers to charge at a trot and gallop from two hundred paces, and smite a target which was set up on a stake. 'All of this demands work, but you won't get anywhere without effort and application... and this is how the ordinary soldiers are managed in the Prussian service. Their superiors treat them with patience, especially the recruits, and they address them as "my lads." When it comes to attacking the enemy you will hear things like: "Boys, now you've got to be heroes, and don't run away. We won't let you down, and don't you let us down either?"'[10]

The Prussian army was therefore impressive in its individual components, but it was more impressive still for the harmony in which the elements worked together. Frederick was aware that change could often do more harm than good, and he was content to exercise a sage inertia in the matter of uniforms and the established routines of the service. The basic tactical evolutions were therefore familiar as well as simple, even if they could be put together in novel and interesting forms.

The army as a whole had been schooled in moving in multi-regimental formations in the peacetime maneouvres, the largest of which were held every year at Potsdam and Spandau and in central Silesia. The army was habituated in moving across the landscape 'by lines' or 'by wings,' and how an individual column could be transmuted into line of combat either by a 'processional' movement of the individual components, or by the fan-like *Deploiren*—all of which procedures were going to be of great value to Frederick at Leuthen.[11]

It is easy to imagine the chaos that would have ensued if the generals had not been trained to judge their times and distances correctly, and Frederick continued the educational process even on campaign. On the spur of the moment he would send an adjutant to order one or other of the wings of cavalry to mount up and place itself at his disposal. 'The King then puts this wing through various manoeuvres, which sometimes extend to an hour's distance to the front or the flank of the army. The cavalry might be made to attack head on, or wheel to take the enemy in flank, or perhaps the design might be hidden by the first line, while the second line moves off to the right, then marches by squadrons to outflank the enemy and attack them. In such a way the generals and commanders are trained in how to exploit the potentials of ground.[12] With an army trained to these standards Frederick was confident that he would be able to put into effect his favourite grand tactic, the 'oblique order,' whereby he marched his troops to an advantageous position on the enemy flank or rear, then launched the main assault with a wing that was heavily reinforced, while he held the weaker wing in reserve to amuse the enemy and cope with unforeseeable eventualities.

All of this was second nature to the Prussian generals by 1757, and Frederick was able to convey his intentions with the minimum of detail. His standing orders before the battle of Leuthen were given at Görlitz on 24 November 1757, and confined to a few lines:

> All generals and staff officers present here today are hereby instructed in how they are to behave in the event of a battle:
>
> 1. The regiments are to advance in compact formation.
> 2. Fire is to be delivered by entire battalions at a time, and at the appropriate range.
> 3. One wing attacks, while the other is held back.
> 4. The officers are to make certain that everyone is well closed-up and kept under control.[13]

The Silesian Wars, the inter-war manoeuvres, and the first campaigns of the Seven Years War had brought forward a generation of officers who were capable of responding to this style of direction. 'As for Seydlitz,' remarked Frederick, 'when he was still a cornet I saw in him the great general and leader. I knew that Czettritz had the makings of a general too, when he was still a peasant. Now can you really say that I don't understand men?'[14]

The Seydlitz in question was Friedrich Wilhelm Baron v. Seydlitz-Kurzbach (1721-73), who was born to a military family then quartered in the garrison town of Kalkar in the Rhineland. While still a child he lost his father, but for the five years from the age of fourteen he was page and virtually adopted son to Friedrich Wilhelm of Brandenburg-Schwedt, deservedly called 'The Mad Margrave' from his wild ways. During this apprenticeship the young Seydlitz already put at risk his neck by feats of crazy horsemanship, his lungs from tobacco, and very much else besides from promiscuous womanising.

Seydlitz began his military service in 1740 as a cornet in his patron's regiment of cuirassiers (No. 5), however his most formative experiences came from his long spell (1743–52) as captain of horse *(Rittmeister)* in the White Hussars (No. 4). Command of light horse was now being recognised as an excellent training for high command, the reason being that survival and success in this branch of the service depended on physical agility, a capacity for independent command, and that instinct for opportunity which was called *coup d'oeil.*

Seydlitz had already been marked out as a cavalryman of exceptional promise. He caught the king's eye again a review on 21 September 1752. Frederick promoted him to lieutenant colonel on the spot, and two weeks later transferred him to the Württemberg Dragoons (No. 12) as commander. Early in 1753 Seydlitz moved in the same capacity to the Rochow Cuirassiers (No. 8), thus having served in all three types of the cavalry in less than a year.

As a full colonel *(Chef)* Seydlitz contrived to get stuck in the mud during his first two encounters in the Seven Years War—at Lobositz (1 October 1756) when the charge of the Prussian cavalry floundered in the Morellen-Bach, and again at Prague (6 May 1757) when he tried to ford the Moldau River and re-join the Prussian army. At the otherwise unfortunate battle of Kolin (18 June 1757) Seydlitz took over the acting command of the brigade of Krosigk, and nearly succeeded in turning the tide in favour of the Prussians. Two days later Frederick awarded him the *Pour le Mérite,* made him major general, and kept him in mind for further advancement. A great deal was invested in promotions of this kind among the cavalry, for a general of horse had it in his power to affect the whole course of a battle.

Otherwise Seydlitz made no attempt to advertise himself, and it is remarkable how a man who was singled out for such a brilliant career had nothing of the careerist about him. His fellow officers without exception were ready to testify as to his straight dealing and talking, and his efforts to secure them advantages before himself. They knew him both as an entertaining comrade off duty, and as a superior who set a terrifying example of proficiency and turnout on parade. One of his people testified: 'Slim and tall, he was the image of warlike splendour. He loved military show, and gave the impression of having been poured into his uniform.'[15]

The standing of Seydlitz among the cavalrymen was only increased by his ineradicable streak of play and irresponsibility. He took the lead in daring tricks, like the one he had learned in his youth of riding through the revolving sails of a windmill. He had little time for the pistol or carbine as weapons for mounted combat, but he was an expert shot with them both. He was able to part the bell rope of the *Rathaus* in Ohlau with a single ball, when he was annoyed by the ringing; he liked to stick one of his long clay pipes in the earth, and trim it down to ground level by successive shots; he had another habit of holding a taler piece between his fingers and inviting another good marksman to shoot it away—a practice which demanded nerve and steadiness by both parties.

Frederick prized Seydlitz amongst other things for his independence of mind, and for that reason the association between king and cavalryman survived a large number of fallings-out. Most frequently the two were at odds on questions of tactics and horsemanship. Frederick himself was a fast but untidy rider, and Seydlitz respected the royal dignity by looking to one side whenever the king found himself dumped on the ground. On such occasions an eloquent silence was commentary enough, as were the posture and expression of Seydlitz when Frederick was giving out his orders at the daily *Parole*.

The French Army

In the second half of 1757 Frederick's Prussia was fighting for its survival. No such compelling reason seemed to be at stake for the French monarchy when it engaged its main military strength to a land war in continental Europe, where a principal army of 105,000 troops overran Hanover, and—more immediately relevant to the present story—a force of rather more than 21,000 combatants was committed to joint action with the German *Reichsarmee*. The French grand strategy, at least until the autumn of 1757, was more consistent than has been generally represented, even if it was the product of competing influences. Who were the people most directly responsible?

Louis XV was drawn by personal inclination to the cause of Maria Theresa and Catholic Austria, but his sense of purpose was vitiated by his style of life. His principal mistress, Jeanne Le Morant, Marquise de Pompadour, was cultivated by the Austrians and supported this connection; she was also credited with exercising a baleful influence on military affairs, which in fact was mostly confined to pushing forward her friends, and especially *cher Soubise,* who was appointed to command the troops who marched to join the *Reichsarmee*. The titular foreign minister, Antoine-Louis de Rouillé, was eclipsed by François-Joachim de Pierres, Abbé de Bernis, who was buoyed up for a time by his success in negotiating the two key treaties with Austria—the defensive First Treaty of Versailles on 1 May 1756, and the offensive Second Treaty exactly one year later. The fragile enthusiasm of Bemis collapsed after the battle of Rossbach, which brought home to him just how formidable an enemy the Allies had taken on in the person of Frederick. Conversely the scarred old Marshal de Belle-Isle was no friend to the Austrians, but he was attracted by the notion of invading Hanover, which promised to be a telling blow against the British-Hanoverian dynastic nexus. In other words, the commitment to the war in Germany extended beyond the circle of Louis and the Pompadour, though it afterwards suited French commentators and historians to pretend otherwise.

After the continental war turned out so badly, there was no lack of people who claimed to be offended by the way the relevant policies had been reached, and by the alleged subordination of French interests to those of Austria. Later in the century a biographer of Marshal Richelieu wrote that

> The conduct and principles of the courts of Berlin and Versailles stood in such stark contrast that the very existence of the first was a damning indictment of the decadent pleasures and indignities that reigned in the other. Frederick accomplished great things with very little, while Louis XV, who had all the resources of France, and the spirit of that nation at his disposal, succeeded in debasing France and the name of the Bourbons... In the war of 1757 the French were governed by a woman [the Pompadour] who was nothing better than a whore, and devoid of any qualities of intellect or character. The army was managed by cowards who acted in the name of a spineless king. A sequence of major disasters was the inevitable outcome... Every project was overthrown by the factions at court. Command appointments were at the disposal of the whimsical and stupid royal mistress, and they were bestowed or withdrawn at the drop of a hat.[16]

It seemed moreover contrary to the natural order of things that France should be a partner in a conspiracy to despoil Frederick of Prussia, who had been an active ally of France in the 1740s, and who was an honorary Frenchman in his intellectual and artistic interests. Moreover Frederick and his army had been upheld in France for years as models of excellence, with the result that the French army in Thuringia was going to be at a moral disadvantage even before it encountered the Prussians in action. None of this was of any help to Lieutenant General Soubise in establishing his authority over his troops in that part of the world.

Charles de Rohan, Prince de Soubise was born on 16 July 1715 to the grandest house in France next to the royal family. His military career opened on 1 May 1732 when as a *guidon* he entered the Gendarmes de la Garde. This red-uniformed elite had accumulated more privileges than any other of the Household troops. The Gendarmes owned the king as their captain, and had the curious honour of accompanying him to his bedside with their standards. Soubise distinguished himself as tactical commander of the Gendarmes at Fontenoy (11 May 1745), which helped to secure his promotion to *maréchal de camp,* and the Pompadour advanced his career further by pushing his marriage to a daughter of the Prince de Condé, which established an immediate connection with the royal family, and secured him the title of *très-haut et très-excellent prince.*

Soubise was unable to establish the military credibility which alone would rid him of the taint of being a protégé of the Pompadour. The Prince of Hildburghausen, as nominal commander of the combined force in Thuringia, wrote on the subject to Maria Theresa and Emperor Francis Stephen: 'Soubise is excellent company—he likes to please, and he knows how to live. But as regards the military trade he is a total ignoramus. The invariable and unavoidable consequence is that he never knows what he ought to do, is incapable of fixing on any resolution, and still less of manoevering an army... his subordinates do exactly what they please, for Soubise cannot bring himself to reprimand anybody, let alone mete out punishment. People just laugh at him.'[17] When the French were in Gotha none of their soldiers were seen to present arms to their officers, or the officers to raise their hats to a general. When Soubise rode past the troops on guard the drummer could not be bothered to lift his drum from the ground, and just beat out the time with the buttons of his cuff.

The French officer corps was of very diverse origins, from the grand *noblesse de cour*—Soubise, the Broglies, Noailles, Ségur and the rest—who found a natural home in the highest ranks, down to the officers of the line infantry, who were divided in turn between commoners *(roturiers),* many of them newly-rich, and the nobles, some of whom had scarcely the money to keep up appearances. The poor nobles defended themselves by reinforcing their caste privileges, and from 1758 the commoners found themselves increasingly excluded from commissioned rank. This made for bad blood during the Seven Years War, and afterwards the resentment of the maltreated commoners was going to be one of the forces driving the Revolution.

Few officers of any kind had as yet undergone formal training in the École Militaire (founded 1750), a deficiency which would not have mattered so much if the young men had received the informal but rigorous schooling which would-be officers had to endure in the Prussian regiments. Idealism, commitment and subordination became rare commodities in the French officer corps, and the troops took due note of the example that was being set by their superiors. Thus the colonel of the Fitz-James cavalry regiment was seen to secure himself a comfortable billet in Gotha town, in open defiance of an order to the contrary, and he escaped with no more than a rebuke.

The rank and file of the French army were raised by 'voluntary' enlistment. There were many criminals and unemployables among the recruits, as in most other armies of the time, but what singled out the French was the disproportionately large numbers of townsmen, amounting to about one-third of the whole, a figure which by itself helps to account for the reputation of the French troops as being turbulent, opportunistic and quick to take advantage of their superiors. The pay of the French soldier was poor, and so were the rations he usually received in the field, which often fell below the stipulated daily one and three-quarters of a pound of bread, and three-quarters of a pound of meat, thanks to the way the system of provisions was mismanaged by the semi-independent fodder agency and the bread contractors. Sheer necessity therefore combined with the decline in discipline to give the French native troops a virtual licence to

Charles de Rohan, Prince de Soubise. He is wearing the uniform of the Gendarmes de la Garde (red coat, with gold lace on black velvet facings).

plunder. In two much-quoted letters Lieutenant General Saint-Germain wrote after the battle of Rossbach that the men under his command were a band of mutinous, cowardly murderers and concluded that 'our nation has lost the military spirit, and feelings of honour are utterly defunct.'[18]

The internal order of a French regiment was often of less concern to its colonel than the task of maintaining the historic privileges of that regiment *vis-à-vis* the other units of the army, which were extraordinarily diverse. The army of Soubise in Thuringia was by no means a cross-section of the French army as a whole, yet it still showed a considerable variety, comprising Irish and Swiss in their historic uniforms of red, German infantry in their blue, and the native French in their baggy coats of light grey. The sheer numbers of the units looked good in the orders of battle, which were computed with sedulous attention to custom (the Swiss, for example, refusing to be brigaded with anyone else). The regiments of horse were on a low establishment of two squadrons each (only the Apchon Dragoons having four). The two-battalion establishment was the norm among the infantry, with the exception of the single-battalion regiments of Royal-Bavarois, Royal-Lorraine, Saint-Germain and the Royal Artillerie, and the four-battalion super-large regiments of Piémont, Mailly and La Marine.

The big Irish cavalrymen of Fitz-James indulged in marauding as enthusiastically as did the native French. However the German-speaking troops of the army (German regiments of Royal Deux-Ponts [Zweibrücken], Royal-Bavarois, La Marck; Swiss regiments of Castella, Diesbach, Planta, Reding, Wittemer) stood aloof from all such demeaning activities, and maintained full military discipline and routine. Piémont was not only one of the largest regiments of native French infantry, but also by its own reckoning one of the best. The citizens of Gotha were unconvinced, having taken stock of the rival armies which had tramped through their town during the campaign, the troops of the regiment being 'badly fitted-out, with some pretty indifferent muskets, and a standard of drill more abysmal than the worst German militia.' The regiment of Brissac was cheerful, noisy but otherwise well behaved, while that of Poitou was genuinely stylish and smart. However the general run of the French infantry was made up of men who were 'poorly equipped and even more poorly disciplined... their long coats flapped along their legs, their cartridge pouches dangled by their calves, their sword belts were slung around their necks, their so-called haversacks were tied on their backs two or three times over, and from the haversacks again were suspended objects like water flasks, field kettles and great metal cooking pots.'[19]

The French infantry tactics as they existed in 1757 were the product of two tendencies, respectively those of shock and firepower. The tradition of the *furia francese* had been renewed most recently through the *Histoire de Polybe* (1727) of Jean Chevalier de Folard (1669-1752). The column was in Folard's view a formation which allied mobility, shock and the national spirit in a way that would make it as formidable weapon for the French as the phalanx had been for the ancient Macedonians, as described by the historian Polybius. Folard's disciples became known as the advocates of the *ordre profond,* and their influence was shown in the successive tactical Ordinances of 1753 (the first of its kind), 1754 and 1755, all of which featured columns of attack, that of 1755 being by platoons or the two-platoon divisions. Doubling of lines was another way of augmenting the concentration of troops, producing formations six ranks deep which could be considered either as thick lines or thin columns.

The Ordinance of 1754 adopted the Prussian practice of marching in step (the *pas cadencé*) and close-order formations, which were certainly compatible with the *ordre profond*. Fire rather than shock action was nevertheless the traditional foundation of the Prussian infantry tactics, and the supporters of firepower and linear tactics (the *ordre mince)* had meanwhile been arguing that the French must improve the speed and discipline of their fire. The Ordinance of 1754 made a concession in their favour by reducing the standard number of ranks from four to three, thus enabling more of the infantrymen to use their muskets effectively. The partisans of a compromise *ordre mixte* began to make their voices heard on the eve of the Seven Years War, but no accord between the two contending schools had been reached by the time the French did battle at Rossbach.

As regards appearances, the French cavalry made a universally favourable impression. When they reached Gotha the Penthièvre Cuirassiers were observed to be 'well set-up men on large, powerful horses,' and 'formed a regiment which lived up to the reputation of the French for having a fine-looking cavalry. We have to admit that the mounted arm of the French is in an incomparably better state than that of their infantry.'[20]

The show and care had actually counted for too much. The captains had been unwilling to risk the fine and costly horses in any strenuous activity in peacetime, or (unlike the case in the Prussian service) provide the necessary supplements in fodder. The French cavalry regulations of 1755 sought to bring home to the regiments the importance of impetus and shock, but the Seven Years War overtook the army before the horses and troopers could be brought into the necessary condition and state of training, even if we suppose that the officers were inclined to put the regulations into effect. When the French cavalry could be persuaded to attack at all, it was seldom at any faster gait than the trot.

The preponderance of the native French cavalry in the army of Soubise was relieved only by the disorderly (and very well-paid) Fitz-James Horse, Rougrave's regiment of *chevaulegers* (light dragoons) from Liège, and the exotic Volontaires de Nassau, a regiment of hussars which had been raised for the French service a few years before in Nassau-Saarbrücken. Colonel Wurmser (brother of the 'Austrian' Wurmser who was to defend Mantua against Bonaparte in 1796) had the reputation of being a good commander of the Nassauers, and his three hundred hussars were decked out most elegantly in blue dolmans and red pelisses. They had their sabres sharpened specially in expectation of their first clash with the Prussians. It arrived on 11 September 1757 and the Nassauers came off badly. The hussars were distinctly out of sorts after a second mauling on the 15th, and later the same day they descended on the innocent village of Friedrichsrode, where they were 'given a hot reception by the local people, who rushed to the spot, beat them up and placed them in confinement. The hussars begged piteously to be released, and the villagers agreed—which was a very bad idea.'[21]

The 450 French artillerymen with the army of Soubise were highly trained, and they would certainly have given a much better account of themselves if they had been equipped with more suitable ordnance. The design of French artillery had been driven to extremes. Each battalion of infantry was provided with one or two close-support cannon on the 'Swedish' or 'Rostaing' models, which seem to have been thin-barrelled 4-pounders, and were certainly too light and too scattered to do more than augment the firepower of the musketeers. The range of field artillery proper comprised 4-, 8- and 12-pounder cannon on the La Vallière System of 1732, which were well made but very heavy, in the style of siege pieces. They could be moved into position only with difficulty at the beginning of an action, and it was not easy to extricate them if the day turned out badly for the French.

The *Reichsarmee*

Francis Stephen who was at the same time Duke of Lorraine, Grand Duke of Tuscany, and the husband of Maria Theresa, was crowned Emperor of Germany in the cathedral at Frankfurt-am-Main on 4 October 1745. He was weighed down by his coronation robes, and on catching Maria Theresa's eye he raised his hands in their mighty gloves in a gesture of mock martyrdom. She could not contain her amusement. If the ceremonial of the *Reich* was laughable to the new Imperial pair, the institution as such was highly needful, for it extended the moral authority of the Habsburgs over the myriad sovereign states which then made up Germany. There were nearly 2,000 of them in all, if we include every last abbey and knightly holding, and a still sizeable 300 or so were represented in the assemblies of the ten Circles *(Creise),* the regional groupings which had been set up in 1521. They included the Habsburg territories of the Circle of Burgundy (the Austrian Netherlands), as well as the Circle of Austria proper and Bohemia.

The system of the Circles survived the Thirty Years War (1618-48), but many other features of the Empire were changed. France and Sweden entered the scene as guarantors of the new arrangements in the Peace of Westphalia. There were safeguards for the religious liberty of Protestants under Catholic sovereigns, and an institutional balance was maintained between the Catholic States (the *Corpus catholicorum)* and the Protestant *(Corpus evangelicorum)* in the debates of the Imperial Assembly *(Reichstag)* which met at Regensburg from 1663. However in the new century Frederick the Great did not hesitate to broker questions of regency and inheritance in a number of the German states, and to that extent he succeeded in undermining the authority of the Empire's supreme court of judicial appeal *(Reichshofrath).* His potential for making trouble was helped by his family ties with Bayreuth, Wolfenbüttel and Württemberg, and he ultimately enlisted forty German princes in his personal masonic lodge of The Three Globes, of which he became Grand Master in 1744.

The military provisions evolved unevenly over the course of several decades. A first set of arrangements was agreed between May 1681 and March 1682. Germany was being threatened simultaneously by the advance of French power across the Rhine, and by that of the Turks up the Danube, but Emperor Leopold I was able to secure a consensus only by devolving control in such a way that reassured the smaller states that they would not be swallowed up by their larger German neighbours. An element of potential chaos was therefore embedded in the military structures from the start. It was agreed on 31 August 1681 that the joint force would be calculated on a 'simple' peacetime paper establishment of a supposed 40,000 troops, of which seven-tenths were to be infantry and the remaining three-tenths cavalry. In 1702 this peacetime *miles perpetuus* was doubled to 80,000, and a tripling of the 1681 quotas brought the wartime footing up to 120,000. Finally the command arrangements were regulated in 1727, and in a way that guaranteed that the appointments would be balanced or alternated between the two religions.

Although the debates and documentation had been of extraordinary length, the *Reichsarmee* as such did not exist in peacetime, and it knew only a limited corporate existence in time of war. The Assembly at Regensburg might agree on a particular step, but that was only the first stage in a tortuous process, for the individual Circles then had to give their approval, and lastly and crucially the individual states had to be willing to raise the actual troops. Co-ordination was more than usually difficult at this level if (as happened in some regions) the relevant Circle failed to appoint a *Creisoberst* to supervise the affair.

The responsibility of providing the troops was sub-divided minutely among the political entities, and there was no obligation to earmark any men in advance of a mobilisation, or to provide them with weapons. It is not to be presumed, for example, that the Abbess of Guckenzell attended sedulously to training her one-third of a cavalryman or her three-and-one-third infantrymen. There were no joint drills in peacetime, no standardisation of the calibres of muskets or artillery, and although a military tax *(Römermonath)* was payable to the central funds of the Empire for the upkeep of the generals and a modest train of artillery, the provisions and the transport remained entirely the responsibility of the sovereigns who provided the individual contingents.

A *Reichsheer* to wage war against an external enemy had been formed against the French between 1689 and 1697, in the War of the Spanish Succession from 1702 to 1714, and again in the War of the Polish Succession from 1734 to 1735. Even in those wars the political unity had not been absolute, for the Bavarians and others had been clients of the French, and accord proved harder still to achieve when it was a question of setting up a *Reichs-Executions-Armee* to enforce a judgement against an offending member inside the *Reich.* The consequent intrigues and arguments at

Regensburg lasted from 14 September 1756 until 17 January 1757, when Austria finally secured the pronunciation of the *Reichs-Execution* against Frederick of Prussia, who had broken the peace of the Empire by invading Saxony. There still remained the business of raising the contingents, and getting them to the scene of operations, which delayed action for several months more.

To some extent the business of the *Reichs-Execution* divided the Empire along fairly predictable lines. The prince-bishops (Cologne, Trier and Mainz) of the Electoral Rhine Circle had been the most enthusiastic from the outset, just as the electors of Brandenburg (Frederick), Hanover (George II of Britain) and Brunswick came to form a bloc of opposition. Beyond this the complications were endless. Military coercion might be decisive. Electoral Saxony and the duchies of Anhalt-Zerbst and Mecklenburg-Schwerin were under Prussian military control and therefore unable to contribute to the *Reichsarmee,* just as on the other side the pro-Prussian rulers of Ansbach, Bayreuth and Gotha were unable to resist the intimidation of Austria and her associates. Loyalty to the Emperor and the institution of the Empire determined the allegiance of the Protestant Landgraf Ludwig VIII of Hesse-Darmstadt, whose regiment of infantry was of excellent quality, just as his second son, Prince Georg Wilhelm, was the finest general of the *Reichsarmee.* His neighbour, Landgraf Wilhelm VIII of Hesse-Kassel, was enmeshed in the opposing political and military system of Prussia, Hanover and Britain.

As a general rule, the better regiments of the *Reichsarmee* were those which represented a single contingent from an individual state, while the worst were the composite Circle regiments which were drawn from all over the relevant *Creise.* Among the extreme cases of the latter we may mention the infantry regiment of Baden-Baden which was cobbled together from 42 contingents, and the 61 contingents which made up the cuirassier regiment of Hohenzollern.

A number of the sovereigns chose to keep back substantial numbers of their best troops from the *Reichsarmee* as such, for it paid them much better and gained more political kudos to hire them out as paid auxiliaries to the Austrians or French. Thus the regiment of Mainz was maintained on the Austrian establishment, along with the Red and Blue regiments of Würzburg. The French were the paymasters of the auxiliary forces of the Palatinate (Pfalz), Bavaria (4,000) and Württemberg (6,000). By creaming off troops in this way the sovereigns inevitably diminished the quality of the support they could give to the *Reichsarmee.* Austria, in its capacity as a member of the Empire, was the biggest defaulter of all. Emperor Francis Stephen claimed that the troops he hired in Germany counted as part of his commitment as head of the Austrian and Burgundian Circles, but even by that reckoning he was still short of his quota by 27,919 men.

The full triple-strength wartime establishment stood at 120,000 men, as we have seen. The number of troops supplied should still have reached 47,565, after discounting the states of the Empire which were in active opposition or under enemy control. The further shortcomings and withholdings on the part of the well-affected states reduced the total which went on campaign in the late summer of 1757 to 25,000, of whom little more than one-third were actually present at the battle of Rossbach.

The forces of the *Reichsarmee* stood under the military command of the Austrian field marshal and full general of the Empire the Prince of Sachsen-Hildburghausen, of whom there will be something to say shortly. Under his authority the *Reichsarmee* was commanded by:

General of Cavalry of the Empire *(Reichsgeneral der Cavallerie):*
Prince August Wilhelm of Baden-Baden

Full Generals of Infantry of the Empire *(Reichsfeldzeugmeister):*
Landgraf Egon Ludwig of Fürstenberg-Stühlingen
Prince Carl August of Baden-Durlach

Lieutenant Generals of the Empire *(Reichsfeldmarschallieutenants)*:
Prince Georg of Hesse-Darmstadt
Ludwig Wilhelm v. Ostein
Franz Johann v. Brettlach (he was the elder of the two Brettlach brothers in the Rossbach campaign).

All of these people were career officers in the Austrian army, in which they held separate field ranks, and without their presence the *Reichsarmee* could not have functioned at all. However the elaborate provisions for the appointments collapsed when it was found that many of the generals in Germany were physically or mentally decrepit, or in open opposition.

The Landgraf of Fürstenberg was valued for political rather than military reasons, for he had his finger on the pulse of the Empire, and kept Vienna briefed on developments there. The most useful of the others was beyond doubt Lieutenant General Prince Georg of Hesse-Darmstadt (1722-82), 'an extraordinarily active individual.'[21] As a young man he had been enthralled by the Prussian military system and by the personality of Frederick, who in 1743 appointed him *Chef* of a new regiment of infantry (No. 47), with the-task of shaping it up to Prussian standards from a draft of men who had been taken over from the service of Holstein-Gottorp. He accompanied Frederick on the Bohemian campaign of 1744, and on 12 September he was injured by an Austrian cannon shot which ploughed through the king's suite on the Ziskaberg outside Prague. Prince Georg and his regiment fought at Kesselsdorf on 15 December 1745, and he would have probably known a brilliant career as one of Frederick's generals if his father the Landgraf had not insisted that he must leave the Prussian service. Prince Georg was made an Austrian lieutenant general in 1752, and a lieutenant general of the Empire two years later. He devoted himself to his new responsibilities with typical enthusiasm, making his regiment the best in the *Reichsarmee,* and becoming Hildburghausen's right-hand man. Not long after the battle of Rossbach Hildburghausen wrote to Vienna: 'That is what comes of not having enough good people. The only one I can rely upon is the Prince of Hesse-Darmstadt.'[22]

Old Franz Johann Brettlach was a full general, but also something of a political animal after the style of Fürstenberg. He was an experienced negotiator on behalf of Vienna, and was considered all the more valuable for having just converted to Catholicism, and being in daily contact with his younger brother Major General Ludwig Carl, who was in immediate command of the two attached Austrian regiments of cuirassiers. The elder Brettlach exercised his skills in an attempt to bring harmony and consistency to Hildburghausen's headquarters, but finally had to desist just before the battle of Rossbach, when the cold weather caused his sore throat to develop into a full-blown quinsy.[23]

Among the junior generals one of the most able was the thirty-two year-old Prince Carl of Stolberg-Gedern, Major General of the Circle of the Upper Rhine. Hildburghausen himself placed a high value on the services of the Würzburg major general Johann Ferdinand Balthasar Baron Kolb v. Rheinsdorf, who had arrived at headquarters ahead of the Würzburg Circle contingent.

An informative commentary on all the doings of the *Reichsarmee* is provided by Franz Rudolph Mollinger, who was secretary to Prince Georg of Hesse-Darmstadt, and wrote frequently to a son of the prince who was staying at home. He noted 'how a good basic education in youth is just as important for great gentlemen as it is for people like me. I have to tell you in confidence that there are a great number of generals and other high-ranking officers here who show only too well that they learned nothing in their younger years. From this you may imagine what a frightful show they make in the army.'[24] At the lower level the officers of the Circle contingents embraced men who, as Hildburghausen testified, were trying to do their best with intractable material, but also included some over-promoted NCOs, and dilettanti who had purchased their commissions and had were devoid of any commitment to the military life.[25]

It would have been contrary to Austrian interests to see the Empire and its army divide along religious lines, and so enable Frederick and his party to represent their cause as a Protestant struggle against Romish tyranny. On 8 June 1757 Vienna's instructions to Hildburghausen told him that no officer, soldier, priest or preacher was to be allowed to say a word tending to religious hatred; on the contrary, the 'chaplains of all denominations are by their teaching and admonitions to promote good Christian conduct, to pray to God for His grace and blessing, to establish and maintain brotherly love and unity among the men of the army, and to discourage blasphemy, swearing, drunkenness, whoring and other vicious behaviour.'[26]

In practice Hildburghausen and his officers found it impossible to dictate to their men how they ought to think and behave. Many of the Protestant troops believed that they had been enlisted in the wrong cause, and an Austrian officer claimed 'that does not apply just to the Protestants, for I have seen men from Bavaria, the Palatinate and Mainz, with their rosaries in their purses and scapulas over their shoulders, who would rather have fought for the King of Prussia rather than against him.'[27] More embarrassing still was the behaviour of those Catholic troops who not only remained loyal, which was desirable in itself, but maltreated the Protestant civilians in the theatre of war. Although the men of the mixed Franconian Circle regiments were notoriously pro-Prussian, their neighbours in the unitary regiment of Blue Würzburg descended on one of the Lutheran pastors of the duchy of Gotha and plundered him unmercifully. The duke complained to Colonel Moser v. Filseck, who called the guilty troops to account, but

> on the following day several hundred other men from this very regiment fell on the same place. They cleaned out not only the pastor's house and the school but the entire village. They made off with the plate and ornaments of the church, wrecked the chancel, the baptismal font and the organ, fouled the sacristy in a disgusting way, and tore up and scattered the bibles and the church accounts and bonds. In the houses they overturned the stoves and smashed them and the windows. They went after the villagers in the neighbouring wood, whither the people had fled in their terror. The pastor had gone there as well, but he now had to take himself off again, for the soldiers were mounting a ferocious hunt for him, and threatened to hang him or cut him in pieces.[28]

Such was the state of ecumenical relations in this part of central Germany.

In the late autumn of 1757 Soubise reviewed the character of the German units, taking into account both their competence and their reliability. On this basis he rated the Hesse-Darmstadt regiment as excellent, seven more as good, six as adequate, seven as bad, and Trier in a category by itself as the worst of all:

Excellent:
Hesse-Darmstadt

Good:
Nagel, Elberfeld, Bavarian, Salzburg, Mainz, Blue Würzburg

Adequate:
Württemberg, Pfalz-Effern, Nassau-Weilburg, Paderborn, Cologne

Bad:
Varel, Ferntheil, Cronegk, Pfalz-Zweibrücken, Baden-Durlach, Baden-Baden, Fürstenberg

Very Bad:
Trier.[29]

Among the five regiments of the Empire cavalry only the Pfalz Cuirassiers were formed from a single contingent. Many of the troopers had never ridden a horse before they went off to war, let alone undergone any military schooling, and the wonder is that they performed as well as they did. Hildburghausen allowed that the cavalry were willing and brave, 'but, for God's sake, there is nobody in charge who knows how to lead them. They are incapable of executing any kind of manoeuvre, and the limit of our training was to get them to make an about turn to the right by fours. In the time it takes for one of their squadrons to form up the Prussians will have covered a league.'[30]

Nothing had been done in peacetime to make sure that the *Reichsarmee* had a ready central reserve of medium artillery. The 12-pounder cannon in the Nuremberg Arsenal now proved to be too long and heavy to be taken on campaign, and so a train of ten lighter 12-pounders and two howitzers had to be rounded up from a number of states. Likewise the necessary gunners would have gone without pay if the newly-elected Bishop of Würzburg, Prince Adam Friedrich v. Seinsheim, 'the friend of mankind.'[31] had not provided for them from his own purse. The regimental artillery amounted to sixty-two pieces, a diverse collection of 3- and 4-pounders which had been raised by the Circles. The two mixed regiments of the Circle of the Upper Rhine had gunners 'who certainly knew how to serve the pieces, but only with blank charges on festive occasions. They had never taken their guns on campaign.'[32]

Hildburghausen applied to Emperor Francis Stephen in the matter of artillerymen, and also to provide him with bridging material, for it had been found impossible to transport the pontoons overland from the Main. 'Your Imperial Majesty will know from Your fundamental knowledge of the art of war that were are unable to carry out any kind of military operation in the absence of pontoons, and especially in lands like these, which are intersected by a multitude of little rivers.'[33] On 29 July the Emperor's officials replied that they were unable to help the *Reichsarmee* in this respect, and it was just the same with the artillerymen, for the Austrian gunners had suffered heavy losses at Kolin. All that the Austrians could have done was sent untrained men, and 'recruits of this kind can be raised just as easily where you are as they can here.'[34]

Concerning transport, the only word from Vienna was a stern admonition, based on the experience which showed that the *Reichsarmee's* officers of all ranks were in the habit of taking into the field not just waggons laden with silver dining services and other luxuries, but their wives and mistresses and sometimes their whole families.[35]

The tents which the contingents extracted from their dusty stores were found to be full of holes, the belts, cartridge pouches and so on were cracked and brittle, and few of the muskets were in working order. Hildburghausen's attempts to provision the *Reichsarmee* were hardly more successful, even though he was aided by two of the most able public servants of the Austrian monarchy—the commissary Johann Georg Baron Grechtler, and Johann Wenzel Baron v. Widmann who represented Austria as minister in Franconia and Bavaria.

Hildburghausen took the precaution of setting up magazines of flour and fodder at Erlangen, Meiningen, Barchfeld and other places along the *Reichsarmee's* routes of march, and he urged the rulers that they ought to centralise their provisioning. The states misconstrued Hildburghausen's efforts as an assault on their independence, and they instead placed contracts with a total of sixty private entrepreneurs to support the individual contingents, thus setting up a corresponding sixty separate systems of supply. Responsibilities were further divided at the unit level, 'so that in a number of regiments every half-company had one or two Jews responsible for keeping it supplied.'[36]

The princes even objected to Hildburghausen making arrangements to supply the Austrian contingent, for he paid his contractors well, and the Circles of Swabia and Franconia complained that 'he thereby made things difficult for them, since their own contractors cited this precedent as grounds for raising their prices, and putting themselves on the same footing.'[37] The states were not to be swayed even after happenings such as that on 13 September 1757, when the Baden-Durlach column struggled into Meiningen and found that the contractor was observing a Jewish holy day and their provisions had been locked away. The troops would have gone hungry if the Austrians had not fed them out of the goodness of their hearts.

The difficulties were compounded when the army came into close proximity with the French, whose marauders swept the country bare, who borrowed far more flour and fodder from Hildburghausen than they ever paid back, and who even snatched an issue of bread rations from Grechtler by force.[38]

Here is probably the most useful place to gain an overview of the forces as they were grouped by Circles, with their ratings as assessed by Soubise:

Circle of the Elector Rhine *(Kurrheinische Creis)*

Mainz Infantry Regiment Wildenstein:	4 battalions, 'good,'
Cologne *Leib-Infanterie Regiment:*	1 battalion, 'adequate'
Cologne Infantry Regiment:	1 battalion, 'adequate'
Trier Infantry Regiment:	2 battalions, 'very bad'
Palatinate Infantry Regiment Effern:	2 battalions, 'adequate'
Palatinate Cuirassier Regiment.	

The Catholic bishop-electors as a tribe were the most whole-hearted supporters of the Allied cause in the *Reich,* and their goodwill, together with French pressure, dragged the Elector Palatine in their wake. Under separate arrangements seven more of his battalions were operating with the French forces in Hanover. All of the regiments of this Circle were formed from contingents from single states, which gave a coherence that was lacking in some of the units from the other Circles. However Johann Philipp the Prince-Bishop of Trier would have been much put out to learn that his regiment had been dismissed as 'very bad' *(vilain)*. He had driven forward the mobilisation of his two battalions as being a matter which concerned so closely 'his name and standing with His Imperial Majesty and the whole Empire'. He had obtained anew almost every item of equipment, down to the iron ramrods, and he had commandeered all the tailors of Koblenz and Ehrenbreitstein, forbidding them to work on anything but the uniforms, and threatened them with severe punishment if they made a botched job through over-haste.[39]

Circle of the Upper Rhine *(Oberrheinische Creis)*

Hessen-Darmstadt Infantry Regiment:	1 battalion, 'excellent'
Pfalz-Zweibrücken Infantry Regiment:	2 battalions (of 33 contingents), 'bad'
Nassau-Weilburg Infantry Regiment:	2 battalions (of 26 contingents), 'adequate'

In spite of its name, this region spanned the middle rather than the upper reaches of the German stretch of the Rhine. Here the lead was taken by the Landgraf Ludwig VIII of Hesse-Darmstadt who was a Protestant, but dedicated to the ideal of the *Reich* (above p. 24). His single-battalion regiment was the best that the *Reichsarmee* proper had to show, and represented something of a sacrifice on the part of Ludwig, for he could have hired it out on very favourable terms to a foreign prince. 'You can imagine nothing more splendid than the sight of the Darmstadt Grenadiers when they come on guard. They are picked, tall and fine-looking men who put the French to shame.'[40] The regiments of Pfalz-Zweibrücken and Nassau-Weilburg were of much less account, having been put together from numerous and often ill-affected contingents.

Westphalian Circle *(Westphälische Creis)*
Münster Infantry Regiment Nagel: 1 battalion, 'good'
Münster Infantry Regiment Elberfeld: 1 battalion, 'good'
Paderborn Infantry Regiment Mengersen: 1 battalion, 'adequate'

The local assemblies of Münster, Osnabrück, Paderborn and Hildesheim were slow to respond to the warlike calls of Clemens August the Bishop-Elector of Cologne, who in his capacity as Bishop of Paderborn and Hildesheim wished to assert his influence in a region of north-west Germany which had been under heavy Prussian and Hanoverian influence. The regiments were nevertheless formed of single contingents, and on the whole were rated highly by Soubise.

Swabian Circle *(Schwäbische Creis)*
Württemberg Infantry Regiment: 1-2 battalions (of 6 contingents), 'adequate'
Fürstenberg Infantry Regiment: 2 battalions (of 21 contingents), 'bad'
Baden-Baden Infantry Regiment: 2 battalions (of 42 contingents), 'bad'
Baden-Durlach Infantry Regiment: 1 battalion (of 27 contingents), 'bad'
Hohenzollern Cuirassier Regiment: (of 61 contingents)
Württemberg Dragoon Regiment: (of 22 contingents)

The Swabian Circle embraced a wide tract of Germany between the Neckar, the Rhine and the borders with Switzerland and Bavaria. All the regiments were assembled from multiple contingents, a circumstance which sapped the morale even of predominantly Catholic regiments like those of Baden-Baden and Fürstenberg. The Württemberg Dragoons fought with some spirit at Rossbach, but the Württemberg infantry were not of the same quality, for Duke Carl Eugen had given priority to rebuilding his auxiliary contingent in the French pay to 6,000 men, after the force had broken up in a violent mutiny in Stuttgart on 21 June (see below p. 93).

Bavarian Circle *(Bayersiche Creis)*
Bavarian Infantry Regiments Pechmann and Holnstein: 3 battalions, 'good'
Salzburg Infantry Regiment: 1 bn (of 12 contingents), 'good'

The Bavarian Circle took in electoral Bavaria proper, together with the states of Salzburg (not yet part of Austria), Passau, Pfalz-Neuburg (Upper Palatinate) and the city of Regensburg. The population was largely Catholic, and the Circle stood under the political domination of Elector Max Joseph II of Bavaria and Archbishop Siegmund of Salzburg. Bavaria (like Württemberg in the Swabian Circle) supplied a large auxiliary contingent (in this case 4,000 troops) directly to the Alliance, but the Bavarian Circle troops were willing enough, and the leadership of a large number of former Austrian officers helped to make up for the lack of experience among the men. Soubise assessed both of the regiments as reliable, though Franz Johann Brettlach was not happy to see the Salzburg Regiment given the important task of securing the Protestant city of Nuremberg, and 'especially because its colonel [Count Orbea] is a weak man, and in present circumstances a great deal depends on having an intelligent commander.'[41]

Franconian Circle *(Fränkische Creis)*
Varel Infantry Regiment: 2 bns (of 26 contingents), 'entirely Prussian in sympathy'
Ferntheil Infantry Regiment: 2 bns (of 20 contingents), 'entirely Prussian in sympathy'
Cronegk Infantry Regiment: 2 bns (of 18 contingents), 'entirely Prussian in sympathy'
Bayreuth Cuirassier Regiment: (of 23 contingents)
Ansbach Dragoon Regiment: (of 21 contingents)

The troops of the Franconian Circle were collectively the least reliable element of the *Reichsarmee*. The splitting-up of the contingents was taken to such an extreme that the companies and squadrons even from the same states were distributed among different regiments. The rulers of Ansbach and Bayreuth contributed men only under Austrian pressure, and disaffection was rife among all the Circle troops proper. Politically the Circle was dominated by Adam Friedrich v. Seinsheim who was Prince Bishop of Würzburg, and from 21 April 1757 Bishop of Bamberg as well, which made him by far the most important Catholic ruler of west-central Germany. He chose to put his best men not into the Circle regiments but into two regiments that were placed directly on the Austrian establishment by an agreement of 27 October 1756. They were uniformed in white, and designated respectively 'Blue' and 'Red' on account of the distinguishing colour of their cuffs and lapels. For a while we lose sight of Red Würzburg (Rot Würzburg) for it marched off to join the Austrians, and shared their fate at Leuthen. Blue Würzburg acted with the *Reichsarmee,* but was not technically part of it. The first battalion was simply the existing regiment of Kolb under a new name. The second was raised entirely from recruits, but the regiment as a whole was commanded by the experienced colonel Gottfried Wilhelm Moser v. Filseck, and despite some indiscipline (above p. 26) Hildburghausen reckoned Blue Würzburg the best unit at his disposal.

The Austrian Contingent

The *Reichsarmee* would have been overtaken by misfortune earlier and more completely than it was if it had not been supported by a contingent of Austrians. Towards the middle of June 1757 the two fine Austrian cuirassier regiments of Brettlach and Trautmannsdorff, together amounting to about 1,900 men, received orders to march to join the *Reichsarmee*. The Brettlach regiment arrived on 12 August, and that of Trautmannsdorff (coming from Hungary) a few days later. They stood under the temporary command of Major General Ludwig Carl v. Brettlach, whose elder brother General of Cavalry Franz Johann had taken a detour by way of Vienna. Once he reached the army the elder Brettlach found that his considerable experience of active service counted for little with Hildburghausen. He wrote frequently about his frustrations to his confidant in Vienna, the *Reichsvizecanzler* Rudolph Joseph v. Colloredo, who was in charge of Austria's relations with the *Reich.*

The cuirassiers alone would have not been enough to meet Hildburghausen's need for reliable cavalry. Vienna had promised to support the French army in Westphalia by two regiments of Hungarian hussars, and in June the regiments of Széchenyi and Splényi were selected for this purpose, forming a brigade under Major General Anton Széchenyi. A French attaché described him as 'a well-motivated individual, who is very keen and most gratified with the responsibility which has been entrusted to him.'[42] The French then decided that they did not want the hussars after all, and in view of Hildburghausen's calls for help the Austrian authorities decided in the middle of August to reassign Széchenyi and his hussars to the combined forces of the *Reichsarmee* and French at Erfurt.

Another good man was Gideon Ernst v. Loudon, who had been operating on the borders of Bohemia and Saxony with an Austrian roving corps of two companies of grenadiers and 4,000 Croatian light infantry. This force too came to operate with the *Reichsarmee*. A veteran of the Russian service, Loudon had been rejected when he had offered his sword to Frederick (who admitted later that he had made one of the worst mistakes in his life). Loudon then threw in his lot with the Austrians, and by sheer ability rose very rapidly in their army. He was promoted from colonel to major general on 22 August 1757, and ended his days in 1790 as a field marshal and the most celebrated commander of eighteenth-century Austria next to the long-dead Prince Eugene.

Feld Marſchall
Joh: Friedrich, Prinz
von Sachſen-Hildburgshauſen.

Field Marshal Prince Joseph Maria Friedrich v. Sachsen-Hildburghausen.
(Courtesy of the Austrian Military Academy, Wiener Neustadt)

A Pomeranian marches until he dies,
A Brandenburger marches until he drops,
A Saxon marches until he is tired,
A Rhinelander marches as long as he is in the mood.

(German proverb)

Notoriety rather than fame was attached to the name of Joseph Maria Friedrich Wilhelm Hollandius Prince v. Sachsen-Hildburghausen (1702-87). He had secured a particular place in the favour of the Habsburgs. The late Emperor Charles VI had seen in him a potential successor to Prince Eugene—a disposition which Hildburghausen encouraged by marrying Eugene's very rich (and very ugly) niece and heiress, and by cultivating the arts (he discovered the musical talents of Carl Ditters v. Dittersdorf (1733-99), and launched him on a brilliant career).

Hildburghausen also succeeded in making his mark with Maria Theresa and Francis Stephen. He militarised the Croatian Military Borders between 1744 and 1749, and he acquired a particular value in the confrontation with Prussia. He was a sovereign prince of the *Reich,* and as a Catholic convert from a Protestant house he was believed (like the elder Brettlach) to have an understanding of both the Catholic and Protestant mentalities.

In physical conformation Hildburghausen was built like a gorilla. His upper parts were so massive that he was able to lift a chair with a seated servant above his head with ease, while his legs were so feeble that he had to be supported when he went out shooting game. He was as eccentric in his way as Maria Theresa's foreign minister Count Kaunitz, and as hideous as Prince Eugene. Unfortunately there was no outstanding record of military achievement to set against his peculiarities. Prince Eugene himself had nicknamed him 'the man who loses our battles' *('der Schlachtenverlierer')* in the War of the Polish Succession (1734-35), and on 4 August 1737 Hildburghausen was defeated by the Turks so badly at Banja Luka that his cavalrymen had to escape across the River Verbas by holding onto their horses' tails. Two years later Hildburghausen was nevertheless promoted to full general *(Feldzeugmeister)* and awarded the Order of the Golden Fleece.

In the campaign of 1757 one of the few sympathetic readings of Hildburghausen's character came from an official of the ducal court of Gotha, who claimed that the man's innate goodness finally overcame the disadvantages of a rudimentary education, overlain by 'Austrian bombast, pride and harshness.' He had come to Gotha as an enemy, 'but he now left us animated by as much friendship as such a crude character was capable of showing.'[43]

Hildburghausen's upbringing and his unfortunate military experiences had left him with a bleak view of humankind. 'The principle of blind obedience has been adopted not just to spare the country from the depredations of the armies, but rather to hold the soldier to his duty in front of the enemy. We will be very much mistaken if we were to suppose that, out of a given 50,000 men whom we lead into battle, there will be more than 10,000 who act out of courage or feelings of honour. What moves them is obedience, and the habit of doing what they are told. The soldier is a material being, a walking machine which can be put into motion only through the application of rigorous discipline.' Good order affected the whole chain of command, and the soldiers would despise the officer who in turn despised his own superiors.[44]

Hildburghausen's inability to communicate in positive terms alienated him from the ordinary soldiers of the *Reichsarmee,* and by all accounts he got on just as badly with its generals. Franz Johann Brettlach wrote to Vienna that 'this prince is totally devoid of what is needed to command an army, and above all an army like ours, which calls for a good deal of patience and a good deal of perception to be able to convey to almost every individual exactly what he ought to do.' Instead, Hildburghausen antagonised the officer corps from the princes downwards by his coarse and hostile ways. He showed also little care for the troops, 'and this failing proceeds

Feld Marschall Lieutenant
Freiherr
Ludwig v. Pretlach.

Major General Ludwig Carl v. Brettlach, commander of the Austrian cavalry in the campaign of Rossbach.
(Courtesy of the Austrian Military Academy, Wiener Neustadt)

mostly from his extreme sloth, for he is entirely out of sorts if he cannot spend ten hours out of the twenty-four in bed.[45]

Out of the senior Austrian commanders, Ludwig Carl Brettlach was preoccupied with his cuirassiers, Loudon and Széchenyi were usually absent with their roving detachments, which left only the old Johann Franz Brettlach, who found Hildburghausen impossible to work with.

Whether through the traits of his character, or a genuine lack of capable subordinates, Hildburghausen had nobody to whom he could delegate even so much as the routine business of command, except possibly his Irish aide-de-camp, Lieutenant Colonel O'Flanagan. The prince could not trust his headquarters clerks to write up so much as a journal of operations unsupervised, and he protested to Colloredo in Vienna that he had not a moment to spare to pen the regular personal reports he was supposed to be sending to the Emperor. He was plagued with endless stupidities from the *Reichsarmee* and the French, and 'now comes a peasant who has had his head smashed, his arm broken, or a bullet through his belly—the work of our marauders. He is followed by a mother who is distraught because her daughter has been raped... It is called the *Reichsarmee*, and that says it all.'[46]

The command arrangements with the French were never properly sorted out, and the French were divided among themselves. Two days before the battle of Rossbach Hildburghausen summed up for his Emperor the experience of trying to work with Soubise. He cited a recent council of war, which was attended not just by the French generals, but their staffs, their clerks and 'God knows what.' The atmosphere was like a 'synagogue' or a 'Jewish school', for everyone felt free to speak out as the inspiration took him. Hildburghausen never knew where he stood. He would be assured that a battalion or squadron would be at his disposal at a particular place, only to find that somebody had posted it somewhere else two or three hours before. He would go back to Soubise and impress upon him how important it was to have undivided command. 'He would be in total agreement, and in fact I have heard him say to his generals and officers: "Well then, *Messieurs,* we have to obey the prince. I am only to glad to do so, and I trust that nobody will find the slightest difficulty in following my example." But the trouble is... that this genial gentleman commands not the slightest authority among his forces, and so it all stays as before. Your Majesty as a master of our profession will be able to judge what would happen if it came to a battle, and I had to order such and such a battalion or squadron to advance, change front, cover a flank or so on, and the commander just replied with a "Nobody told me so !"'[47]

It would be difficult to think of a more unhappy connection than that between Hildburghausen, bad-tempered and disordered during his waking hours, and the pliant, evasive Soubise. The decisions which emerged from these tangled counsels were usually bad; worse still, they were never carried through with the brute conviction that could have still have retrieved something good from a wrong-headed course.

II

The Gathering of Forces

To Eisenach

We left Frederick in the high summer of 1757, by when he had lost the initiative he had snatched by irrupting into Bohemia in the spring and early summer of that year. He was now north of the border hills, and immobilised by the Austrians, who had planted their main army at Zittau, on the borders of Saxony and Silesia. In the operational sense he was also looking over his right shoulder, towards the considerable if ill-assorted enemy forces which threatened to emerge on the theatre of war from the west.

Two of the hostile armies were French. The larger force, that of an initial 105,000 troops under Marshal d'Estrées, represented in part France's treaty obligation to come to the help of the Austrians. Much more interestingly, from the French point of view, it would bring considerable forces to bear against the Anglo-Hanoverian House of Hanover where it was most vulnerable, in the Electorate of Hanover. If Hanover came under French domination, it could be used as a bargaining counter against Britain, whose ascendancy at sea was more difficult to challenge. The Austrian foreign minister Kaunitz had tried to keep Hanover out of the war, along with the smaller north German states of Hesse-Kassel, Lippe-Bückeburg, Brunswick, and Saxe-Gotha-Altenburg, but the French demands on Hanover were pitched at such a high level that negotiations were broken off early in May 1757, and Hanover and its associates could now be regarded as being in the Prussian camp and legitimate targets.

In the middle of July d'Estrées led his army across the Weser at Höxter, and on the 26th at Hastenbeck he beat the Duke of Cumberland's 'Army of Observation,' composed of the Hanoverians and their German friends. Marshal Richelieu took over the command of the victorious French, and drove the Hanoverians so hard that they ran out of land, and, with his back to the estuary of the Elbe, Cumberland was forced to sign the treaty of Kloster-Zeven (10 September), whereby the Army of Observation was to be dissolved. Richelieu now appeared to be well placed to resume the eastward march and arrive on the central centre of war in the neighbourhood of the key Prussian fortress of Magdeburg on the middle Elbe.

The other French army, that of Marshal Soubise, was sent on the personal initiative of Louis XV, as an earnest token of his support for his ally Maria Theresa, who was in a bad way after her main army had been defeated outside Prague (6 May) and was blockaded in the city. This generally welcome news was debated in a conference in Vienna on 25 June. By then Austria's immediate crisis in Bohemia had been resolved when Field Marshal Daun beat Frederick at Kolin (18 June) and went on to relieve Prague. It was now a question of how Soubise could best contribute to operations of an offensive kind.

Vienna's first thought was to bring the forces of Soubise by a roundabout route via Würzburg and north-west Bohemia into Saxony, where they could join German auxiliaries and Austrian cavalry to form a respectable army of 50,000 troops. Such a force would inevitably have come under Austrian control. From the French point of view it would be much better to have Soubise and his troops operating on the north German plain, and acting with the *Reichsarmee* 'according to circumstances, whether in Thuringia, towards Leipzig or towards Dresden.'[1] This would secure the right flank of Richelieu, and reinforce the French presence in northern Germany. In theory at least the French would still be at liberty to advance against Magdeburg, which would keep the Austrians happy. The war minister Paulmy issued the necessary instructions on 25 July, and on 5 August news reached Vienna that the army of Soubise was to move not by way of Würzburg, which was on the way to Bohemia, but to make for Erfurt 150 kilometres to the north-east beyond the Thüringer Wald. Emperor Francis Stephen therefore ordered the Prince of Sachsen-Hildburghausen to move the *Reichsarmee* across the Thüringer Wald in time to reach Erfurt before the French, 'as is also demanded by Your Excellency's own prestige.'[2]

Through a final adjustment, two corps of German auxiliaries in the French pay, namely 6,000 Württembergers and 4,000 Bavarians, were reassigned in the middle of August from Hildburghausen's command to the main Austrian army, where we shall take up their harrowing story in due course. Hildburghausen was glad to be rid of them both, and especially the Württembergers, who were Protestants and a potentially unreliable element. The shortfall in Thuringia was to be made up by drawing a contingent under Lieutenant General Broglie from Richelieu's army in the north, which would build up Soubise to a strength of 48 battalions, 40 squadrons and 32 heavy field pieces, approximately 30,000 troops with an unquantifiable number of non-combatants on top.

To sum up, the main Austrian army had carried the war north from Bohemia, and was confronting Frederick at the gates of Silesia. To the west, two armies were seemingly making ready to advance towards the middle Elbe on two axes—on the left or north the victorious 'Hastenbeck' army under Richelieu, and on the right or south the combined army of the *Reichstruppen* and the French of Soubise. Vienna knew that Richelieu was an energetic individual, who was driven on by the desire to outdo Soubise, and it was hoped that the rivalry would produce happy results—a mild foretaste of the race between Zhukov and Konev to reach Berlin in 1945.

The coming-together of the allied forces in Thuringia was a long drawn-out process, but not devoid of episodes of bizarre interest. Marshal Soubise set out for his army on 26 July 1757. Four days later he was at Strasbourg, supervising the passage of his regiments across the Rhine, and their further march down the right bank. Soubise left Hanau on the Main on 16 August, and on the 20th he reached Eisenach, which had already been occupied by his leading infantry, the regiment of Piémont. Eisenach was a sizeable town of between 1,200 and 1,300 houses, and had played a key role in the German Reformation. The surrounding wall was a feeble medieval thing, and the high-perched Castle of Wartburg nearby commanded nothing in particular, but the 'situation of this town demands particular attention, being situated at the exit of the hills which continue all the way from Fulda, which have to be crossed in order to reach the Thuringian plain. It is of importance for both offensive and defensive purposes… during the short time he spent here Soubise reconnoitred the various positions which the army might have to take up, as dictated by circumstances.'[3] Eisenach became a nodal point for French communications with the Main and the Rhine in one direction, and Hesse in the other, and the military hospital which was established there soon had to accommodate the many soldiers who were out of condition and had been struck down by the heat in the course of the march from France.

Parties of French cavalry were already ranging ahead into the Duchy of Saxe-Gotha-Altenburg, which had supplied a battalion to the Hanoverians, and could therefore be treated as hostile territory and forced to yield up 'contributions' in cash and kind. On 21 August the Due de Crillon's six-horse carriage swept into the great courtyard of Schloss Friedenstein above Gotha town, escorted by fifty of the Volontiers Liègeois under Colonel Rougrave. These horsemen with their great bear-skin caps were marching with carbines balanced on their hips or drawn swords at the ready, and rode directly to the Schloss, where they posted themselves outside the Arsenal, to the great terror of all the townspeople.[4] In the palace chapel the congregation had just finishing singing '*Liebster Jesu wir sind hier'*. The sermon should have followed, but the good people brought the service to a hasty end by singing *'Gott sei uns gnädig und barmherzig!'* ('Be gracious and merciful to us, O God!'). It turned out that Crillon had come to pay his respects, and no harm was done.

Soubise arrived in Gotha at eleven in the morning of 22 August, and he was accompanied by his personal baggage, which in addition to the carts and the spare riding-horses, comprised twenty-two heavily laden mules, which were adorned with nodding plumes and coverlets embroidered

The March of the
Reichsarmee

with the Soubise coat of arms. This was to be the way of all the French generals, and 'people who saw this army, and knew how frugally the Prussian army was fitted out, and how the king himself lived in the field, were reminded of what the historians tell us about the contrasting styles of the armies of Alexander and Darius!'[5] The Duke of Gotha was allowed to retain his Palace Guards, and he held free table for Soubise and all the other French officers, with whom he was on excellent social terms, despite their political differences.

On 25 August Soubise and his heads of columns reached Erfurt, which was the appointed rendezvous with the *Reichsarmee*, but Hildburghausen and his Germans were still far distant on the far, or southern side of the massy woods of the Thüringer Wald.

The Austrian authorities knew from the outset that political considerations had spoken for mobilising the *Reichsarmee*, 'but we would be would be sadly mistaken if we allowed ourselves to think that we could rely on it in the slightest for direct military operations against Prussia.'[6] The *Reichsexecution* had been pronounced against Frederick on 17 January 1757, but with the best will in the world it would have taken many weeks for the states, statelets and Circles to gather in and organise their contingents, and to forward them to the assembly point, which was first designated as Kitzingen near Würzburg, then at Fürth just to the west of Nuremberg. Elector Max Joseph of Bavaria and the Protestant city of Nuremberg itself were not the most willing patrons of the *Reichsarmee*, and for a time they were even frightened into offering their neutrality to the Prussian lieutenant colonel Johann v. Mayr, whose raiding party of 1,400-odd troops had wrecked Austrian magazines in Bohemia, then turned west and was in the process of coursing through Franconia. The spirited Bishop of Würzburg took the lead in organising a response, and after an action at Vech (north of Fürth) on 9 July Mayr knew that it was time to end his successful spoiling operation and rejoin the king. Elsewhere in the Empire the marching troops were secure from armed disruption of this kind, but not from muddle, obstruction and ill-will.

Some of the experiences of the Upper Rhine contingent will serve to illustrate the whole. For the sake of appearances, the Nassau-Weilburg regiment had been placed at the head of the column as a tribute to the City of Frankfurt, from where seven of its companies had been drawn. The Prince of Stolberg had been hoping for a quick passage through the city, so that the march through the stifling streets could be completed before the day got too hot. He found the gates shut against him, and he was able to negotiate the transit only by allowing each of the battalions of the column to be escorted by detachments of the city militia. The troops emerged on the far side only in the middle of the afternoon. The city authorities were evidently content to have made life difficult for the contingent, and done all they could to encourage the troops to desert.

Nobody in particular was responsible for co-ordinating the marches of the *Reichstruppen* as they made for Fürth, and for a number of days in the middle of July the headquarters lost contact entirely with the further march of the Upper Rhine contingent up the Main: 'If the bringing-together of the *Reichsarmee* proceeds at this rate, it looks like the last column will be arriving on sledges.'[7] The regiment of Hesse-Darmstadt was the best of the *Reichsarmee*, yet the secretary of its Prince Georg was happy to record that by 29 July it had lost 'only' 116 men from desertion.

Hildburghausen had been sworn in as commander of the *Reichsarmee* by Francis Stephen in Vienna on 8 June. On the 28th he reached Nuremberg, and began to issue more specific orders for the gathering at Fürth nearby. The location was well chosen, for it stood at the convergence of a number of valleys which snaked up from the Main and the Danube, and it was screened to the north and north-east by the ridges of the Thüringer Wald and the Böhmerwald. On 9 July, however, everything was 'still in the direst confusion and disorder.' Individual officers and even small contingents were appearing without notice, and nothing had been heard of the Prince of Stolberg.' That is pretty typical,' reported Hildburghausen to the Emperor. 'It makes me shudder to think of what is involved in the command which has been entrusted to me.'[8] Hildburghausen concluded that there was no point in marching from Fürth until all the expected 24,000 troops

Schloss Friedenstein, Gotha.

had arrived and undergone a critical inspection. Even this measure was opposed by the Trier and Mainz contingents, for they suspected that the Austrian officials harboured 'secret aims that would tend to our prejudice.'[9]

By 11 July scarcely 3,000 men had arrived of 'our *Reichs-Executions* or rather *Reichs-Confusions Armee.*' Prince Georg's secretary Mollinger commented that it was worth paying for the entertainment that was on offer when the troops were at drill, for then they would step off with the right foot, make about turns to the left and right simultaneously, and contrive to face front in all directions.[10] The lack of numbers and training was not the worst of it. The men from Hildesheim arrived under a colour which bore the less than the ferocious motto: *'Da pacem Domine in diebus nostris' ('Lord, give us peace in our days!'),* and many of the rest muttered that they were serving in the wrong cause.

Most of the troops were assembled by the end of the month, though as late as 6 August so-called generals were still turning up with no accreditation from the *Reich* or Circles, but only the authority of their own sovereign. Prince Georg of Hesse-Darmstadt, who was truly indispensable, took the precaution of equipping himself with a new lieutenant general's patent with the date of the promotion left blank, so that he could fill it in as necessary and claim that he was senior to all the rest.

On 28 July the senior generals already present had submitted generally unfavourable reports on the state of proficiency and morale of their contingents. On 7 August Hildburghausen issued a *Disziplinärpatent für die Kaiserliche und des Heiligen Römischen Reichs Executions-Armee.* The thirty-seven articles forbade swearing, blaspheming, poaching and gambling, while they stressed the importance of paying the correct honours. Few of the provisions were obeyed, but they created at least the illusion that the *Reichsarmee* enjoyed a corporate existence.

Hildburghausen also set great store by the day of 11 August, for it marked the departure of the first significant element of the army for Thuringia. The troops in question numbered some 6,800 men under the command of Prince Georg. It had been intended to make a good start before the heat of the day, but Hildburghausen insisted that he must first see the troops on parade, which delayed the departure until eight in the morning. Prince Georg took up musket, knapsack and field kettle and marched on foot to show solidarity with his suffering troops, but by seven in the evening, when the column arrived at Möhrendorf north of Erlangen, thirty men had died of heat exhaustion, and 2,000 more were lying prostrated on the way. During the night the transport horses were scattered by a cloudburst.

Altogether three columns made their way up the narrow, tortuous paths of the Thüringer Wald. Prince Georg's command was designated the advance guard, and (after picking up a force of Würzburgers on the way) it made up a body of eleven battalions and five squadrons, with a total of 8,398 troops, of whom 6,256 could be considered serviceable. He took a route by way of Bamberg, Coburg, Eisfeld and Schleusingen, crossed the highest point of the ridge between Frauenwald and Ilmenau on 25 August, and reached his assigned destination at Arnstadt in Thuringia on the 26th. He had made all reasonable speed, which did not save him from being criticised by Hildburghausen for having galloped ahead, and then for slowing down to a tortoise pace.

The first division or line of the main army (ten battalions and eleven squadrons, or 8,607 troops) under the Landgraf of Fürstenberg set out from Fürth only on 24 August, with the ultimate destination of Erfurt. Fürstenberg followed in the tracks of the advance guard as far as Bamberg, then veered out to the west or left by way of Ebem and Trappstadt to Meiningen, where he arrived on 6 September. On the 8th the column was on its way between Schwarza and Mehlis, and was still short of the ridge of the Thüringer Wald, when it received the order to turn about, retrace its steps to Meiningen, and make its way to a new assembly point at Eisenach. The new route (screened almost all the way by the Thüringer Wald) took the division by way of Wasungen and Barchfeld to reach Eisenach on 15 September.

The corresponding second division or line (ten battalions and eleven squadrons under the Markgraf of Baden-Durlach) departed from Fürth on 26 August, made its way to Bamberg like

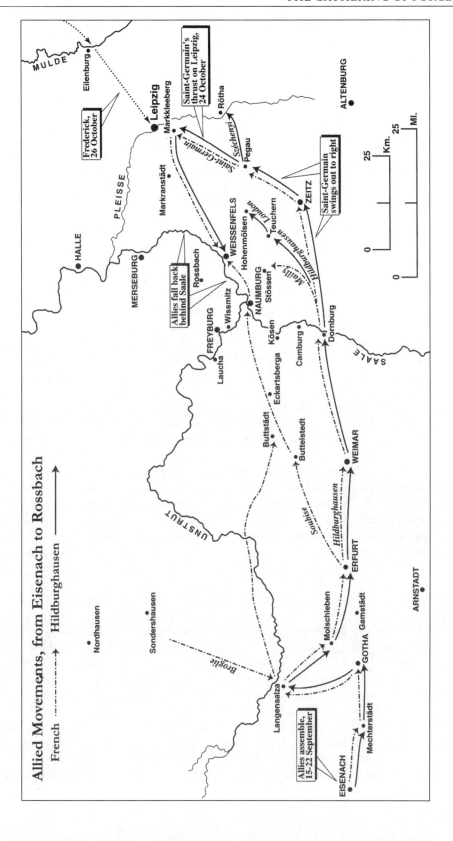

Allied Movements, from Eisenach to Rossbach

French ·······▷   Hildburghausen ——▷

Saint-Germain's thrust on Leipzig, 24 October

Frederick, 26 October

Saint-Germain swings out to right

Allies fall back behind Saale

Allies assemble, 15-22 September

the others, then swung to the right or east through Lichtenfels and Judenbach. It was overtaken by the order to change course on 8 September, when it was between Reichmannsdorf and Saalfeld. The column had to turn sharply left, cross the track of the advance guard at Eisfeld, continue by way of Themar to Meiningen, and follow the route of the first division to Eisenach, arriving there on 17 September. The advance guard under Prince Georg had meanwhile left its exposed position at Arnstadt on 10 September, and marched smartly west to reach Eisenach three days later.

The distance from the original assembly point at Eisenach to the newly-designated rendezvous at Erfurt was only thirty-five miles or fifty-five kilometres by the most direct route along the fringe of the Thuringian plain, but the change of destination had involved some very hard marching for the main columns of the *Reichsarmee,* which were halted in their tracks by the new orders, and had to make their way across the grain of the southern slopes of the Thüringer Wald, where the rain-sodden paths were very quickly ploughed up by the two-wheeled carts of the supply train. In effect the whole axis of the *Reichsarmee's* progress had switched westwards, and this was the result of the entirely unexpected appearance of Frederick of Prussia and his army in Thuringia.

The beginning of the campaign of Rossbach may be traced to 25 August, when Frederick first responded to the news that Soubise and a French army were on their way to the central theatre of operations. The tidings came at a singularly inconvenient juncture, when the king wished to have his hands free to beat or, at least pin down the powerful main force of the Austrians in the neighbourhood of Zittau, on the approaches to the province of Silesia.

On 24 August Frederick told the Duke of Bevern that he must take command of the 41,000 men who were to remain to fix the Austrians, and he himself would take off with all the disposable troops to have words with the French. Frederick departed on the 25th with eighteen battalions and twenty-three squadrons. He wrote afterwards that 'all the pillaging by those wretched troops [the French] did me no harm; the trouble was that they kept me busy while the real damage was being done by the Austrians.'[11] The king was careful not to betray his concern at this time. A spell of splendid weather helped to create the impression that everything was under control, and Frederick rode at the head of his Gardes du Corps, passing amiable remarks to whatever officer spurred up to join him.

On 29 August Frederick reached the Elbe at Dresden, and learned that the French had occupied Merseburg and Gotha, and that Loudon's light corps of Austrians was raiding in the neighbourhood of Leipzig. Frederick's own forces, including those who had joined him on the Elbe, now numbered about 25,000 men. He set out from Dresden with an advance guard on 20 August, trusting that the main army behind would be able to live on the eighteen days' rations which it carried in its bread bags and waggons. It was no longer possible to conceal how urgent matters were. He reached Tannenberg near Lommatsch on the 31st, Döbeln on 1 September, Colditz on the 2nd, and Grimma on the 3rd, and this cracking pace cost him 3,000 men through desertion over the last three of those days. The weather had broken, and the heavy rains continued well into September.

The first clash of the campaign occurred on 7 September. Frederick had just crossed the Pleisse above Leipzig and Rötha, while Seydlitz, pushing on to the Weisse Elster with the cavalry, encountered Loudon's two regiments of Austrian hussars (Splényi and Széchenyi) at Pegau. Seydlitz ignored the conventional wisdom that attacking towns was none of the business of cavalry, and he caught the Austrians off guard when they were still in the place. He ordered fifty of his Székely Hussars to dismount and break in the gate with baulks of timber, while the rest of the regiment waited on horseback out of musket shot. As soon as the door was beaten in, the hussars rode into the town at full gallop, and captured 106 of the Hungarians who failed to escape in time. The episode caught Frederick's imagination. He employed the same technique two months later, just before the battle of Leuthen, and he was still commending it to his generals in 1770.

The only immediate obstacle in front of Frederick was the river Saale, which he decided to cross at and near Naumburg. He arrived in the town on 10 September, wet and muddy from the unceasing rains, but he summoned up the patience to listen to the address of the town fathers who greeted him in the Rathaus. He replied with total hypocrisy that 'nothing can disturb the neighbourly friendship of the Saxons and Prussians. What Saxony owns Saxony will keep; and it will suffer nothing through the agency of my men, who are entirely different creatures from the French.'[12]

The action at Pegau was a small thing in itself, but the timing was crucial, for it was the first encounter of the campaign and it put the Prussians at a moral advantage. The allied commanders had assumed that Frederick was somewhere on the far side of Saxony, and they had no inkling of what was about to befall them when they met for the first time at Erfurt on 29 August. Hildburghausen had posted ahead of his columns, which were still struggling towards the Thüringer Wald, and he arrived at Erfurt uncertain whether Soubise would be willing to accept his directions, despite an agreement which had been made between the courts of Vienna and Versailles. He did not know the extent to which his authority had already been compromised by the underhand dealings of the foreign minister Kaunitz. Soubise greeted Hildburghausen in a polite but non-committal way, and he was encouraged in his attitude by a letter he had received from the Comte de Stainville, the French ambassador in Vienna, explaining that everyone there had been surprised that the *Reichsarmee* (in spite of all the delays) was still on the way to join the French, which would cause dire disorder in the matter of supplies. However Stainville had agreed with Kaunitz 'that Soubise should pile on the difficulties about the outstanding clauses of the convention [regulating the command], so that the issues would still be unresolved when the time came to march. This would justify the Emperor in ordering the *Reichsarmee* to stay behind.'[13]

In due course Soubise received instructions direct from France (from the war minister Paulmy, 30 August and 10 September) telling him that there could be no question of a combined army and a shared command. Soubise was to take orders from Hildburghausen when it was a question of joint operations, but he was to remain in direct command of the French, who were to operate as far as possible independently of the *Reichsarmee*.

More immediately both Soubise and Hildburghausen had to take stock of the reports which were arriving from Loudon from 30 August, to the effect that Frederick had arrived at Dresden with an initial 25,000 troops, and was set on continuing his march to the west. That was difficult to believe, but on 4 September the allies learned that Frederick was still on his way, and was picking up further troops in Saxony

If Frederick held on his course he would arrive shortly at Erfurt, the very place the allies had designated for their rendezvous. In fact only the leading elements were able to arrive in the neighbourhood—twenty-four battalions and eighteen squadrons of French, and Hesse-Darmstadt's force of 8,000-odd nearby at Arnstadt. All the rest of the French were strung out on the march from Fulda, while the main force of the *Reichsarmee* was still labouring towards the heights of the Thüringer Wald. Hildburghausen did not like the idea of beginning the campaign with a retreat, but Soubise, more realistically, was already casting about for a safer assembly area to the west. Lieutenant General Saint-Germain and the experienced staff officer Pierre Bourcet were dispatched 'without the knowledge of the officers of the staff'[14] to reconnoitre the surroundings of Gotha, which was nearly half-way along the road west to Eisenach. Gotha too turned out to be untenable, and Soubise was therefore advised to abandon the neighbourhood of Erfurt and fall back to Eisenach. From the tactical point of view the wooded and broken ground in this part of the world would offer the allies protection against the superior Prussian cavalry, which would have had the advantage in the open country around Erfurt. Operationally, the French could form up in security much closer to the base at Fulda, while the great bulk of the Thüringer Wald would now cover the whole extent of the *Reichsarmee's* line of communication from Fürth.

By Bourcet's account this proposal occasioned three days of debate between the allied commanders. However the issue was decided for them by the news of the clash at Pegau, which was less than four marches short of Erfurt. On 8 September the two main columns of the *Reichsarmee* received the order to make for the western end of the Thüringer Wald at Eisenach, and two days later Prince Georg of Hesse-Darmstadt extracted the advance guard from Arnstadt as part of a general retreat of the allied forces on the northern side of the ridge. Towards noon on the 10th Hildburghausen arrived at Gotha with his adjutants, who were totally disorientated. The Duke of Gotha offered him quarters in the rock castle of Tenneberg, but the prince continued to Walthershausen, evidently to avoid being cut off and captured. He was followed by Hesse-Darmstadt's command, which seems to have gone to pieces.

Hildburghausen reached Eisenach on 11 September. Soubise joined him there on the 12th, and the rest of the French from Gotha arrived in incessant rain in the course of the 13th. Only the light corps of Loudon and the hussar brigade of Széchenyi (regiments Splényi and Széchenyi) were left behind to screen the retreat and hold up the Prussians as best they could. Gotha awaited its liberation by Frederick, but was not yet entirely free of the allies. Loudon made a final sweep of the town with his Croats on the 14th, and sent one hundred of his men to Schloss Friedenstein to wreck the ducal Arsenal. They found that the establishment had already been smashed by the heroes of the Volontiers de Nassau, who had dismounted the cannon and broken the gun carriages. 'The duchess was overcome by one fainting fit after another, being convinced that the Croats were intent on plundering the palace. But this was doing them an injustice, for in general they are very well behaved, and their commander [Loudon] is a perfect gentleman.'[15]

From 2.15 in the afternoon of 15 September the Austrian brigade of Széchenyi came under pressure from Prussian hussars advancing from the direction of Erfurt. The skirmishing continued for half an hour, and ended when Széchenyi's people were driven over the Gallows Hill. Frederick watched the last stages in person, then turned into Gotha by way of the Erfurt Gate. His coming was unannounced, but doors and windows now sprang open, and enough people turned out to form a kind of alley for his progress all the way to Schloss Friedenstein, while his escort of the Meinicke Dragoons stationed themselves in the Market Place below. The troopers wore coats of blue, turned up with red, and both men and horses were impressively large and robust.

The king had not had a proper meal for four days, and he ate like a healthy man. Gotha could now take in its saviour, with 'that pair of fine, great, blue eyes, all shining with animation; the straight, narrow and well-formed nose; the full and friendly mouth, and the intelligence that it conveyed when he spoke, even if the two lines which marked his brow told of his concerns.'[16] Late in the afternoon Frederick returned to Gamstädt, and was content to sleep on a bench in an inn until his camp bed arrived. Lodgings of this kind were his favourite quarters, and it was recalled that when Soubise had first stayed in Gotha he had chosen to rest in Schloss Friedenstein, where his servants installed a double feather bed complete with a coverlet bearing the princely arms.

So far the Prussians had made an almost unresisted progress against the French and the *Reichstruppen*. Frederick's soldiers were confident that their master would lead them on to Alsace, and the king, as a master play-actor, did nothing to suggest the contrary. They did not know what the effort was costing him, for he had to steel himself against bad news that was now arriving almost every day. On 10 September he learned that the army of Field Marshal Lehwaldt had been defeated by the Russians at Gross-Jägersdorf (30 August), and that East Prussia was open to invasion. In the north of his kingdom the Swedes were across the Peene and into Prussian Pomerania.

Frederick in Thuringia was near the desirable western limit of his own operations, and on 14 September he found it prudent to make two substantial detachments—Prince Ferdinand of Brunswick taking off with six battalions and eleven squadrons, or about 4,000 men, to cover the area of Halberstadt against the army of Richelieu, and Prince Moritz of Anhalt-Dessau marching away with ten battalions and ten squadrons to secure the middle Elbe against the Austrians.

The king's force in Thuringia was therefore reduced to thirteen battalions and eleven squadrons, or about 11,000 men, which was far too few to be able to do anything of consequence against Soubise and Hildburghausen, who had slipped out of his reach, and were now, as he learned on 15 September, digging themselves in at Eisenach. Moreover disquieting rumours had been circulating for a number of days to the effect that his confidant Lieutenant General Winterfeldt, who had an important command under Bevern in Lusatia, had been beaten and possibly even killed by the Austrians at Moys on 7 September (p. 98). Frederick dispatched a letter to his friend, as if this would hold death at bay, but a matter of hours later he learned that Winterfeldt had indeed lost his life. The 18th brought irrefutable confirmation that the army of the Hanoverians and their German associates, his only continental friends, was to be dissolved in virtue of the Treaty of Kloster-Zeven (10 September), which liberated the army of Richelieu to act against the Prussians. It was fortunate that Frederick did not yet know that an Austrian raiding corps under Lieutenant General Hadik was making for Berlin (p. 102).

The columns of the main force of the *Reichsarmee* wound their way down to Eisenach between 15 and 17 September, and the last of the French were expected to arrive on the 22nd. 'And now,' reported Mollinger, 'all the allied forces are coming together. We, that is the Germans, have encamped on the far side of town facing Gotha. Our *bons amis* have their camp on the near side, and cover our backs in the direction of the Rhine. The town is in the middle, *comme de raison*. Redoubts and cannon have been planted on all the neighbouring hills… all these mighty preparations indicate that we are prepared to await the enemy attack with stout hearts.' Frederick must surely give way before the weight of the alliance, 'so all that is left to him now is to bow his head beneath the crucifix, and beg pardon for his sins.'[17]

The Contretemps at Gotha, 19 September 1757

When time was working for them, probably the best course of action for the allies at Eisenach would have been no action at all. The French troops were eager enough, but Soubise and his generals had 'too little confidence in the men of the *Reichsarmee* to wish to take our chances with them in any operations which called for mobility.'[18] Ever susceptible to the impressions of the moment, Hildburghausen was nevertheless fired up by a report from Colonel Széchenyi, who from his viewpoint at Mechterstädt reckoned that the Prussians had left all their infantry behind in Erfurt and that they had at the most only 4,000 of their cavalry in their forward position at Gotha. It was undeniably important to have further confirmation, and against his better judgement Soubise decided to support Hildburghausen in an undertaking that was a compromise between a coup de main and a reconnaissance in force. On the evening of 18 September the allied commanders led a body of French and *Reichstruppen* to a rendezvous at Mechterstädt, where they joined Loudon's advance corps—the two regiments of Austrian hussars, the Volontiers de Nassau and 1,500 Croats. The force now comprised 5,125 infantry (Croats and French grenadiers) and 4,794 horse, which made up just over 10,000 men including the gunners. The Prussians in and around Gotha numbered about 2,500 dragoons and hussars in twenty squadrons, which was even less than Széchenyi had calculated.

At six in the dark and foggy morning of 19 September the allies set out in two columns, headed by the hussars and the Croats. The commanders hoped to take the enemy by a pincer movement on both sides of the town, the main forces advancing to the right or south, while the combined cavalry and hussars swept around to the left. Seydlitz was too alert to be caught in this way, and at eight in the morning he extracted the Meinicke Dragoons from Gotha before they could be cut off. His hussars to the north were nevertheless taken by surprise, at least according to the French account, for in the murk they mistook the mass of the advancing enemy force for the routine probing by the Austrian hussars. The violent skirmishing on this side broke out at 9.30, and it continued until noon, when the Prussian hussars fell back on the Meinicke Regiment, after which the hussars and dragoons retreated together east to Tuttleben (the 'leben' in this and similar place names signifies a clearing in the former forest).

The Prussians had therefore evaded the blow, and their whereabouts were unknown, but the allies were in seemingly unchallenged possession of Gotha, where they began to take their ease. They left their security to Loudon's Croats, who were ensconced in the ducal Thiergarten, and the two regiments of Austrian hussars, which were posted out to the east at Siebleben. The heavy cavalry, however, made back to Eisenach, while the French grenadiers, having assembled to sounding music in the Market Place in Gotha, were left to consume the bread and beer provided by the town authorities, or disperse to the taverns. The Austrians brought in seven captured Prussian hussars, and towards noon thirty wounded Austrian hussars were assembled outside the inn *zur Schelle* (the House of the Little Bell). 'Some of them had had their noses cut from their faces, or their teeth from their jaws, which was a frightful sight.'[19] The officers gave a glass of wine to those who were capable of drinking. The princes and generals meanwhile repaired to Schloss Friedenstein at the invitation of the duke, and at 12.30 in the afternoon they sat down to await the meal that was being prepared for them. Hildburghausen left Gotha for Eisenach about an hour later, for he was dissatisfied with the way the operation had turned out.

Seydlitz was still making his way in the military world, and if the enemy had known him better they might have been alert to one skill in particular, which was to disengage his troopers from an action cleanly, reassemble them under cover, and bring them on again from an unexpected direction. On the present occasion he ordered up the Katte Dragoons from Gamstädt to join the Meinicke regiment on the highway at Tuttleben, then brought the two regiments north around the Lindwurmsberg, and reformed them at Friemar. At the same time he sent one of his dragoons to Gotha to play the part of a deserter, and announce that Frederick was on the way with his whole army. At the same time the Prussian hussars were on the move again from the east, as could be seen plainly from Schloss Friedenstein.

The allied generals bade a hasty farewell to the duke without having had a bite to eat, and ordered the drums to be beaten in the Market Place to rally the grenadiers. The troops, or at least those who heard the summons, were marched out of town to the west and were arrayed in battle order to the south of the Gallows Hill. Seydlitz accordingly brought the Meinicke and Katte regiments down from Friemar at 2.20, and deployed most of them in a single rank. 'The dragoons had neither infantry nor cannon with them, but Seydlitz took the precaution of dismounting half of the men, who were now to march on foot and spread themselves out. Seen from a distance it appeared that at least 6,000 men were on the advance, whereas they numbered scarcely 1,500.'[20] This show succeeded in fixing the greatly superior enemy infantry by the Gallows Hill.

The Prussian hussars were now pushing back the Croats and the Austrian hussars, and the crackling of skirmishing fire all around Gotha should have told the allied personnel still inside the town that it was high time to leave. They failed to respond, probably trusting in the fact that the east-facing Siebleben and Erfurt Gates were locked and barricaded. All of a sudden the Erfurt Gate burst open, and several hundred of the Prussian Székely Hussars galloped through the town to the Market Place, from where they went in search of prey. In the tavern *zur Schelle* their captives included Hildburghausen's adjutant-general Lieutenant Colonel Eisenberg, the Warzburg major Gutenberg, and a senior French commissary. 'The hussars brought them out... robbed them of their purses, watches, swords and effects, in fact everything they had, and then, ignoring their protests, conducted them on foot out by the Erfurt Gate.'[21] The hussars proceeded to hunt down officers, soldiers and other unfortunates in almost every street, and drag them along by the hair. The total haul came to about 190. 'And in addition there fell into the hands of the hussars a mass

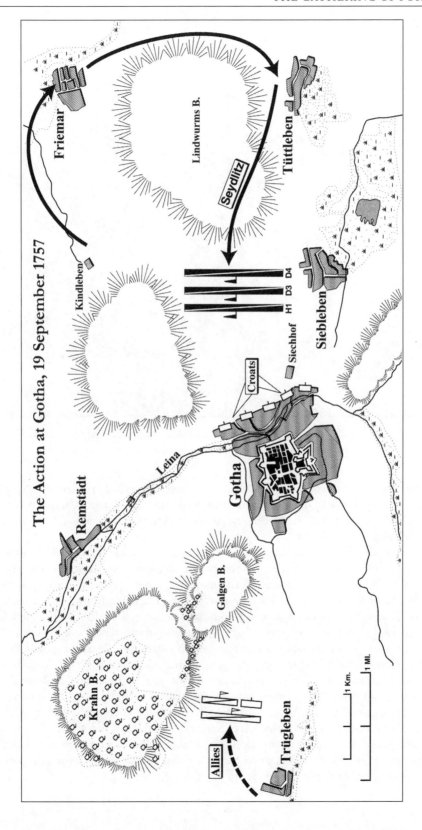

The Action at Gotha, 19 September 1757

Prussian hussars disporting in the baggage of the 'decadent' French at Gotha.

of secretaries, valets, commissary officers, chaplains, entertainers, lackeys, hairdressers, cooks, and purveyors of luxuries—not to mention the women of pleasure… as also a great quantity of dressing gowns, wig bags, parasols, lace, night-dresses, parrots and the like, which had been brought along to please the ladies of Gotha.'[22]

By four in the afternoon the rest of the allied force was streaming back to Mechterstädt, and at six Seydlitz and his victorious officers sat down to a fresh meal of up to twenty-four covers in the Friedenstein (where the cooks must have been among the busiest people in the campaign).

The estimates of the respective losses vary wildly. The Prussians admitted to thirteen prisoners and twenty-three killed or wounded, which sounds reasonable. The allies by the French account lost between twelve and fourteen men,[23] which is plainly much too low, and they claimed the operation as a success, for it enabled them to establish where the enemy were, namely Frederick in person at Gamstädt, and his infantry in camp at Bittersleben near Erfurt. Together with the relatively small complement of dragoons and hussars the whole was put at 17,000 men.

The events at Gotha on 19 September have a wider interest. On the tactical plane the assault by the Székely Hussars on the Erfurt Gate looks back to the action at Pegau twelve days before, while the way Seydlitz brought the two regiments of hussars around the Windswurm hill anticipates the sweep of his cavalry on a much larger scale at Rossbach. Well over a century later the description of the luxurious booty taken in the town came to stand in 'patriotic' German histories for the decadence of the French nation as a whole.

When the Cat's away... the Allied Advance to Leipzig

For the next few days Gotha stood in a kind of no-man's land in which neither party could feel secure—the Prussians because they could not afford to commit themselves in force so far to the west, and the allies on account of their ragged nerves. Seydlitz evacuated the place on 21 September, and the advanced troops of the allies were once more in possession, when, on the 25th, they were overtaken by a false alarm. They flooded out of the gates in panic, and the townspeople climbed to their roofs to see what was going on. 'Large pickets were on the march along the roads to Langensalza and Goldbach. There was marching and counter-marching on all sides. Officers were riding out on reconnaissance. On every hill there were men looking about them. Orderly officers and adjutants were galloping back and forth, and of the enemy, the Prussians, as far as the field of view allowed, and the eye could see—well, there was nothing.'[24]

On 27 September Frederick withdrew his army from Erfurt to a new camp north of Weimar at Buttelstedt. He had re-positioned himself one march nearer the Elbe, and by leaving the highway uncovered in this way he hoped that he might even now tempt the main force of the allies forward. He wrote to Maurice of Anhalt-Dessau: 'I am waiting here to see what is going to happen. I take Hilspershausen [i.e. Hildburghausen; Frederick was not good at spelling] to be a fool, and I hope he might come after me. In that case I'll draw you to me and go for this throat.'[25]

On 1 October the French advance guard duly occupied Erfurt, but the rest of the allied forces were content to settle down around Gotha. Hildburghausen accommodated himself in Schloss Friedenstein, where the staff were by now accustomed to providing for a rapid succession of grandees of the warring parties. Down in the town a tremendous brawl broke out in a beer house between French and German soldiers. The guard was called out to separate the combatants, but the French fought on, knocked down the duty captain, and made good their escape.

On 3 October Frederick withdrew his army from Buttelstedt a couple of hours' march further north-east to Buttstädt, and had still not entirely given up hopes of bringing on a decisive action in Thuringia. Back in Gotha the allies proceeded to commemorate the name-day of Emperor Francis Stephen. 'It was not indeed to celebrate the victories we have won—no, we are too modest for that—but to register our deepest pleasure at the fact that His Imperial Majesty is called "Francis." It was also important to make certain that the various states of the Empire did not get back all the gunpowder they had given their troops to take into the field... so it was that at six in the evening all the artillery and small arms of the two armies gave forth a triple salvo. Now that was thunder for you! It was such a pity that the King of Prussia, our hereditary enemy, was not around to hear it. He would have heard that we can shoot as well, admittedly not in such fine order as his own troops, but that we can fire nevertheless.'[26]

In the second week of October Soubise was able to persuade Hildburghausen that they must guarantee a safe reception for Lieutenant General Broglie, who was bringing a powerful reinforcement of twenty battalions and eighteen squadrons, or 12,000 troops, on a potentially dangerous trek from the army of Richelieu on the far side of the Harz Mountains. On 10 October the allies therefore extracted themselves from Gotha amid considerable and protracted commotion, and marched the twenty kilometres north-east to Langensalza.

The move to Langensalza was out of the usual east-west axis of operations, and Frederick drew the false conclusion that the allies were making for winter quarters and would be out of his reach for the foreseeable future. He believed that he had been hanging around too long already in this part of the world. Affairs elsewhere had deteriorated so badly that his Westphalian provinces, along with East Prussia, the duchy of Halberstadt and much of Pomerania and Silesia were now in enemy hands, and were now lost to him as sources of revenues and recruits. Berlin itself was now reported to be in danger from a substantial Austrian force advancing from Lusatia.

On 11 October Frederick accordingly terminated the initial phase of the campaign in Thuringia by making his first march from Buttstädt to the middle Elbe to confront the Austrians. On the 14th the reached Naumburg, and entrusted Field Marshal Keith with the command of seven battalions and six squadrons, with which he was to defend the line of the Saale if the allies showed signs of life and tried to force that river. Still making in the direction of Berlin, the king and his depleted forces reached Leipzig on 15 October, Eilenburg on the 17th, and Torgau on the Elbe on the next day. He learned from Prince Moritz of Anhalt-Dessau on the 18th that the Austrians corps was already in Berlin, but he was now spurred on by the ambition to cut it off before it could escape.

On the 19th Frederick left Torgau and prosecuted his march on the far side of the Elbe by way of Annaberg to Schweinitz. He was now among the forests of Brandenburg, but he stopped there, just over fifty miles short of Berlin, for he was informed that the Austrians had left the capital and were out of his reach on their way back to Lusatia. It now transpired that the enemy force had been no more than a lightly-equipped detachment under Lieutenant General Andreas Hadik, which had been launched from Marschall's corps in the neighbourhood of Bautzen (see p. 99 for the detail of Hadik's raid on Berlin). Frederick allowed his troops some rest on the Schwarze Elster after their forced march, and took up his quarters in the abandoned palace of Grochwitz, a residence of one of his particular enemies, Count Heinrich Brühl the prime minister of Saxony. We shall leave him there, taking stock of the magnificence of his surroundings, and return to the doings of the allies in Thuringia.

The 15th of October found the main forces of the French and the *Reichsarmee* still in Langensalza, and celebrating Maria Theresa's name day in the same style as they had marked that of Francis Stephen, 'and indeed it was only proper that our rusty and tarnished weapons should once again have the experience of being fired.'[27] Frederick was still drawing away in the direction of Berlin, and the confirmation of this 'retreat' had its predictable effect on Hildburghausen, who now urged a full-blooded pursuit. Hildburghausen had been disappointed in his hopes of acting in concert with the 6,000-strong Austrian corps of General Marschall, who was now immobilised beyond the Elbe at Bautzen, but he remained confident that the allies would be able to defeat the isolated Prussian detachments in Saxony one by one.

Soubise pleaded that the lack of provisions prevented him from moving, but, according to Hildburghausen, the reason why the French refused to march with him 'is exactly the opposite from what they claim. Now, if we have managed to provision the *Reichstruppen,* in spite of the dismal arrangements for their supply, how the hell can the French say they are short when they have double what they need? No, the root cause is something I have mentioned already, that everyone is in charge except the man who is supposed to be in charge, and those *Messieurs* are so fond of their billets and their comforts that they... have persuaded Soubise that they are utterly incapable of marching.'[28]

Hildburghausen therefore took off with the *Reichsarmee,* reaching Moschleben on 16 October, and Erfurt on the 17th. It struck Franz Rudolph Mollinger as curious that the Hesse-Darmstadt Regiment was now within less that four hours' march from Arnstadt, from where it had set out more than five weeks before, and he compared its progress since midsummer with that of a snake, or the wandering Israelites in the desert.[29]

Hildburghausen believed that if the French had now come up on his left flank, he could have anticipated Frederick beyond Leipzig at Eilenburg, and that Soubise with his existing fifty battalions and forty squadrons could have been able at the very least to prevent Ferdinand of Brunswick from joining his royal master. He wrote after the battle of Rossbach that 'instead of destroying the detachments of the King of Prussia, of beating them in detail, or at any rate of preventing them from joining up, we just put our hands in our pockets, we let them come together in a mass, and finally we let ourselves be routed.'[30] On October 17 Lieutenant General Broglie with the reinforcements from Richelieu arrived on the Thuringian theatre of operations, but the troops had suffered badly on their march through the snowy Harz Mountains, and they were so badly off for tents and even shoes that they did not become an effective part of the army until the end of the month.

On 19 October we witness what was to become a typical feature of this campaign, namely one of the commanders taking it into his head to march off with his contingent, leaving the other to trail reluctantly in his wake. In the absence of agreement between Soubise and Hildburghausen this was often the only way the allies ended up by doing anything at all. On this day the main force of the French finally left Langensalza, one of the columns marching down the left bank of the Unstrut, and the other down the right. The *Reichsarmee* was moving from Erfurt to Weimar, and so the general movement took the form of an advance on parallel axes, with the French to the left or north, and the Germans on the right.[31] However Broglie's footsore soldiers were unable to set out from Langenzsalza until the 23rd.

On 22 October the main force of the allies reached the line of the Saale, the *Reichsarmee* and the attached corps of Mailly (four battalions and eight squadrons) crossing to the right bank at Dornburg and Camburg, and Soubise making for Weissenfels. In the course of the following day the forward detachments closed in on Leipzig from the south: Saint-Germain with the advance guard proper penetrated to Pegau, Loudon to Hohenmölsen, Mailly to Stössen, Széchenyi with his hussars to Rötha. Lest this should be thought particularly bold it should be mentioned that the mobile forces by themselves probably enjoyed a decisive advantage in numbers against any one of the scattered formations of the Prussians—Frederick was still at distant Grochwitz with 9,000 men, Prince Moritz of Anhalt-Dessau at Baruth with 6,000, Ferdinand of Brunswick in the area of Magdeburg with 4,200, and Field Marshal Keith with just 4,600 at Naumburg and the other very exposed posts along the Saale.

Hildburghausen and *le brave et admirable Loudon* were concerting a plan whereby the advance detachments were to turn the left flank of Keith's troops along the Saale and block their retreat to Leipzig, which was a substantial walled town. Loudon believed that the Prussians could now have been mopped up 'with no great effort'[32] but the scheme fell apart when the advance guard under Saint-Germain, instead of keeping the Prussians in sight, swung well out to the right by way of Zeitz, Pegau and Markkleeberg and came at Leipzig from the south. Hildburghausen reported scathingly to Emperor Francis Stephen that on the day in question (24 October) Saint-Germain's (mainly Austrian) hussars had done nothing more than discharge their pistols and carbines at the garden walls of the suburbs from a range of three or four hundred paces, and that by leaving the western approaches uncovered they allowed the Prussians under Keith to disengage from the Saale and throw themselves into Leipzig. 'I can scarcely begin to describe to Your Majesty how much I am affected by all these upsets. On the one side critics say that I have any army of forty or fifty thousand men under my command, and expect me do what might be anticipated from such a powerful force; on the other side I have to work with people I cannot bring to execute what I know has to be done. That means that we lose one opportunity after another to attack the enemy in detail, and so doing something really effective.'

The first summons was made to Leipzig on 24 October, and a second on the next day, by when the city had been reinforced, and Keith was in a position to reply:

> 'The Prince of Hildburghausen knows that I am Scottish by birth, and a Prussian from incli
> nation and duty, and that I will defend the town in such a way that no Scot or Prussian will be
> ashamed of me. My master the king has ordered me to defend the place, and defend it I will.'[34]

III

To Rossbach

The Line of the Saale and the Action at Weissenfels

The sequence of events which led directly to the battle of Rossbach has its origins on 21 October, which was the day when Frederick received a report from Keith that the allies were advancing towards the Saale. It was just possible that the enemy might be bold enough to cross the river and continue their advance towards him, and so give him the chance to bring them to battle after all the frustrations of the last few weeks. He put off his planned march to Silesia, and ordered the scattered Prussian corps to concentrate. By the 24th it was clear that the allies were still on their way, and on that day Frederick made his first march to encounter them, reaching Torgau on the Elbe.

As late as the night of 25/26 October we find Hildburghausen still urging Soubise to come up on the left wing and fall on the corps of Ferdinand of Brunswick at Halle, or, if nothing else, to join the *Reichsarmee* in the attack on Leipzig. However the same argument that was being put forward by Hildburghausen—that the Prussian forces were about to unite—was the one which Soubise now advanced to justify his refusal. Frederick had meanwhile hastened ahead of his main force with an advance guard consisting of the mounted Garde du Corps, the Meinicke Dragoons, the infantry regiment of Itzenplitz and two battalions of grenadiers. He reached Eilenburg on 25 October, and on the next day he entered Leipzig. On encountering Keith he remarked: "Well now, has Prince Hildburghausen already gobbled you up?" "No Sire," answered the imperturbable Scot, "but he would have, if I didn't know what I was about."[1]

Frederick's brother Prince Henry reached Leipzig with the main body at noon on the 27th, and the corps of Ferdinand of Brunswick arrived a matter of hours later, having marched from Magdeburg by way of Dessau and Delitsch. Moritz of Anhalt-Dessau had meanwhile left Berlin on the 22nd, hurried through Mittenwalde, Baruth, Dahme, Torgau and Eilenburg and reached the rendezvous at Leipzig on the 28th. The concentration had been effected in five days, and brought together a force of 23-24,000 men, of whom 21,600 could be reckoned effectives, 'but what is the most surprising and pleasing at the same time is the spirit the soldiers showed on this occasion; they had marched upwards of twenty-five English miles a day for three or four days successively, and at the moment they arrived they desired to be led again against the enemy, expressing great dissatisfaction with the order they received to go into quarters, saying there was still day enough to go on…'[2]

The arrival of the Prussians precipitated days of turmoil among the allied high command. Mollinger records that 'every day I pass by the house where they are holding their councils of war, but I still cannot comprehend what we hoped to achieve by anything we have done so far, unless it is to waste the campaigning season, and wreck half the army by running it into the ground. If this is our aim, we have fulfilled it admirably'.[3]

Up to now, and in spite of all their disagreements, Hildburghausen and Soubise had shared the basic aim of liberating Saxony from the Prussians in the course of the present campaign. The war minister Paulmy endorsed this ambition in a letter to Soubise of 21 October, and commended Hildburghausen's idea of effecting a junction with the Austrian corps of Marschall.

Hildburghausen, after pulling the *Reichsarmee* to Teuchern, returned to his scheme with more enthusiasm than ever. He still suspected the motives of Soubise, but nothing prepared either commander for a total volte face in the policy of Versailles, which Paulmy disclosed to Soubise in a letter of the 23rd, namely that the French must now terminate their pursuit of the Prussians and consolidate on the line of the Saale.[4]

According to the Austrian minister Widmann, who was with Hildburghausen, 'the contents of this letter gradually became general knowledge, and gave rise to much speculation, and even to the suspicion that Prussia and France had made peace, or at least entered into negotiations and settled on an armistice.'[5] With hindsight we can see that the restraining order was probably the first indication that the French cabinet was abandoning its commitment to aid the Austrians in central Europe, and that it would now concentrate on its narrower interests in north Germany.

Soubise himself was taken aback, and in his reply of 29 October he admitted that he did not know how to break the news to Hildburghausen, for 'to re-cross the Saale, having advanced to Leipzig, and being superior in force to the King of Prussia, will inevitably be construed as a feeble and dishonourable retreat.'[6] On the same day the Prussians provided the excuse for which Soubise

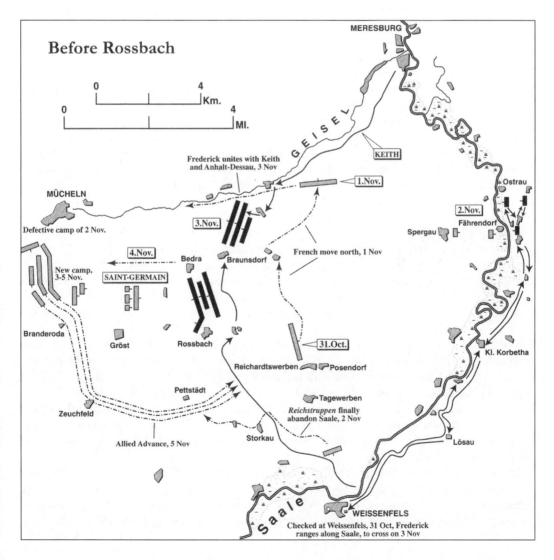

Before Rossbach

0 — 4 Km.
0 — 4 MI.

MERESBURG

GEISEL

Frederick unites with Keith and Anhalt-Dessau, 3 Nov

KEITH

1.Nov.

Ostrau

MÜCHELN

2.Nov.
Fährendorf

Defective camp of 2 Nov.

3.Nov.

Spergau

4.Nov.

Bedra   Braunsdorf

French move north, 1 Nov

New camp, 3-5 Nov

SAINT-GERMAIN

Branderoda

Kl. Korbetha

Gröst   Rossbach

31.Oct.

Reichardtswerben   Posendorf

Pettstädt

Tagewerben

Zeuchfeld

Reichstruppen finally abandon Saale, 2 Nov

Storkau

Lösau

Allied Advance, 5 Nov

Saale

WEISSENFELS

Checked at Weissenfels, 31 Oct, Frederick ranges along Saale, to cross on 3 Nov was searching. Colonel Széchenyi's command of two regiments of Austrian hussars and 1,000 heavy cavalry had been reposing comfortably in billets in Markranstädt and other villages to the south-west of Leipzig in the way that Hildburghausen deplored. They were therefore unable to offer much resistance when on the 29th a powerful body of Prussian horse debouched from the city and barged through their cantonments. Frederick so far kept his forces bottled up inside the walls of Leipzig, and the allies did not at first grasp that his united army was coming up behind the screen of cavalry. In the evening Soubise and Hildburghausen were in conference when reports came from all sides which put it beyond doubt that the Prussian army was in full march from Leipzig. Soubise was secretly delighted, for he now had all the justification he needed to insist that the allies must retreat to the left (west) bank of the Saale and put that river between the Prussians and themselves.[7] The French and the *Reichstruppen* were at once ordered to march for the Saale at Weissenfels, the Germans setting out at midnight on 29/30 October.

Hildburghausen's coach overtook the marching columns in the darkness, and deposited him at first light on the 30th outside the French headquarters in Weissenfels. Soubise and his staff were still asleep, though most of the French troops were drawn up in the market squares. Once Soubise had bestirred himself the commanders conferred briefly, and by eight in the morning all the French and German troops had passed the single congested bridge, apart from a rearguard which was left in the town on the right bank to guard the crossing (below).

On the left bank of the Saale, the army of Soubise, according to a standing agreement, took up position to the left of the *Reicharmee,* in this case downstream towards Merseburg, where Broglie now joined with twelve battalions of his badly-equipped infantry. Soubise took up his headquarters beside the Saale at Gross-Korbetha. The *Reichsarmee* was quartered to the right (south), and Hildburghausen planted himself at Burgwerben immediately below Weissenfels. Even now there was no effective concentration of forces. A substantial part of the *Reichsarmee* (the division under the Prince of Baden-Durlach) had been posted upstream since the 28th to guard the crossings at Naumburg, Kösen, Camburg and Dornburg, and the regiments of the main armies were billeted in the villages around their respective headquarters, 'which was contrary to the urgent desire of the prince [Hildburghausen], who knew how dangerous enemies the Prussians were, and wished to keep the regiments under canvas.'[8]

Most of the allied forward detachments managed to make their way behind the Saale, but Loudon was left stranded at Zwenkau, having received the order to retreat only at 3.30 on the afternoon of the 30th. He reached Pegau one-and-a-half hours later, only to find that Saint-Germain had already departed, and had left no indication as to where he was going. Loudon's patrols now informed him that the Prussians were already across the direct route to Weissenfels and Naumburg, and only through some swift marching by way of Zeitz was he able to rejoin the main forces on 2 November.

The hasty re-arrangements had a disastrous effect on the logistics of the *Reichsarmee.* To avoid overloading the bridge at Weissenfels, which was encumbered with the baggage of the French, the comparable train of the Germans (with all the tents) was directed upstream to Baden-Durlach's sector, and from there by routes which actually took it further and further from the troops it was supposed to be supporting. The able Austrian commissary Baron Grechtler was cut off and lost to sight when he was trying to arrange supplies from Zeitz, while an important convoy carrying bread from that place ran into the enemy on the 31st and was captured. The *Reichstruppen* would now have to go cold and hungry.

On the evening of 30 October Seydlitz reported to Frederick at Lützen not only that the allies were retreating over the bridge at Weissenfels to the far bank of the Saale, but also, and more encouragingly, that the crossing was unlikely to be completed before morning. Here was a chance for action. While Keith led his corps downstream against the bridge at Merseburg, Frederick set out at three in the morning of the 31st with fourteen battalions, thirty-five squadrons and eleven heavy pieces. The king's force made slow progress through the heavy rain, and threatened to stick fast at the crossing of the Rippach stream at Posterna. Frederick therefore left the main body under the charge of his brother Prince Henry, and he and Seydlitz took off in the direction of Weissenfels with a fast-moving force of two grenadier battalions, the Mayr free battalion, and all the dragoons and hussars. They were opposed only by the Austrian Széchenyi Hussars under their Colonel Anton Széchenyi, who by his own account, kept the advancing enemy under constant observation, and exchanged shots with them all the way to Weissenfels. However Soubise, Hildburghausen, Widmann and Brettlach senior all complained that no useful reports of any kind reached them from the hussars, and that the appearance of the Prussians at Weissenfels came as a complete surprise.

The fine wooden covered bridge spanning the Saale at Weissenfels had been built in 1733 after a much-admired prototype at Torgau. The French and the *Reichstruppen* now quartered on the far or western bank were dispersed among the villages over a distance of more than three hours' marching. The walled town on the eastern bank was overlooked by a fine ducal palace which now provided accommodation for fifteen companies of French grenadiers. The rest of the garrison consisted of the two battalions of the regiment of Pfalz-Zweibrücken and the two battalions of the Bavarian regiment of Holnstein, which together made up the brigade of General Rosenfeld. The 31st had been designated a rest day, so no particular vigilance was observed either by the Palatines (providing the central *Hauptwache)* or the Bavarians who were responsible for guarding the gates *(Torwache).*

Just one Bavarian lieutenant was on duty with the *Torwache* when, just before 7.30 in the morning of 31 October, the Austrian hussars were driven back on the town, and, moments later, the Prussian grenadiers and the ruffians of the Mayr free battalion burst in the gates and overcame the guards. The French grenadiers at once descended from the palace hill, pushed through the narrow streets and escaped across the bridge. The Germans, braver or slower-moving, formed up in the market square and tried to offer some resistance, but came under an intolerable fire of musketry and canister from higher ground.

The Austrian minister Baron Widmann had spent the night in the building which housed Hildburghausen's headquarters above the river at Burgwerben. 'All of a sudden a commotion broke out in headquarters towards eight in the morning... Not the slightest report had come from our hussars or outposts, but from my windows you could see plainly enough how the Prussians were marching up on the far side of the Saale, and taking possession of the heights which extended from opposite my room to the riding school at Weissenfels. They proceeded to bring up artillery to the high ground, and opened fire both against the town, and our troops who were gradually forming upon this side of the Saale. Very soon afterwards the sound of small arms fire... carried from Weissenfels.'[9]

Hildburghausen was writing a report when an officer crashed into his room to tell him what Widmann had seen, whereupon the prince pulled on his boots, called for his horse to be got ready, and repaired to Widmann's chamber, which filled rapidly with the officers of the staff. The sight of the Prussian artillery deploying and opening fire was a sign that something serious was afoot, and Hildburghausen and his officers dashed off, mounted horse and galloped for the bridge.

> I cannot begin to describe the confusion [wrote Hildburghausen] ... Hussars, baggage carts and French grenadiers were all mixed together, and when I tried to lead the grenadiers back to the bridge they merely replied 'We haven't any orders!' Through my eloquence and all kinds of devices I finally got four or five companies of them to go down with me... Just ask O'Flanagan [his aide-de-camp] what I had to do, not just to get them to march, but to make them listen to what I was telling them. At every wretched cannon shot they crouched down by entire companies... which meant that I had to go through the whole process twenty times over.[10]

The Ducal Palace at Weissenfels.

Hildburghausen planted some cannon in an enfilading position on the near side of the bridge, while his orderly officer Baron Mengen ransacked the locality for hay, candles and anything else that would burn, and had the mass piled on the bridge ready to set alight. Prince Georg of Hesse-Darmstadt had accompanied Hildburghausen to help in any way he could, and 'acted like an authentic Caesar,'[11] leading the French grenadier companies of Beauvoisis and Saint-Chamond across the bridge to cover the Bavarians and Palatines who were falling back from the town. The combined forces held back the enemy until Mengen was ready to fire his pyrotechnics, and they then retreated before they were caught in the conflagration. Prussian troops rushed forward under Frederick's eye to try to save the bridge, but they were all cut down by allied infantry firing from behind the cover of walls on the western side of the Saale. The bridge was in flames from end to end in less than five minutes, and Prince Henry, who was bringing up Frederick's main force, could see the great cloud of smoke and knew what it must betoken.

Frederick rode up to the Weissenfels Bakery *(Bäckerhaus)* and took in the sight of the bridge as it was being consumed (it was not rebuilt until 1780). The mounted figure was espied by two French officers who had been posted on an island by the Duc de Crillon, the nominal commander of the French grenadiers, to observe the bridge. They decided that the personage must be a senior officer, and presumably Frederick himself, to judge by the deference which was being shown to him, and one of the officers reported to Crillon (who was enjoying an al fresco breakfast) that it would be easy enough to pick him off from the island. 'Crillon knew that Brunet was a well-meaning man. He handed him a glass of wine, and sent him back to his post. He told him that he and his comrades had been placed there to see whether the bridge was burning properly, and not to kill a general who was on reconnaissance, let alone the person of a king, which must always be held sacred.'[12]

An artillery duel across the Saale prolonged the action until after three in the afternoon. Keith was having no better luck downstream at Merseburg, for Broglie had moved to secure the bridge with nine of his battalions, and he held the Prussians at bay with a cannonade until the structure burned down. The bridge at Halle was likewise put to the torch.

The allies had been caught very badly off guard at the opening of the action at Weissenfels, and the men who were captured in the town account for most of the 190 troops who were lost by the Bavarians and the 440 by the Palatines. The Prussian losses were low, but in all other respects Frederick had suffered a major check, and the allies had been granted a not entirely deserved respite.

'It is a miracle that this little affair did not lead to a rout,' exclaimed Hildburghausen, '...my skin crawls when I think how badly we would have been placed if the Prussians had passed the river.'[13] He put the blame on the French for having scattered the troops in billets, and on this point at least old Brettlach agreed with him.[14] Hildburghausen observed that the Germans in general had done better than their allies at the affair at the bridge, but now there was no end to the boasting of the French. 'Some of those impudent gentlemen not only demanded that I should testify to deeds they had never done, or even refused to do at my orders, but told me to write to our ambassador in Paris on their behalf.'[15]

Frederick awoke in the Schloss above Weissenfels on the morning of 1 November, and saw that the *Reichsarmee* was drawn up in battle array on the far side of the Saale. He withdrew his troops behind the crest on the near side, and so out of sight of the allies, and ordered Captain Gaudi to prepare to bridge the river at the seigneurial mill *(Herrenmühle)* at the Klingen suburb just below Weissenfels, where the work would be difficult to see from the enemy side. However Frederick had no news of the doings of Keith, he had no standing bridges available to him on his own stretch of the river, and he spent the night of 1 November at Dehlitz in a state of angry dissatisfaction. He did not suspect that the allies were about to give him a free passage of the river.

In retrospect the actions of the allied chiefs seem predictable. On 1 November Soubise shifted his army downstream to a new camp, which had its right leaning on the Saale, its left extending towards Runstädt, and its front protected by a marshy stream which entered the river below Merseburg. The position covered only the crossing from Merseburg, and not very effectively at that. The allied forces were now more scattered than ever, and for a time Hildburghausen lost all confidence in the passive strength of the Saale as a protection for the coming winter quarters. He therefore represented to Soubise that the allies must either bring on an action or retreat to somewhere altogether more secure. If it came to a battle 'we have to choose the best position we can and stand firm there, but above all we must leave the ways open to the enemy. Thus we would have all our forces together instead of scattered here and there by platoons. The enemy will see that we are not afraid to receive them, and we will not run the risk of being beaten in detail.'[16]

Soubise thereupon assembled five of his generals in a council of war. They decided to fall back from the Saale opposite Merseburg and take up a new camp at Mücheln, as a central position from which they could await any Prussian forces which came across the river.[17] This was exactly what Hildburghausen had wanted, but in a matter of hours he awakened to the implications of what he had done, for by abandoning the defence of the Saale and committing himself to join the French he would expose the *Reich* to invasion. To guard against that eventuality he had already left the division of Baden-Durlach on the upper Saale, and backed it up by the regiments of Nassau-Weilburg and Pfalz-Effern which he had dispatched to Freyburg on the lower Unstrut on the evening of 31 October. He was aware that he had thereby weakened the forces at his immediate command (which stood at only eleven battalions, nineteen squadrons and thirteen heavy pieces, making up just 10-11,000 troops even with the addition of the Austrian contingent and Loudon's roving force).

Another consequence was to separate the *Reichsarmee* from its supplies. The transport train with the tents and heavy cooking pots began to arrive from 3 November at Erfurt, and considerable magazines of fodder and flour had been built up both there and at Jena. Nobody bothered to tell the commissary officials where the army was now going, and so they had no idea as to where they ought to forward the tents and provisions.

In something like panic Hildburghausen wrote to Soubise at two in the morning of 2 November to tell him that the Prussians were preparing to throw a bridge of boats across the Saale from Weissenfels, and to beg him to send troops to help him to defend the river bank.[18] A little reflection told him that it was too late, and he ordered Prince Georg of Hesse-Darmstadt to lead the *Reichstruppen* from Weissenfels to the new French camp. They arrived there in a state of fair disorder in the course of the 2nd and 3rd. Brettlach senior remained in position with a small mixed rearguard until Georg was well on his way, then set off after him at noon on the 2nd. The Prussians were left in peace to build their bridges, and on 3 November they made unopposed crossings of the Saale at Weissenfels, Merseburg and Halle, on a total frontage of thirty-five kilometres.

Frederick and Prince Henry brought the main forces across the new bridge of boats from the Klingen suburb at Weissenfels, while the cavalry waded by means of a nearby ford. The passage began at four in the morning of 3 November, and was complete by two in the afternoon, upon which Frederick ordered the bridge to be broken up—not as a symbolic 'burning of boats,' but to prevent it being used by the enemy to come at his rear. Frederick now learned from Prince Moritz of Anhalt-Dessau that the allies were retreating under cover of a rearguard (Brettlach's force), whereupon the king directed the march towards Kayna. One of Henry's adjutants records that 'after just half an hour I caught sight of some tents. I tried to draw the attention of the others, but they could not make them out—either because their eyes were bad, or because they did not wish to see them. But after another half hour there was no mistaking the enemy camp, even if it occupied such a peculiar position that we could make out only a part of it.'[19] Frederick was in the lead with an escort of cavalry, and halted on the heights of Schortau. The Székely Hussars contrived to snatch some Frenchmen from their tents, and the king saw enough to convince him that the allies were facing north, and that if he came at them from the east he would be able to roll them up by their right flank.

The corps of Moritz meanwhile crossed at Merseburg, and was followed by that of Keith, and by seven in the morning the greater part of the Prussian army had assembled in a camp between Braunsdorf and Neumark. Prince Ferdinand's corps, coming from Halle, had much further to go, and was still on the march when night fell. Veering too far to the west, he ran into enemy troops at Crumpa, and was able to find his way to the camp only after exchanging fire with the main force. Frederick established his headquarters in the vicarage (Pfarrhaus) at Neumark, and there he briefed his generals on the attack he was going to carry out on the next morning.

The allied camp at Mücheln was deplorable in every way. The trees and fields of the neighbouring villages were strewn with feathers from the beds which had been ripped up by the French marauders, who also plundered the provisions so thoroughly that there was nothing left for the Reichstruppen, who had not eaten for four days. Hildburghausen explained to the Reichsvizecanzler Colloredo that from the technical aspect 'I have seen some bad camps in my life, but I swear to Your Excellency that I have never encountered anything as deplorable as this. All through the evening of the 2nd I raised loud protests and put up all sorts of objections, and all without effect. Then—would you believe it—on the next morning Soubise sent me a note in which he proposed moving the camp, as if the idea had just occurred to him, and I had never opened my mouth.'[20]

The French were even now disinclined to uproot themselves before the next day. Fortunately for the allies, Colonel Széchenyi was on his mettle after he had failed to give warning of the attack on Weissenfels on the 31st. Very early on the morning of 3 November he was careful to inform Soubise that spies had told him that the Prussians intended to attack in three columns, namely from Weissenfels, Merseburg and Halle, and that he had sent out three detachments to verify the reports.[21] It was scarcely light before the patrols were pushed in by columns advancing in just the way which had been foretold, and Szechenyi went at once to the headquarters of Soubise in Mücheln. 'When I arrived I found His Excellency [Soubise] at table with Prince Hildburghausen. "How are the enemy advancing?" Prince Hildburghausen at once enquired. "The enemy are coming in three columns," I answered. This was in an under-tone, so that the other people at table could not overhear. But at that moment an NCO from my outposts came in and announced that an enemy column was on the advance from Weissenfels, which confirmed the report I had made in the morning.' Further intelligence made it clear that this was one of the three columns with which the enemy intended to deliver their attack.[22]

This was the spur which finally persuaded the French that the allies must get on the move. The new alignment was generally agreed to be excellent. It faced east, and therefore confronted the most likely direction of the enemy attack. The ground on that side fell away in three hollows, separated by spurs, which would split up any Prussian advance in a useful way. The French, as always, took up station on the left, being technically 'auxiliary' troops, and their formation as a whole assumed the shape of a half-moon, with a gap left in the middle sufficient for twenty-six squadrons to counterattack through it. Their left wing adjoined Mücheln, and was covered by a valley and a pond. Two battalions of Swiss occupied an earthwork on the French right, while the Austrian cuirassiers and the cavalry of the Reichsarmee maintained the connection with the main force of the Reichsarmee on the allied right. This wing too was anchored securely, for the Hakenholz and Taubenholz woods to the front and east of Branderoda were furnished with abattis, and garrisoned with the regiments of Blue Würzburg, Kur-Trier, Hesse-Darmstadt and (less impressively) the infantry of the Franconian Circle. The Saale in that direction was too far away to offer any cover, but the ground between the river and allied right flank was a mass of little woods and hills and was considered impassable to the enemy.

One providential but unintended result of the sluggishness of the French was that the march from the old camp to the new was accomplished during the night, long after Frederick had returned from his reconnaissance. 'All the units and officers familiarised themselves with their positions. We wanted the Prussians to come, and Soubise was determined either to await them there, or go over to the attack as circumstances indicated.'[23]

On the night of 3 November the French huddled around their fires, while a large number of the *Reichstruppen* were set to work to build the redoubts on the right wing. At midnight exactly a number of Prussian detachments (quite possibly Prince Ferdinand's command) probed towards the allied left, and opened up with artillery against the camp fires, 'without doing any real damage, even if the French showed considerable annoyance and unease.'[24] Hildburghausen adds that the entire personnel of his own headquarters took to their heels, leaving him without secretaries, pen or paper. To Pastor Schieritz at Neumarkt it seemed that the Prussians were signalling the junction of their three columns, and the shots sounded so loud 'that we all staggered about the room, not knowing what was happening to us. Then we heard the challenge of the sentries coming from the Prussian camp: *"Wer da ?!"* A ghastly sound.'[25]

The firing had died away by the time Frederick rose at two in the morning of 4 November. The night was unseasonably warm, and the landscape was illuminated by a three-quarter moon which seemed to favour the enterprise still further. 'At daybreak on this 4 November the Prussians at once set themselves in march against the French, intoning the morning hymn "Awake my Heart and Sing!" [*Wach auf mein Herz und singe*], giving special emphasis to the last three verses. Then we heard them take up "In Thee have I hoped, O Lord!" [*In Dich hab' ich gehofft, Herr!*]. This carried far and wide through the air to God, and was most moving to hear.' The regiments halted to receive a short address from their chaplains, and set themselves in march again to the accompaniment of another hymn.[26]

The Confrontation of 4 November

Towards six in the morning the Austrian hussars and Croats stationed in front of Gröst reported that the whole Prussian army was approaching along the road from Merseburg. At eight o'clock the allies saw Frederick and an officer of cuirassiers (Seydlitz) appear on the crest of the Schortau Heights. Only now did the king discover that the allies had changed position overnight, and that instead of arriving at an uncovered flank, he was confronted with field fortifications, bristling abattis, and the right wing of a fully-prepared enemy army. Frederick rode off to his right, but what he saw from there merely confirmed that the French and the Germans were present in greatly superior force, and that they were ready to meet him.

On their side the French had 'resolved that we would let the Prussians approach to within a certain distance, and then move against them. Our motives were partly to take advantage of the more favourable ground which lay three or four hundred paces ahead, and partly because this advance would be compatible with the spirit and desires of our nation. This movement was executed with a vigour and exactitude which moved all those who witnessed it. Never have our men been more eager to close with the enemy.'[27] The centre of the infantry had been reinforced by seven large columns, with bodies of dragoons at the tail of each column, and four small cavalry columns on the wings of the first and second lines of infantry. The columns were not full-blown attacking formations in the style of Folard, but this interesting arrangement shows that the French were anticipating the celebrated *ordre mixte* which Broglie was going to employ at Bergen on 13 April 1759.

Between nine and ten in the morning the Prussians began to disengage from the confrontation by making a series of left about-turns. The infantry moved first, and negotiated the narrow passage across the water meadows to take up a new camp between the villages of Rossbach and Bedra. The cavalry remained on the Schortau Heights until Franz Johann Brettlach came on against it with the entire horse of the allied right wing. Six heavy French cannon were sent to join Brettlach on the heights, and he advanced them to a suitable battery site under the escort of six squadrons of cavalry and six hundred or so infantry. Brettlach opened a cannonade, while the allied main army gave itself up to celebrations. By Frederick's account 'their full complement of musicians, trumpeters, drummers and fifers resounded as if they had won a victory. It was not particularly pleasant for men like us, who had never turned our backs on the enemy, but as things were all we could do was to match the high spirits of the flighty French with a display of German composure.'[28] The Prussian cavalry fell back under Brettlach's fire to form a third line behind their infantry, having lost by Bourcet's calculation just ten horses.[29]

Loudon was one of the few allied senior officers who preserved a sense of proportion, and concluded rightly that the king had just been making a reconnaissance. After the allies fell back to camp, the two princes and the generals dined in the open air next to the line of the Brettlach Cuirassiers. There was much debate, and Hildburghausen rejected altogether a probably over-ambitious plan from Loudon to come at the enemy overnight and attack from the two flanks the next morning. 'The Prince told me [Loudon] that the French did not like marching in the night time, and I believe that was the reason why my proposal was not taken up.'[30] Sensible old Brettlach argued that time was on the side of the allies, and that they could not do better than wait in their present position, but 'by the end of the dinner the princes had still arrived at no decision, for they kept changing their minds from one moment to the next.'[31] Brettlach is a reliable witness, and his statement corresponds with the complaint from the *Reichsarmee* by Ludwig Egon Fürstenberg that 'the battle was undertaken without consultation.'[32]

As things stood late on 4 November we can therefore talk about predispositions rather than resolutions. Hildburghausen knew that the starving and shelterless *Reichsarmee* was near its end as a fighting force, but he was a man who was as easily elevated as cast down, and by temperament he would respond to any display of apparent weakness on the part of the enemy. He was going to be primarily responsible for launching the allies into an outflanking move on 5th November, and then converting it into the headlong dash which precipitated the battle.

Afterwards it was natural for the French to distance themselves from the ultimate decision to fight. This did not necessarily correspond with their mood on the evening of the 4th, after Frederick had backed away from the confrontation, and when, according to Mollinger, the French were 'absolutely full of themselves, and even proposed to attack the enemy alone, and without the help of the *Reichsarmee*.'[33] Both Saint-Germain and the Comte de Revel (younger brother of the Duc de Broglie) were counted among the bellicose party, and they made their feelings known at some decisive moments on the 5th. The Saxon representatives too were pressing for positive action, as the only means of liberating their land before the end of the year.

Soubise himself was confident that the French had established a moral preponderance—a supe-riority which corresponded with the already-evident advantage of the allies in numbers. As far as the balance can be reconstructed now, it stood as follows:

French:
48 battalions; 40 squadrons of horse (34 of cavalry, 4 of dragoons and the 2 squadrons of the Volontiers de Nassau); 32 heavy pieces. About 30,000 men.

Reichsarmee:
11 battalions; 39-42 squadrons; 2 carabinier companies; 13 heavy pieces. Total 11,464 at full establishment, but more probably no more than 9,900.

Austrians:
2 regiments of cuirassiers (3 squadrons each); 1 regiment of hussars; Loudon's corps of 3 battalions of Croats and 3-400 hussars. Total very approximately 3,850.

Allied Grand Total: Very approximately 44,750.[34]

These figures are subject to a wide margin of error, but even the lowest possible estimate would give allies a comfortable numerical advantage over their enemy.

Prussians:
27 battalions, 45 squadrons, 18 heavy pieces, with 16,200 infantry, 5,400 cavalry and 400 gunners.

Prussian Grand Total: 22,000.

Well-informed men throughout Europe had long been aware of the disparity in numbers. To Count Henri de Callenberg in Brussels it seemed scandalous that Hildburghausen and Soubise had done so little with the forces at their disposal, 'and we shall know in a few days whether these gentlemen have it in them to direct a battle, now that they are within reach of the enemy and are under an obligation to fight.'[35] At this point Callenberg had to put down his pen, for news had come that the princes had been overtaken by some kind of catastrophe.

IV

The Battle of Rossbach

The Ground

On a single point the allied commanders were agreed, that if they were to go for the enemy it could not be directly from the west, for the Prussians were looking in that direction, and on that side they were protected by the marshy meadows of the Leiha stream, which wound lazily through Rossbach, Leiha village, Schortau and Bedra. Behind this rivulet the Prussian camp was situated along the line of villages, just where the ground began to rise to form a low and open ridge, which extended for some five kilometres to the east, and reached its highest points at the gentle eminences of the Janus Hill and the Pölzen Hill (for the sake of clarity we shall call these heights the 'northern ridge'). Frederick had probably registered the tactical potentials of these features as a matter of routine.

If the allies were to move at all, it would be almost inevitably by their right. Less than an hour's normal marching to the south would bring the heads of columns to where the paths forked at the village of Zeuchfeld. If the commanders just intended to cover their line of communications, they could halt there and so protect the path which led south-west under the wooded hills to the Unstrut at Freyburg. If, however, the generals were bent on mischief, they could direct their forces further to the right and along the axis of a curving track which led to the summit of a further ridge, which was marginally higher than the northern ridge, and followed the same west-east alignment. A march in this direction would take the army past the left or southern flank of the Prussian camp, and clear of the obstacle of the Leiha stream, and so open the possibility of doing interesting things in the enemy rear. Between the two ridges extended a plain some three kilometres in width. The ground was open and cultivated, and devoid of obvious features except a pair of villages (Tagewerben and Reichardtswerben) to the east. They were poorish affairs of thatched houses, and offered no defensive potential.

Nowhere on the field was there anything which could be considered an obstacle, apart from the Leiha stream and a deeply-cut stretch of the road which led from Reichardtswerben north to the Janus Hill. Conversely a great deal was going to depend on the screening effect of the otherwise remarkable ups and downs. From the highest point of the southern ridge, near the Luftschiff ('Airship') Inn above Pettstädt, an observer had an excellent prospect over the Leiha stream and its villages, and on a clear day could make out Merseburg and even distant Halle. However the ground behind the northern ridge was out of view, and as the observer descended towards the plain still more of the landscape (such as the low-lying surroundings of Tagewerben) escaped from sight. Infantry would be at a relative disadvantage in such terrain, for the artillery could be positioned on a number of excellent battery sites, while cavalry could assemble behind the cover of the low hills and gentle declivities, and launch surprise attacks in great force across the open ground.

The Allied Flanking Move

Some time early on 5 November Hildburghausen persuaded Soubise that the allies must bring forward the turning movement, which the Frenchman had by no means rejected in principle, but which, as he had just written to Versailles, was originally intended to be launched on the 6th. The detachments of Saint-Germain and Loudon, which had functioned as roving advance guards earlier in the campaign, now took up assigned positions, Saint-Germain with his eight battalions and twelve squadrons on the heights of Schortau, and Loudon with his three battalions of Croats and his hussars on the rounded Gallows Hill *(Galgen-Berg)* to the south. Their immediate task was clear—to command the attention of the Prussians and fix them in position.

Even as daylight came on this dull, overcast day it was not evident to the troops in the main allied armies what the commanders had in mind. At eight the units were summoned by the thundering of the *Générale* in the French camp and the *Generalmarsch in* the comfortless bivouacs of the *Reichsarmee*. The sound was calculated to stir the blood, but instead of getting his regiments on the move as formed bodies, Soubise decided that it would be a good idea for the officers of his general staff to reconnoitre the approaches to the enemy camp, and meanwhile allow large numbers of his troops to go out foraging. Not surprisingly the men concluded that the allies were about to retreat.[1]

Towards nine in the morning it appeared that the enemy might even snatch the initiative, for Seydlitz marched towards the positions of Saint-Germain and Loudon with Mayr's free battalion and the combined Prussian hussars, making a reconnaissance in force 'in the same manner as on the day before.'[2]

Saint-Germain opened a cannonade and Loudon advanced his Croats, whereupon the Prussians fell back with speed, but not before they had put Hildburghausen in a state of great alarm for his communications. The best counter-move appeared to him to be to shift the army smartly to secure the approaches to Freyburg, and place the army in a position to threaten the Prussian left flank.

View from the 'southern ridge' north-northeast over Pettstädt to Rossbach.

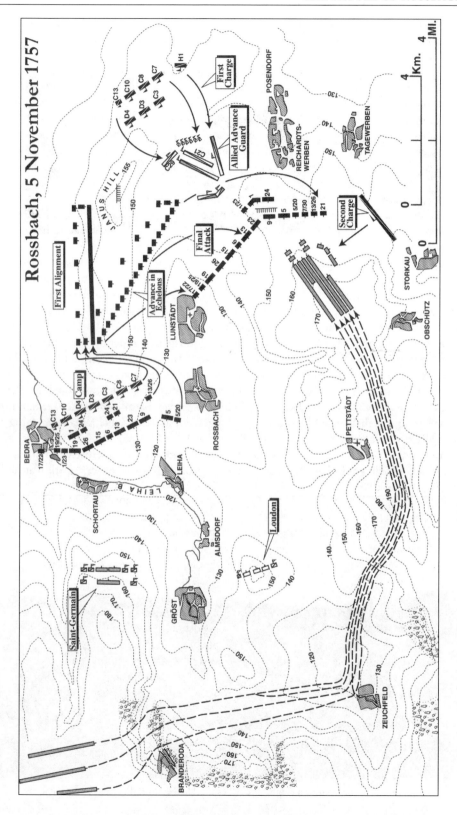

Rossbach, 5 November 1757

'Hildburghausen assembled a council of war at the head of the army. The gathering found his proposal admirable, and nobody imagined that the march would bring on a battle in the course of the same day.'[3]

However a more aggressive tone was sounded in a note which Hildburghausen sent to Soubise shortly before or afterwards. 'I believe that we must waste no time in taking the initiative, and going out to attack the enemy. They will not come at us, as we saw very clearly yesterday, but there is good reason to fear that they intend to sever our communications with Freyburg, and so cut us off from our supplies. I am of the opinion that we must be the first to get on the march, and gain the heights at Schevenrode so as to attack from that side. The warning order must therefore be sent to the regiments, and the foragers recalled without delay.'[4] It is doubtful whether Soubise grasped the full import of the message, or whether he or anybody else assumed that they were committing themselves to anything more than an outflanking manoeuvre.

The allies lurched out of camp in a process which extended from ten in the morning to one in the afternoon. The Austrian cuirassiers, the cavalry of the *Reichsarmee* and the right wing of the French horse set out ahead. The German infantry should have followed next, according to the established order of precedence, but they still had to be extracted from the abattis and redoubts which covered the camp. For that reason they waited for the French to trail past them, and finally took up station at the rear of the army. According to the Austrian Colonel Széchenyi the allied infantry as a whole was marching in column by platoon frontages, and the cavalry by column of squadrons, but in the event the proper intervals were lost very soon.

Hildburghausen claims that 'so it was we advanced in the best order by two columns, the first line forming the first, and the second the other column.'[5] The good order did not last for long. The French reserve corps under Broglie (eight battalions and ten squadrons) surged ahead and inserted itself between the train of heavy artillery and the column of the second line, though for that there might have been a good reason (below p. 75). When the eleven battalions of the German infantry came up they found their way blocked by the congestion around Zeuchfeld, and swung to the right to avoid the village.

The original two columns of the allies therefore contrived to divide themselves first into three, then into four, which would have been acclaimed as a brilliant piece of staff work if it had been

Panorama of the 'southern ridge.' The Allies marched from right to left as we see it.

part of the original design. In the present circumstances it resulted in the army being packed together in multiple columns on a frontage of only some 400 metres, namely (from left to right):

First Line—Broglie's corps
Second Line—Infantry of the *Reichsarmee*

The confusion was augmented when a large number of the French horsemen returned from their foraging expeditions, and now had to be re-inserted in their parent regiments. It was in any case a bad idea to have assigned the heavy artillery to a route between the two original columns, for the guns would have to barge through the column of the first line before they could get into action. By the Prussian practice the heavy guns would have been marching on the side nearest the enemy, which in the present case would have been to the left of the column of the first line, from where they would have had a clear field of fire from the outset. All the time the screening force of cavalry drew gradually ahead of the main force of the army. The two Austrian cuirassier regiments of Brettlach and Trautmannsdorff headed the column until late in the morning, when the Széchenyi hussars took the lead.[6]

Now that the whole army was in motion, the two senior commanders found that they could not agree on what to do next. Once substantial forces had reached the neighbourhood of Zeuchfeld, Hildburghausen could be confident that he had eliminated the perceived threat to the line of communication from Freyburg, and he returned to the notion of turning the flank of the Prussians and attacking them, or as Bourcet put it, not altogether accurately,

'it was during the march, towards one o'clock, that Prince Hildburghausen had the bad idea of attacking the enemy without delay.'[7]

Hildburghausen at that time was up with the advance guard, and Soubise further back and probably on or near the Stein-Berg — a low hill just beyond Zeuchfeld which commanded a view of the Prussian camp, the villages along the Leiha stream, and the forward slope of the northern

Branderoda and the allied camp lay beyond the wooded heights on the far right.

ridge. Soubise was inclined to think that the army had done enough, or nearly enough for that day, and the Comte de Mailly (commander of the left wing of the French cavalry) urged that the allies should continue their progress only as far as the nearest village (probably Pettstädt), consolidate there, and postpone any further action until the next morning. 'This proposal received almost unanimous support.[8] Soubise accordingly sent ahead one of his most experienced staff officers, Pierre Bourcet, to find Hildburghausen and present four objections to prolonging the march further to the east:

1. Frederick would thereby have the opportunity to occupy the former camp of the allies at Mücheln,
2. From Mücheln the king would be well placed to pounce on Freyburg, and thereby cut the allies' only path of retreat,
3. The allies would then find themselves jammed in the angle between the Unstrut and the Saale, with no bridges available to them to cross either of these rivers,
4. It was already past two in the afternoon, and almost two hours more would be needed to reach the point of Hildburghausen's intended attack.

In the view of Soubise the best course would therefore be to anchor the joint army with its left flank on the wooded hills towards Freyburg, and its right on an inn (almost certainly the Luftschiff above Pettstädt) from where the allies could cannonade the open flank of the Prussian camp on the following day.[9]

Hildburghausen would have none of it, and told Bourcet to inform Soubise that the march must go on. 'Hildburghausen was blind in his over-confidence... the leading troops were in pursuit of the Prussian rearguard, and he believed that they could not go fast enough. That is why he did not bother to observe the proper intervals between the lines, and why he neglected the precautions he would certainly have taken if he knew that he was so near the enemy.'[10]

Soubise responded by convening one of his notorious 'synagogues.' The Marquis de Custine had been one of the officers who were sent by Soubise to reconnoitre the intended encampment, and when he returned he was astonished to find that the army had come to a halt and that the generals were engaged in discussion. Soubise himself noted that the debate was conducted on horseback, and that no less than fifty officers were within earshot. By now Prussian cavalry could be seen trailing away from the enemy camp. 'At that moment Prince Hildburghausen came up in a state of great excitement, and asked what had been decided. Prince Soubise told him, which displeased him mightily. He rejoined in an insulting tone: "That's just like you French, isn't it? When the enemy advance you go back, and when we ought to attack you stick fast." Immediately afterwards the Comte de Revel returned from a reconnaissance, when he had seen the Prussian cavalry in apparently full retreat. He spoke out in favour of the pursuit, and 'the Duc de Broglie, who has a soft spot for his brother, supported his proposal to attack without loss of time.'[11]

Prince Georg of Hesse-Darmstadt, as a veteran of the Prussian service, warned that the enemy would fight hard, and all the more so because they were commanded by the king in person. 'But Prince Hildburghausen, with rather more fanaticism than suited a commanding general, drew his sword, stretched out his army and shouted: "'I'll show you how to beat the Prussians!"'[12]

The First Prussian Response

From the tall manor house *(Herrenhaus)* on the southern edge of Rossbach village it was possible to see the steepish slopes of the southern ridge between Zeuchfeld and the Luftschiff inn. Frederick's young *Flügeladjutant*, Captain Gaudi, was stationed in the attic, and had removed a number of

The village of Rossbach.

bricks or tiles to give himself a better view, and by two in the afternoon he had seen enough of the enemy movements to convince him that the enemy were bent on turning the Prussian left flank. He reported as much to the king, who was lunching with Prince Henry, Seydlitz and a number of senior officers in a chamber below. If there was anything Frederick disliked more than having his monologues interrupted, it was signs of panic in a junior officer. With an ill grace he climbed to the attic, surveyed the ridge through a telescope, and told Gaudi very firmly that he had been mistaken. Not long afterwards Lieutenant Colonel Mayr made a report to the same effect, and was sent away with a flea in his ear.

The Prussian camp had been put on no particular state of alert, and following the routine inspections in the morning the officers settled down to enjoy a leisurely meal. In one of the tents in the second line Prince Henry's adjutant announced to his friends that goose was on the menu. Major Friedrich Wilhelm v. Kleist (later the celebrated Major General 'Green' Kleist) had no intention of missing the treat, but as a precaution he had a hole cut in the wall of the tent so that he could keep an eye on the doings of the allies. 'Having taken this precaution we awaited the roast goose, but at the third appetizer Kleist cast his napkin away, and threw himself into the saddle with the comment: "Now things are getting serious!" That was the cue for us to do the same.'[13]

Before long many of the troops could see the enemy movements for themselves. Seydlitz was still incarcerated at lunch with the king, but he contrived to get some messages to the cavalry to get ready to leave, and the sight of the horsemen saddling up was enough to persuade the artillerymen to limber up their pieces. Major Biedersee, the commander of the mounted

The Herrenhaus at Rossbach.

Feldwache, saw that the allied columns needed only to wheel into line in order to be able to roll up the Prussian army from its left, and he sent the impressively tall Lieutenant Viereck of the Gensd'armes to carry the message to Frederick. According to one account the young officer's arrival prompted Seydlitz to stand up, go to the attic to take in the view, and stride off without making his apologies to the king.[14]

Whether Seydlitz departed in such a dramatic way is unlikely. He must at least have stayed long enough to learn from Frederick (persuaded at last that the Prussians were under threat) that he was now in charge of the entire Prussian cavalry, and that he must swing it far enough to the left to head off the allied horse, and throw himself on the enemy columns before they had time to form into line. Seydlitz galloped away, summoned the senior officers of the cavalry, and although he was the most junior of the generals he had the royal authority to announce: 'Gentlemen, I obey the king, and you will obey me!'

In effect Seydlitz was leading a countermove of the entire Prussian army, save the light command of Lieutenant Colonel Mayr (the Mayr free battalion, together with five squadrons of the Székely Hussars and another seven of the Seydlitz Hussars), which was to remain in position at Schortau to observe the combined corps of Saint-Germain and Loudon on the hill opposite. If the Prussians could march quickly enough, they would be able to make up for the time that Frederick had lost at his over-long lunch in the *Herrenhaus*. More crucial still was the element of surprise, as represented by the dead ground behind the long northern ridge, which could permit the Prussians to form unseen at right-angles to the advance of the allied columns, so enabling Frederick to 'cross the enemy T,' by analogy with naval warfare.

Seydlitz signals the charge at Rossbach.

The first task of the massed thirty-eight squadrons of the Prussian cavalry was to move smartly over the nearly five-and-a-half kilometres which separated them from the slopes behind the Janus and Pölzen hills of the northern ridge. The march was headed by the remaining five squadrons of the Székely Hussars [H1], which were probably under orders to prevent the allied horse from gaining the crest. The main force of the Prussian cavalry followed, and during the march it was re-made by Seydlitz from three ranks into two, so as to form a wider frontage when the squadrons wheeled from column into line. There were fifteen squadrons in the first line (from right to left the Czettritz and Meinicke Dragoons and the Leib Cuirassiers [D4, D3, C3]), and eighteen in the more widely-spaced second line (the Gardes du Corps, the Gensd'armes, the Rochow and Driesen Cuirassiers [C13, C10, C8, C7]), with the Székely Hussars extending the line to the left. Seydlitz himself took station on the crest, smoking a long-stemmed Dutch pipe, but a commotion drew him back down the slope to where a captain of the Leib Cuirassiers was unable to control his horse and was throwing his troopers into confusion. Seydlitz exploded in wrath: 'Why don't you bugger off!'

Colonel Moller had brought up a powerful contingent of heavy artillery (twelve 12-pounders, four short 24-pounders, and two howitzers) immediately behind the cavalry, and was about to position these pieces across the Janus Hill. The infantry had set off to the left by two columns of platoons, and re-formed into to south-facing lines, with the left flank on the Janus Hill, and the right on a rough alignment with Lunstädt, which was out of sight on the far side of the ridge. The entire leftward shift of the Prussian army had begun at about 2.30 in the afternoon, and was accomplished an hour later.

The Cavalry Combat

The last we had seen of the allied army was when its leaders had gathered in their chaotic council of war near Pettsädt, and when Hildburghausen had overruled all protests and resumed the onward march. Colonel Anton Széchenyi had been designated to lead with his regiment of hussars, as had been noted. He records that 'we made a brief halt, so I took the opportunity to go to the princes Hildburghausen and Soubise and report for further orders. Prince Hildburghausen merely replied: "I have more important things to think about than the hussars. Just get on with the march!"'[15]

For a little way Széchenyi was accompanied by the Volontaires de Nassau, until those exotic gentlemen were ordered to stay behind to guard the left flank of the main columns. The Széchenyi Hussars [H32] now inclined towards the northern ridge, drawing further and further ahead of the two Austrian cuirassier regiments of Brettlach and Trautmannsdorff [C29, C21]. These regiments led respectively the columns of the first and second lines of the right wing of the *Reich* cavalry:

- the Brettlach regiment being followed by the Palatinate (Kurpfalz) Cuirassiers (three squadrons), the Swabian Hohenzollern Cuirassiers (four squadrons), and the Swabian Württemberg Dragoons, and
- the Trautmannsdorff regiment heading the Franconian Cuirassiers (four-and-a-half squadrons) and the Franconian Dragoons (another four-and-a-half squadrons).

As the unsupported Austrian hussars drew nearer the northern ridge, Colonel Széchenyi espied what he took to be six squadrons of Prussian hussars (actually the five squadrons of the Székely regiment) standing on the crest, whereupon the enemy fell back out of sight, leaving only a few troopers within view. Széchenyi continued on his way with his 300-odd hussars, and passed by the left flank of the Prussian camp. It was only a distance of two cannon shot away, but all the tents were still standing and there was no sign of any response.

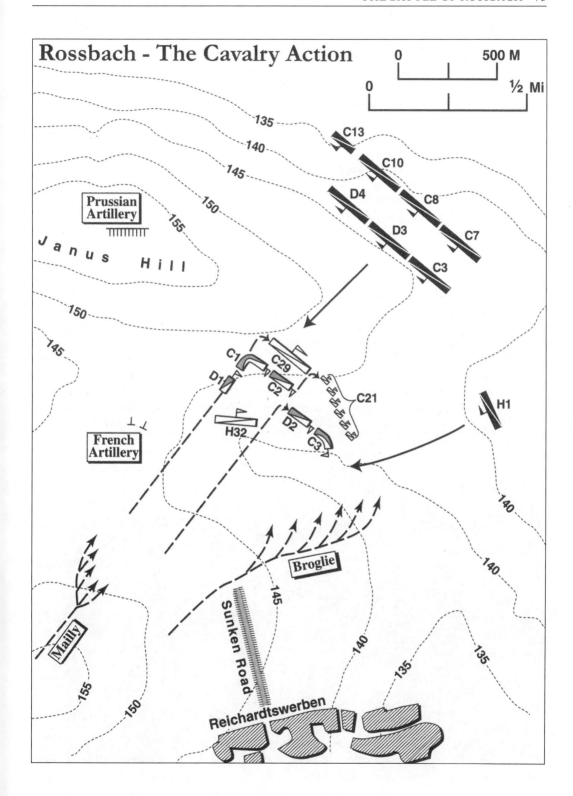

Rossbach - The Cavalry Action

0   500 M

0   ½ Mi

135

140

145

C13

C10

150

D4

C8

155

Prussian
Artillery

C7

J a n u s   H i l l

D3

C3

150

145

C1

C29

D1

C2

C21

French
Artillery

H32

D2

C3

H1

Broglie

140

145

140

Mailly

Sunken Road

140

135

135

155

150

Reichardtswerben

To observers in the main allied army the lack of enemy reaction had seemed no less strange, for the only activity which had been detected so far had been that of the Prussian cavalry, whose initial movement had been a tight left turn out of its encampment, after which it had disappeared in the direction of Merseburg. 'But in less than two minutes all the tents lay collapsed on the ground, as someone had pulled a cord to bring off a theatrical effect, and their whole army was in full march. This sudden transformation made us believe that they were afraid of us, and intended to retire to Merseburg. Cries of victorious jubilation began to be heard, and our courage redoubled in keeping with our pace.'[16]

Captain Zarnoczay (a Hungarian in the Dutch army, now serving as a volunteer with the Austrians) rode ahead of the Széchenyi regiment and discovered that the enemy were moving in force against the allied right wing. Colonel Széchenyi at once sent his colonel commandant Baron Stephen v. Vecsey to investigate. Vecsey verified the report, whereupon Széchenyi sent Zarnocsay off at a gallop to carry the vital news to Hildburghausen, who was riding with the Austrian cuirassiers. 'The prince just answered: "How can that possibly be?"… then, after a moments thought, he told the captain: "You hussars are useless! A waste of the rations the Empress gives you!"'[17]

The first enemy force to show itself above the skyline was the Prussian heavy artillery. Allowing for the standard two-pace interval between his guns and howitzers, and the three paces occupied by the pieces themselves, Colonel Moller must have spread his ordnance across about 250 metres of the 'Prussian' ridge. The allied columns appeared like a black cloud when they descended from the further ridge, but Moller reserved his fire until the hats of the enemy horsemen could be seen bobbing up and down. The Prussian artillery opened the battle at 3.15 in the afternoon, and to Pastor Schieritz in Neumarkt it seemed 'like the end of the universe. The ground trembled under our feet, and the worst thunderstorm was nothing in comparison.'[18]

Hildburghausen and Soubise evidently took the outburst of fire as cover for the Prussian retreat, and for a few minutes the allied cavalry continued on its way amid the howling roundshot and

View from the road between Reichardtswerben and Lunsttädt, looking northeast towards the 'northern ridge' and the face of the advancing Prussian infantry.

crashing shell. There was a pause in the cannonade at 3.30, and then, according to Széchenyi, 'the enemy cavalry came trotting over the hill, closed up so tightly that there was no interval between the squadrons.'[19]

Soubise grasped at once that the Prussians were committing the whole of their cavalry on this sector, and also that Hildburghausen was making not the slightest arrangement to meet them, for the two regiments of Austrian cuirassiers continued to march in column. Soubise at once sent word to Lieutenant General the Duc de Broglie to bring up the ten squadrons of the cavalry of the French reserve (the two-squadron regiments of Penthièvre, Saluces, Lameth, Lusignan and Escars).

It would still have been too late, if Colonel Vecsey, having failed to impress his warning (above) on the high command, had not encountered Broglie, and urged him to throw two battalions of his infantry into a 'nearby village' (Reichardtswerben) as an anchor for his cavalry, which must cover the right flank of the Austrians along the line of the sunken road which led to the north. Thus Broglie got his forces on the move even before the order came from Soubise, and 'we had just enough time to put ourselves in battle order, so as to close up the intervals and deny the plain from the right flank of the Austrians as far as the village of Reichardtswerben. We had scarcely formed up before a wall of Prussian cavalry attacked with incredible speed.'[20]

This sequence of events is contradicted only by the unconvincing justifications which Hildburghausen later proffered to Vienna. By Hildburghausen's account Soubise had told him that he had been up with the hussars, and seen them skirmishing with a few of their Prussian counterparts, but otherwise he had detected 'neither hide nor hair' of the enemy.[21] Firm arrangements were supposed to have been made on the 4th for both the cavalry and infantry of the reserve under Broglie to be stationed on the right of the Austrians, but on the day of battle Hildburghausen sent his adjutant O'Flanagan no less than four times to ask for Broglie's cavalry to be brought up, and on every occasion without success. Hildburghausen ascribed Broglie's recalcitrance to an episode in a campaign in Italy, when 'I surprised his father on the Secchia river [night of the 14/15

The Janus Hill (now dug out) rose to the right of the picture.

September 1734], and forced him to flee from bed in his night shirt.'²² If Broglie had been where he was supposed to be, the allies would have overcome the unsupported first line of Prussian cavalry, and unfailingly won the battle.

In the moments before the impact Major General Ludwig Carl Brettlach had just time to wheel his regiment into line and swing to the right to face the attack, though the Trautmannsdorff regiment [C21] was caught before it could complete the manoeuvre, and had to fight in an improvised array of staggered columns. Frederick was watching from his viewpoint close to a gigantic old elm tree at Lunstädt, and long afterwards he asked the Prince de Ligne if he could identify the Austrian officer who had acted as an inspired madman at the outset of the combat. It turned out to be the Marquis August Voghera, colonel commandant of the Brettlach Cuirassiers [C29]. He got ahead of his troopers, selected a regiment of enemy horse as his target, and saluted its commander as if on parade. The Prussian returned the compliment, whereupon they set to like berserkers. 'I like the man's style,' exclaimed Frederick. 'I'd like to meet him, I'd shake him by the hand.'²³

Hildburghausen had been riding on the left flank of the Brettlach regiment, and I witnessed something I had never seen in my life before—two bodies of cavalry fighting it out head-to-head for an extended period of time.'²⁴

While the Austrian cuirassiers got to work, Hildburghausen ordered the two columns of the *Reich* cavalry into the battle, which necessitated a wheel to the right by their successive squadrons. The Palatinate Cuirassiers [C2] began the manoeuvre of the intended first line, followed by the Hohenzollern Cuirassiers and the Württemberg Dragoons [Cl, D1]. The Bayreuth Cuirassiers [C3] under Colonel Gladis led the Ansbach Dragoons [D2] in the attempt to form a matching second line.

More and more troopers were being fed into the scene of the mounted combat. The first clash had been staged about 300 metres to the south of the Janus Hill, but the Austrian cuirassiers lived up fully to their nick-name of 'the Smashers' *(Schmeisser),* and pushed the first line of the Prussian horse to within thirty paces of the summit, to judge by the mass graves which were discovered in that location in the 1840s. The evidence of a French sword blade that was found at the same time indicates that Broglie had not been content to extend the French cavalry reserve in the direction of Reichardtswerben, but had joined in the counterattack directly.

On the Prussian side the brunt of the action had been borne by the first line of cavalry (the Czettritz and Meinicke Dragoons and the Leib Cuirassiers [D4, D3, C3]) and the Székely Hussars. They got the worst of the encounter until the eighteen squadrons of the second line breasted the ridge and intervened in the fight. The cavalry of the *Reichsarmee* was still trying to shake itself from column into line, but lacked the necessary training, cohesion and space to complete the evolution before the Prussians were upon them.

The Prussian Székely Hussars were responsible for most of the damage, when they cut in behind the Austrian cuirassiers and rolled up the German cavalry from the right. Two of the cuirassier regiments (Hohenzollern and Bayreuth [Cl, C3]) collapsed, leaving the Palatinate regiment [C2] to fight on, together with the Württemberg and Ansbach Dragoons [D1, D2]. The Austrian Széchenyi Hussars [H32] were in support, but through a tragic accident the hussars mistook the blue-coated Württemberg regiment for their identically-uniformed Prussian counterparts, and hewed into their formation, capturing a standard.

Further out on the allied right Broglie's cavalry seems to have been most immediately engaged against Seydlitz's second line, where the cuirassier regiments of Rochow and Driesen had been recruited from Pomeranians [C8, C7]. Tempelhof records that 'they were calling out to each other in good Low German, *Bröderken gah to!!* ['Lads, go to it!']. This, the French assumed, must have been a reference to a cavalry regiment with the curious name of 'The Cakes.'²⁵

The allied senior officers found themselves caught up in the thick of the mêlée. Major General Brettlach, Colonel Voghera and the Marquis de Castries all sustained wounds, while Brigadier de Saluces was overpowered and captured in a hand-to-hand combat with Count Friedrich v. Schwerin, the commander of the Prussian Gensd'armes. One of Schwerin's troopers nearly managed to capture Soubise himself, but the great man escaped with a cut in the ear. 'It is remarkable that the prince did not appear in the battle in uniform, but concealed himself in a grey coat, so that he might be mistaken for one of the mob of the servants who accompanied the French army.'[26] Hildburghausen lost contact with Soubise and Brettlach and all but one of his adjutants. Perhaps it was then that a Prussian hussar dealt him a bruising blow across the shoulders with the flat of his sabre.

In the turmoil Soubise managed to send an order to Lieutenant General the Comte de Mailly to bring up the remaining French cavalry, that of the left wing. The idea was good, but by the time Mailly came up on the left rear of the cavalry battle the issue had already been decided—Major General Ludwig Carl Brettlach attributed the final blow to 'an enemy dragoon regiment [probably Meinicke] which had concealed itself in a village [Reichardtswerben] on the enemy left wing, and which cut into us from the rear and forced us to give way.'[27]

Mailly in person rode ahead in an attempt to rally the collapsing *Reich* cavalry. He was unable to make his way through the fugitives, and he returned to his command, hoping now that his force could take the pursuing Prussian cavalry in flank, 'but the rout was so speedy that the intermingled enemy and friendly cavalry swept like a whirlwind around the left flank of these two brigades, leaving them behind on the field of battle, where the Comte de Mailly stood isolated at their head under the fire of thirty-three [sic] pieces of cannon… and yet these two brigades (made up of the regiments of Bourbon, Beauvoisis, Fitz-James and Rougrave) stood manfully in their position, with not a trooper leaving his rank.' Such was the example of 'a leader who is courageous, experienced, and knows how to keep his head in the most trying conditions.'[28]

A knot of one hundred shaken cavalry under Brettlach rallied on the French brigades, and the sight of a line of horse approaching at a trot aroused hopes that further allied cavalry might be retrieved from the battle. Mailly ventured out to investigate, and barely escaped with his life when it transpired that the strangers were the Prussian Gensd'armes. The French got the better of the first tussle, at least by Mailly's account, but the fight had carried them further and further from the main force, and a renewed Prussian attack caught the two brigades when they were partly in line and partly in column. 'In the course of this mêlée the Comte de Mailly took a sword thrust on his cuirass which forced him back in his saddle. He drew himself upright, but received a further thrust in the head which threw him to the ground. He lay there unconscious until two enemy officers grabbed his arms, raised him up and made him prisoner.'[29] Seydlitz disengaged his triumphant cavalry, and began to reassemble it where the ground fell away gently towards Tagewerben.

The Infantry Combat

The twenty-four battalions (15,000 men) of the Prussian infantry were meanwhile marching half-left over the northern ridge, and becoming more and more teased out in the process. Frederick had entrusted almost all his cavalry to Seydlitz, which left the thirteen battalions of the right wing potentially vulnerable to the Franco-Austrian corps of Saint-Germain and Loudon, now standing on the heights of Schortau. It was probably for that reason that Frederick ordered Prince Ferdinand of Brunswick to hold that wing clear of the battle on the plain, and in the event his long line executed a massive right wheel, with the Kremzow Grenadiers on the far right pivoting on Lunstädt and Nahlendorf, and the regiment of Forcade at the other extremity striving to keep contact with the fast-stepping left wing.

The king had assigned the left wing under Prince Henry with a much more active role, which was to exploit the victory of Seydlitz by presenting itself in line at right angles to the heads of the columns of the allied infantry. The first line was not long enough by itself to prolong the array in front of Reichardtswerben, and so Frederick ordered up a first instalment of four battalions of the second line to extend the array to the left (grenadier battalions of Jung-Billerbeck, Lubath and Finck; first battalion of Hülsen). This was still not enough, and Frederick accordingly sent Field Marshal Keith with the five or six battalions of the depleted second line marching straight for Reichardtswerben. The Prussian array was therefore reduced to a single line, of which only about 4,200 troops were going to be in close contact with the enemy, and it was fortunate that Colonel Moller had brought his heavy battery down from the Janus Hill to lend some badly-needed fire-power. Prince Henry now executed a one-eighth wheel to the right in front of the village, producing a pronounced kink in the line where his wing met the right wing under Ferdinand of Brunswick.

Three columns of French infantry were approaching in a closely-packed sandwich no more than three hundred metres across. The left-hand and right-hand columns (i.e. the undeployed first and second lines) were headed respectively by the powerful four-battalion regiments of Piémont and Mailly [1, 3]. Between these two columns Broglie inserted the eight battalions of his reserve corps, led by the two-battalion strong regiment of Poitou [2].

By Hildburghausen's testimony 'during the whole time of the cavalry skirmish (sic) my good friend Soubise did not have the sense to get his infantry to deploy and form; in fact he did nothing at all.' Now that the Prussian infantry was so near Hildburghausen consented to the plea of the colonel of Piémont to be allowed to attack with the bayonet.[30] The French were advancing in column only through force of circumstances,[31] though observers drew the mistaken conclusion that it was a deliberate attack à la Folard.

With extraordinary composure the Piémont regiment continued marching on a frontage of five files and without firing a shot until it reached a distance described variously as between fifty and twenty paces of the enemy. Frederick had been so absorbed in his calculations that he was caught between the Prussian line and the French columns, and a voice from the regiment of Alt-Braunschweig [5] had to call out: 'Father, get out of the way! We want to shoot!' At this range the closing troops would have been able to distinguish not only their opponents' faces but their very expressions before the sight was extinguished in fire and smoke. It was four in the afternoon, and the location was the field called Fürstermarker some three hundred metres to the north-west of Reichardtswerben.

Under the murderous volley a grenadier company of Piémont fell almost to a man, with disastrous effects on the morale of the left-hand column. Mailly's column on the right was being shot up by the extremity of the Prussian infantry line which was swinging like a door against it, and further threatened by the mass of Prussian cavalry lurking near Tagewerben. All three columns were being furrowed from end to end by the murderous enfilade of Moller's battery, and ranks were being snatched away by the remainder of the Prussian heavy artillery, which was firing from in front of Lunstädt. 'If Chevalier Folard had known how it would turn out, he would has cursed his sacred columns.'[32]

The allied artillery was unable to offer an effective reply. Before the allies' thirty or so heavy cannon could get into action they first had to be dragged through the left-hand column and clear of the infantry. On the far side they were scattered in seven batteries, and 'the lie of the ground was such that it was possible to make out only the tops of the wheels of the Prussian gun carriages … the French artillery in particular did its utmost, though with indifferent results, for it was firing at extreme elevation in an attempt to reach the enemy on the high ground, and many of the shots went… astray.'[33]

Hildburghausen relates that he ordered another regiment (probably Saint-Chamond) to support Piémont, but it advanced no more than ten paces. He then pleaded with a regiment of French horse to throw itself into the enemy flank, and he trotted ahead of it for a short distance before he found that an unknown French officer had ordered it back, and that he was facing the enemy alone.[34]

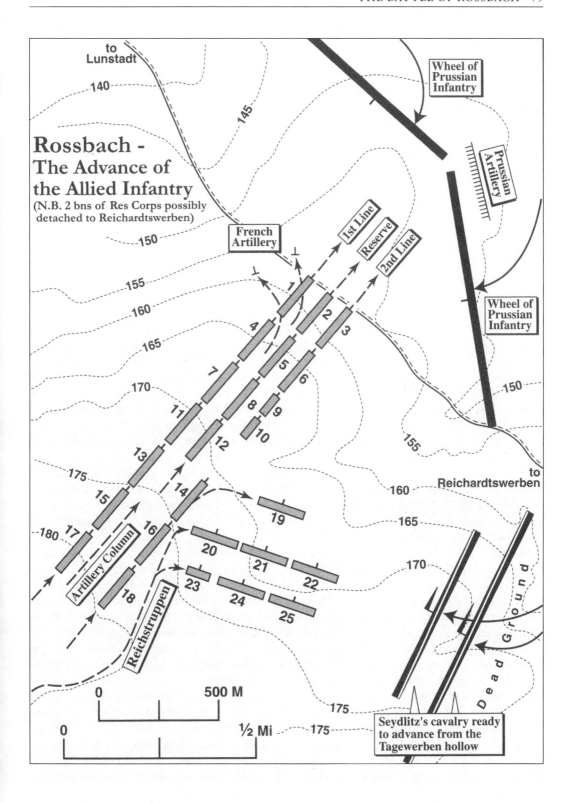

Rossbach –
The Advance of
the Allied Infantry
(N.B. 2 bns of Res Corps possibly
detached to Reichardtswerben)

to
Lunstadt

140

145

150

155

160

165

170

175

180

French
Artillery

1st Line

Reserve

2nd Line

Prussian
Artillery

Wheel of
Prussian
Infantry

Wheel of
Prussian
Infantry

150

155

160

165

170

175

to
Reichardtswerben

Dead Ground

1

2

3

4

5

6

7

8

9

10

11

12

13

14

15

16

17

18

19

20

21

22

23

24

25

Artillery Column

Reichstruppen

0   500 M

0   ½ Mi

Seydlitz's cavalry ready
to advance from the
Tagewerben hollow

With its advance at an end, the regiments of the left-hand column (Piémont, Saint-Chamond, Brissac, Deux-Ponts, Royal-Roussillon and the Swiss regiments of Reding and Planta [1, 4, 7, 11, 13, 15, 17] tried to form as best they could. Their drums took up the continuous rumble of the *Charge*, which was the signal that they must take aim, and hold themselves ready to fire when the beating ceased. 'General Planta commanded one of the brigades (the Swiss). He was deafened by the drumming, and ordered his drummers to stop. The drums of Piémont at the head of the column fell silent also, and their example was followed by the whole line of infantry.'[35] The French gave a general discharge, but then noticed that the Prussian infantry was working around them, and they began to give way.

Broglie sought to check the advance of the regiment of Alt-Braunschweig with a few remaining squadrons of his cavalry reserve. The bluecoats were waiting under the immediate command of Frederick, who called out: 'Now give them something to chew on!' The French were beaten off by blasts of musketry, and finally swept out of contention by Seydlitz, who emerged from the hollow of Tagewerben with his two reassembled lines of horse.

All of this time Prince Georg of Hesse-Darmstadt had been bringing up the eleven battalions of the *Reich* infantry on the right rear of the French columns. The Germans had been spared the first shocking encounter, but now 'the allied cavalry, which had already been in combat with the enemy horse, came surging down towards us. I therefore had to deploy my troops…'[36] The manoeuvre was intended to wheel the troops out to the right in two lines, at right angles to the line of march. The first line was anchored on the regiment of Blue Würzburg [22], which was as good as any unit which fought on that day, but the centre and left of the line were composed of the less than rock-like regiments of Kronegk and Trier [21, 20]. The best of the units of the second line was the battalion of Hesse-Darmstadt [23], which had the support of the dependable Swiss brigade of Wittemer (regiments of Wittemer and Diesbach [16, 18]) towards the tail of the 'French' right-hand column. The rest of the line inspired little confidence, being made up of the regiment of Varell [24] in the centre and that of Ferntheil [25] on the exposed right.

The Würzburgers not only withstood the fire of Moller's artillery (the only *Reich* infantry to undergo this ordeal) but repulsed a first onset of the Prussian cavalry. According to a young officer on the staff of the Bavarian general Holnstein 'this brought an end to the pursuit. The regiment in question stood with admirable composure under the hostile fire. It withheld its own musketry, but its four regimental pieces discharged canister deep into the enemy array from a range of thirty paces. The result was that the enemy, who had been bent on making our better acquaintance, now all of a sudden fled as fast as they could.'[37]

While Blue Würzburg held its immediate ground like a breakwater, panic and collapse spread to its left and rear. Major General Sylvius Christian v. Ferntheil afterwards wrote in defence of the officers of Kronegk that 'they did all they possibly could to keep it in order. However the action was already in full swing, with our cavalry being pressed back before the regiment could deploy, and some of the French infantry giving way. Remember also that the regiment was mostly made up of raw recruits, and so it is not surprising that it fell into disorder and retreated.'[38]

The regiment of Ferntheil itself was attempting to form up in its vulnerable station on the right of the second line, where the beaten allied cavalry was streaming past its open flank. Lieutenant General Reinhard v. Drachsdorff relates that the first battalion (unlike the second) was able to deploy, but then 'a troop of our defeated cavalry came up to the first platoon and one of the horsemen—nobody knows which—called out: "Friends, get away while you can! It's all up!" Upon this the whole battalion made an about turn to the right and sank into dire confusion, without having seen any hostile forces to the front. Drachsdorff and his officers were able to restore the battalion to some kind of order, 'however a number of Prussian cannon shot rang out, and the left wing of the first line simultaneously became disordered, whereupon the battalion turned about for a second time and ran.'[39]

When Drachsdorff alluded to the failure in the left wing of the first line he was writing of the panic in the regiment of Trier, whose commander Colonel v. Coll describes how 'the Prussian musketry was continuous, and not delivered by volleys on command. The regiments of Würzburg, Kronegk, Ferntheil and Trier had been standing in the first line, but all of a sudden Würzburg and Trier found themselves alone, and therefore exposed in this weak state to the Prussian fire. Major Lombardius was shot through the shoulder, Ensign Trapp wounded in the head, Captain Kalkum and Ensign Lohr shot through their coats and waistcoats, and Corporal Blez through both his legs.'[40]

Out of its combat strength of about 1,040 personnel the regiment of Trier actually suffered no fatalities, and only twenty-seven identifiable wounded, but the shock and the sense of isolation were overwhelming. The troops fired a single volley, then fled into the regiment of Varell in the second line, carrying away all but sixty-three of its files. All three of the regiments of the Franconian Circle (Kronegk, Varell and Ferntheil) were now out of the reckoning, together with Trier.

The Flight

The battle as a contest was over. According to Széchenyi 'there was no longer any question of getting the army to stand. I saw only about four regiments of infantry which were able to retreat in closed-up formation under continuous fire.'[41] Quite likely he was writing of the regiment of Blue Würzburg, the disciplined and intact battalion of Hesse-Darmstadt, and the Swiss regiments of Wittemer and Diesbach which not only retained all their colours, but retrieved a colour of one of the regiments which had fled. Young Lieutenant Kalckreuth of the Prussian Gardes du Corps espied one of these potential trophies in the column, which was retreating in an orderly and dignified way. 'The enemy were so near — 150 paces at the most — that I could count them one by one. I had a troop of the Gardes du Corps under my command, made up of thirty-six men and six NCOs. I ordered them to take the colour. They could not have been more enthusiastic, and we set off at a sharp gallop. I was twenty paces from the French column when my NCO on the right wing, an extremely brave individual, called out: "Herr *Lieutenant!* There's nobody with us! All the others fell back a long time ago!" I answered "We have gone so far, we can't go back now. Let's grab that *aide-major* by the side of the column!" We got him. He delivered up his purse and watch to the NCO, and I brought him back prisoner to my troop.'[42]

These scenes were unfolding before the eyes of Prince Georg's secretary Mollinger. He had positioned himself in his light open carriage on a nearby hill, from where he could see both armies from end to end, and count every cannon shot. 'All the same, neither I nor anybody else could find words to described what really happened. Even now I find it difficult to convince myself that what I saw was not a dream. I can say… without boasting that I was one of the last to run. I stayed in my carriage at my viewpoint until the whole of the cavalry, all the French artillery and a good part of their infantry had already gained a fair lead, and until the Prussian cannon shot began to whistle around my carriage, telling me that it was time to turn about.'[43]

The battle had lasted less than one and a half hours. On that date and on that latitude the sun set over the Luftschiff on the southern ridge at 4.45 in the afternoon, and Hildburghausen reported to his Emperor that 'it was a stroke of the utmost good fortune… that night fell, otherwise, by God, nobody would have escaped.'[44]

The allies lost seventy-two cannon, most of them French. The Czettritz Dragoons captured the baggage of Soubise intact, and hung themselves about with the Orders of Saint-Louis which the prince had intended to award to his victorious officers. Other Prussian horsemen were intent on hunting down the fleeing allies. One of the hussars captured three officers who had hidden in a cellar, but a number of his comrades were held at bay by a grenadier of Piémont, who had his back to a tree and absolutely refused to surrender. Frederick rode up, exchanged a few words with the hero, and allowed him to return to his regiment.

The captives could consider themselves lucky, for 'many more French were cut down in the pursuit than lay on the field of battle.'[45]

The allies were saved from something worse not just on account of the darkness, but because the combined detachments of Saint-Germain and Loudon had marched south from the Schortau Heights to intercept the pursuers, which gave rise to a final outburst of firing in the murk. Saint-Germain had eight battalions and twelve squadrons under his command, and Loudon 3-400 hussars and nearly 2,000 Croats. They had been facing only the little command of Mayr (one battalion and seven squadrons), and Loudon, by his own testimony 'remained a passive spectator during the whole affair.'[46] Loudon was almost certainly following strict instructions. Saint-Germain's many enemies in the French army later accused him of sluggishness or even worse, but in the present circumstances it was uncommonly useful for the allies to have a fresh and uncommitted force to cover the only path of retreat, which lay through the wooded hills to Freyburg.[47]

Something like 20,000 troops crowded into the little town of Freyburg during the afternoon and the following night. Some of them belonged to units which had been pulled away from the Unstrut and the upper Saale and came too late to take part in the battle. Contingents of Bavarians, Mainzers, Palatines and Isenburgers arrived between three and four in the afternoon, 'but they had scarcely entered before the news arrived that the French and the *Reichsarmee* had been beaten, and that the King of Prussia was the victor. The French and the other troops already in the town beat alarm, which caused everyone there to fall into total confusion.'[48] The corps of grenadiers (above p. 54) arrived from Kosen, and received orders to make for the main army, but before they could set off Major General Brettlach presented himself, and the first of the fugitives of the cavalry came streaming in behind him. Brettlach called out to the grenadiers: "'Gentlemen, where do you think you are going?" "To the army!" "Stay here" he rejoined, "we don't need you any more... things are bad enough as it is!"'[49]

The beaten infantry poured into Freyburg for hour after hour, and Prince Georg of Hesse-Darmstadt reached the town at ten at night. 'He at least had stuck it out to the end. He did not abandon his flock, like many other shepherds.'[50] The two chief 'shepherds,' Hildburghausen and Soubise, both arrived at Freyburg in a battered state, and had their bruises bathed and their cuts patched up. Soubise and his suite of three hundred personnel lodged in the Post House *(Posthaus)*. Hildburghausen put up in the house of the administration *(Amtshaus)*, and ordered the citizens to set up lights and lanterns both inside and outside their windows, to alleviate something of the confusion among the men who were milling about the town.

Frederick had meanwhile ordered his cavalry to take what shelter they could in the villages. There was little protection against the cutting night wind for the infantrymen, who bivouacked in the open fields of Markwerben, but the troops were able to cheer themselves by building fires from smashed musket stocks, and singing hymns in gratitude for their staggering victory. At six in the evening Frederick repaired to the Schloss of Herr von Funke in Burgwerben, and found that the place was full of captured and wounded French officers. Rather than disturb these unfortunates he greeted them with a few affable words, and resorted to a servant's room in an outhouse, from where he sent the Order of the Black Eagle to Seydlitz and wrote briefly to his foreign minister and to his sister Wilhelmine: 'I can go to my grave in peace, knowing that the reputation and honour of the nation have been saved. We may be overtaken by future misfortunes, but we will never be disgraced.'[51]

The Cost

It took several days to clear the wreckage from the battlefield and the neighbourhood. 'The roads were littered with French cuirasses, great riding boots which had been thrown away… and with lost hats. The sunken road by Markwerben [sic] was full of hacked-about Frenchmen.'[52] The fugitives had thrown 10,000 muskets into the Saale, and the abandoned artillery was 'entirely new and quite splendid. Most of the pieces were French, or from Nuremberg, various Imperial cities and Ansbach, along with a number which the French had taken from the arsenals at Weimar and Gotha.'[53]

On 7 November forty of these cannon were brought to Merseburg, which served as the collection point for the material and human debris. Many of the wounded prisoners were dying there every day. The officers were deposited in individual coffins, and borne away to a cemetery on a bier, accompanied by eight bearers in black cloaks. The ordinary soldiers were taken off in a kind of open box, borne by a couple of labourers or local women. Among those who expired was Broglie's brother, the Comte de Revel, who had been one of the Frenchmen who had promoted Hildburghausen's headlong chase after the 'fleeing' Prussians. All possible consideration was being shown to the victims by Frederick's brother Prince Henry, who had been wounded by a musket shot in the shoulder, and by Field Marshal Keith. In the course of his correspondence with Hildburghausen the Scotsman had occasion to write: 'I must render my most humble thanks to Your Highness for the appreciation you have shown for my way of thinking about the treatment of prisoners. I can assure you that I shall do everything in my power to make their misfortunes as tolerable as possible.'[54]

Out in the fields near Tagewerben the dead were being heaved into mass graves. For the next two springs the cereals over the sites assumed the tall, dark and prospering aspect which earned them the title of 'the black men.' There were further grisly manifestations nearly a century later in 1852, when many skeletons came to light during a programme of straightening roads, levelling hillocks, and filling in sunken paths.

The gruesome sights and the dramatic nature of the events combined to conjure up visions of a wholesale massacre. The more measured assessments showed that such was not the case. If total allied losses from all causes probably exceeded 10,000, most of them were made up of the prisoners and missing.

The Austrian cuirassiers recorded 312 personnel as killed, missing or captured, and 111 wounded men who had been carried off by the two regiments. The Austrian Széchenyi Hussars had no losses among their officers, and just two of the troopers killed, along with eleven wounded and twenty-six captured, which brings to total Austrian losses to 462.[55]

On 9 November the French put together their provisional lists, which showed that their cavalry had 64 officers killed, wounded or missing, with the highest numbers being shown by the regiments of Saluces (sixteen), Penthièvre (fifteen) and Bourbonbusse (eleven). The Fitz-James Regiment had lost two standards and its drums (probably from being among the last to leave the field, as at Culloden in 1746), and Penthièvre and Saluces one standard each.[56] The numbers of the lost troopers are not listed.

Out of twenty-seven of the French battalions which had been in action there were 290 officers and 4,201 soldiers killed, wounded or missing, and five colours lost. The figures for the remaining twenty-four battalions were still being put together, and only fourteen of them had been in combat.[57] If those fourteen battalions suffered losses in proportion, the total would stand at about 440 officers and 6,380 men.

At a rough estimate, therefore, taking account of the provisional figures lodged on 9 November, and the unknown losses among the ordinary troopers, the artillery and the staff, the battle of Rossbach cost the French about 7,000 personnel.

The other figures are no more than approximations, since the Saxon peasants put the dead below ground with all possible speed, and many of the *Reichsarmee*'s missing were men who rejoined their regiments weeks later, or who walked straight back home. The official list of the *Reichsarmee*'s losses presents the total at 2,335, including 1,526 from the Franconian regiments. About nine-tenths of those 1,526 were registered as missing, of whom the greater number were probably deserters.

The number of infantry colours lost by the allies is described as 'many,' but the other trophies can be listed confidently enough at 21 cavalry standards, 3 pairs of cavalry kettledrums, and 72 pieces of ordnance (French: 19 heavy cannon, 41 light. *Reichsarmee:* 2 heavy cannon, 10 light).[58] In other words the allies lost more than 70 per cent of their artillery, and nearly 22 per cent of their total forces. These figures by themselves were by no means high by the standards of battles at the time: what marks them out is the enemy suffered so little in comparison,

The price the Prussians paid for their victory came to just 7 officers and 162 men killed, 23 officers and 356 men wounded, and one verifiable prisoner. The total loss of 549 amounted to 2.40 per cent of their forces. The only unit losses of any significance were sustained by the regiment of Alt-Braunschweig, where the Colonel Commandant Johann Christoph v. Priegnitz had been killed, and about 100 of his people were casualties. Prince Henry of Prussia had been shot in the shoulder, as we have seen, and Seydlitz sustained a couple of wounds which were of little account to begin with, but became infected and put him out of action for the rest of the year. Friedrich Albrecht v. Schwerin, the eccentric commander of the Gensd'armes, went about in a night shirt and bandages, claiming to have been wounded. He happened to have been in genuine hand-to-hand combat, but he put on the same show after every battle, and so nobody took much notice on this occasion.

The Parsonage at Reichardtswerben where Seydlitz was treated after the battle of 5 November His campaign bed is still to be seen inside.

All told the imbalance of the losses was such that 'the King of Prussia could justifiably count this victory as the most economical—but at the same time the most remarkable… and rewarding—ever attained by his arms.'[59]

The Battle Won: The Battle Lost

'The reasons why the battle was lost were very simple. The King of Prussia had seen everything in advance, and made his arrangements accordingly. On our side it was just the opposite. There was a total absence of precaution and organisation.'
(Soubise, at table, 18 November 1757. Philibert de la Cour de Gardiolle, 1883, 23).

Frederick had laid the groundwork for his victory by bringing the scattered elements of the Prussian forces together on the left bank of the Saale in what proved to be a decisive concentration. The basic idea—that of moving by separate corps, then concentrating them for action—looked back to his invasion of Bohemia in the spring of 1757, and forward to Moltke's invasion of the same kingdom in 1866.

On the field of battle Frederick could call on the resources of a finely-tuned army of highly-motivated troops, who were thoroughly versed in a repertoire of requisite manoeuvres, and responsive to a system of command which was technically proficient at the brigade level, and that and a good deal more in the higher reaches. As for the infantry, Prince Ferdinand of Brunswick, Prince Henry and Field Marshal Keith accomplished the difficult crab-like movement of the units with speed and precision. However scarcely more than a couple of the battalions had actually engaged with the enemy, and an official French evaluation pointed out that the Prussian musketry 'killed few of our people, though it inflicted many wounds.'[60]

Essentially the battle was won by a most unusual combination of artillery and cavalry. Here the credit must be shared equally between Colonel Moller, who transported his great battery to the two locations from which it could do the most damage, and Seydlitz, who used his new authority to carry out the most difficult of feats for massed cavalry—to bring it into action twice over. The result was that the Prussians were able to bite off the allied army at his head, and continue the chew their way down the multiple columns.

An officer with Seydlitz testified that 'from that day on the Prussian cavalry grasped just how superior it was to that of the enemy. It was aware that it had been the principal instrument of victory, and that awareness was inevitably accompanied by growing self-confidence.'[61]

All of these elements were combined by Frederick to great effect, once he came to himself after his over-long lunch. He could have had no opportunity to reconnoitre the terrain in detail, but he visualised immediately how the dead ground created by the northern ridge would enable him to interpose his forces across the axis of the allied march, and utilise the swiftness of his cavalry, and the still greater speed of shot, canister and shell to bring a greatly superior destructive power to bear against the successive elements of the allied formation. It is perhaps worth mentioning that a merely competent commander, instead of the aggressive individual represented by Frederick, would have been prompted by the allied flanking march (a genuinely threatening move) to extricate himself from the scene rather than launch himself at the enemy.[62]

At no level did the allies make effective use of their great advantage in numbers. On the strategic plane the French had committed two armies to the German theatre—that of Richelieu on the northern axis through Hanover, and that of Soubise in Thuringia. If we except the transfer of Broglie's corps from Richelieu to Soubise, there was no co-ordination between the two groups of forces. Most crucially, the advance of Richelieu's army had come to a halt well short of the middle Elbe, while Soubise and Hildburghausen were still proceeding with their broken-backed campaign in Thuringia. It was not paranoia on the part of Hildburghausen to suspect that his work was being sabotaged—in fact by Chancellor Kaunitz from Vienna, and by the lack of commitment on the part of the French ministry.

Soubise and Hildburghausen ultimately had 60,000 troops at their disposal, counting the original army of Soubise, the *Reichsarmee* and the newly-arrived corps of Broglie. They had more than enough force to hold the Prussians at bay from behind the Saale. They chose instead to let the enemy across the river, which as the Prussian staff officer Gaudi says, was not necessarily a bad decision. 'For the sake of convenience we passed the river by widely-separated corps on a frontage of four *Meilen* [thirty kilometres]. How was it that the allies, having reached their resolution, did not fall on each in turn?'[63]

The morning of the battle found many of the best troops of the *Reichsarmee* guarding the crossings of the Unstrut and the upper Saale—a point worth making when it comes to apportioning the blame for the disaster. The astute Landgraf Ludwig Egon of Fürstenberg, as Full General of Infantry of Swabia, states that the troops of his Circle were not at Rossbach. 'If the eleven battalions which were present at the battle gave way, it was only following the example of the defeated cavalry which was coming back towards them, and that of the entire first line [i.e. the left-hand column of infantry], which was made up entirely of those French who a moment before had despised the Prussians, and dismissed them as being of no account. The defeat of the *Reichstruppen* should not have occasioned any surprise. At every council of war the generals of the *Reich* drew attention to the lack of training of their men, and to the mistrust which reigned in the combined army, and they declared that it would be far too risky to commit their troops in open country against the Prussians.[64] Fürstenberg could have added that the *Reichstruppen* at Rossbach had been without food or any kind of shelter for four days.

When the allies set themselves in march on the 5th some 6,000 of the French were absent marauding or foraging, which was the product of a more general malaise. According to Bourcet 'our troops were so indisciplined, and so bent on plunder, that there was no prospect of achieving anything that would redound to the advantage of our nation, or to uphold the glory of our arms… I have been serving for forty-eight years now, and have never seen anything like it.'[65]

Hildburghausen protested that he had asked repeatedly for more Austrian cavalry to be sent to his army, and that he had only 1,200 cuirassiers at his disposal on the fatal 5 November.[66] These valuable men were nevertheless not used to the best effect, for they went too fast to keep in contact with the main forces behind, but not fast enough to beat the Prussians to the crest of the northern ridge.

Few voices were heard even among the French to defend their own infantry. However the French cavalry liked to think that it had performed much better than the foot soldiers, and that 'if it was beaten, it was only through the great superiority of the enemy; we could engage only bit by bit, due to the speed of the Prussian cavalry. If we had not charged when we did, whenever we could range a few squadrons in line, and if we had not charged as vigorously as we did, it is fair to say that the Austrian cavalry and all our infantry would have been surrounded and lost.'[67] Broglie reported in the same vein, though Caulincourt adds that 'a lot of trouble could be avoided if the junior officers observed more discipline and silence, and kept themselves on the alert. Then it would be possible for the senior officers and squadron commanders to make themselves heard.'[68]

In this respect the French artillery showed well in comparison, for 'it is busy [training] in peacetime, and therefore surprised by nothing that happens in war.' At Rossbach the heavy artillery never recovered from the disadvantage of being sited in scattered batteries in low ground, but Pierre Bourcet, in his capacity as commander of the artillery, was impressed by the 'steadiness of the gunners and the diligence of the officers. They begged me to let them get off a few rounds more, even when the enemy came within thirty paces.'[69] It was counted as something of a miracle that at the end of the action the artillery was able to bring off sixteen of its heavy cannon and two mortars.

The central issue for the allies on 5 November remained the decision to give battle in the first place. In an impassioned protest to Emperor Francis Stephen on 7 November Hildburghausen rightly pointed out that for weeks he had stressed the shortcomings of the *Reichsarmee* and the French. Less convincing, however, was his assertion that he had been forced into action by pressure from Vienna.[70]

Soubise was just as eager to disclaim responsibility, writing to his War Minister that 'one hour before the battle fifty officers witnessed the discussion I had with him [Hildburghausen] from the saddle, when I urged him to slow down the march, and put off the action until the next day. But he was being egged on by five or six Saxon officers who were appalled at seeing Saxony abandoned. They did everything they could to commit us, and they finally succeeded in persuading Hildburghausen—who at heart did not wish to fight, but wished to give the impression of wanting to do so.'[71] In fairness to Hildburghausen it must be mentioned that bellicose noises also came from officers of the French General Staff,[72] and that it had become a habit among the French to speak slightingly of the enemy: 'Yes, the King of Prussia had never been beaten; but he still has to meet the French!'[73]

Once the battle was in full swing the allied senior commanders were caught up in the events at the head of their columns, with the result that they lost the wider picture. Hildburghausen was particularly sensitive to criticism on this head, and he represented to Maria Theresa that people should not presume to tell him his business, 'having served Your Majesty's House for forty years now, during which time I have been in many bloody battles, and not just as a captain or lieutenant, but as a general in command of whole wings, whole lines, and respectable independent corps of 6,000, 10,000, 20,000 or 30,000 men.'[74]

Soubise made a marginally better showing. He at least sent word to bring up the cavalry of the French reserve corps and the French left wing, and afterwards there was a ring of true nobility in his report to his Minister of War: 'I know that you, as my friend, will be thinking of my situation after this sad turn of events, but what matters above everything else is to do what we can to save the honour of the nation, and to put all the blame on the generals... I tender whatever sacrifices which may prove useful to service of the King.'[75]

After the Battle

Frederick's victory took on an altogether wider dimension in the days immediately following the action, when it became clear that the allies were not only retreating with disorderly speed, but separating. That was more important to him than beating the enemy on the field of battle, however gratifying that might have been.

By Hildburghausen's account, he and Soubise had agreed at Freyburg on the evening of the 5th that the allies would put up a coherent defence of the river lines, with the French occupying the Unstrut, and the *Reichsarmee* the adjoining stretch of the Saale. Hildburghausen states that to put the matter beyond any doubt he had sketched the positions with a pencil for the benefit of the French aides-de-camp, 'but I had scarcely arrived at my first station when the report reached me that all the French had gone to Laucha, and just after that it was confirmed that they had made a further lengthy march... and had therefore abandoned us completely.'[76] The river lines were now untenable.

Soubise claims that the fault was Hildburghausen's, for failing to turn up at the rendezvous which had been agreed. However the documentation makes it clear that the French had taken the initiative in breaking contact, and that the only concerns of Soubise were to put as much distance as he could between himself and the Prussians, and to allow his army to rest and come to its senses.[77]

The French were making off north-west by way of Sonderhausen and Nordhausen to their ultimate quarters behind the Main. For the first couple of days the fugitives were spread widely over
Thuringia. The officers did not attempt to command obedience, and the men pressed on as if the
Prussians had been at their heels: 'many of them were wounded… and dragged themselves most
painfully along until they collapsed from exhaustion and their torments. Most of them carried no
weapons, and many had no hats. The greater part of the cavalrymen had lost their horses, and as
it was impossible for them to progress in their big boots, they had discarded them and were going
about in their stockings… We saw no insignia or colours—all were lost, except for a pair of drums
which were guarded by a party of fifteen or so men. They had a captive with them, a Meinicke
Dragoon who had shot off by himself in an attempt to seize the drums, and had been made prisoner. They had not dared to take his horse. He rode it still, grinding his teeth with anger, and his
enemies were so intimidated that they treated him with great circumspection and honour, and led
his horse by the reins.'[78]

The leading Prussian dragoons and hussars arrived outside Freyburg at seven in the morning of
6 November. The allies had burnt the covered bridge behind them, abandoning all but one of the
French baggage carts in the town on the right bank of the Unstrut. The Prussians proceeded to
clear parties of French from the outlying gardens and track down marauders in the town. Three
hours later Frederick arrived with his main force on the river just below Freyburg at Wissmitz.
There he found a bridge that had been built by the French a few days before, and which they had
made a half-hearted attempt to burn down. It would take an hour or more to restore the crossing,
and the king and his troopers sprawled on the ground to rest. In 1832 the ninety-one year-old
clockmaker Christian Jahn was asked what he could recall of the episode, and described how the
town councillors had come to greet Frederick with a speech, but that he had told them that he
would much rather have something to eat. He was presented with bread and butter and cold roast
meats, and he invited the generals to share the meal with him.

The cavalry was already fording the Unstrut nearby, and at about noon the infantry was able to
begin its crossing as well. Frederick brought together eleven battalions and thirty-two squadrons
on the right bank of the river, and dispatched Colonel Lentulus with the free battalion of Mayr,
and five squadrons each of the Székely Hussars and the Meinicke Dragoons to pursue the allies,
even if there was understandable uncertainty as to where they were heading.

At about the same time Hildburghausen reached Kösen, and picked up a considerable body
of the left-behind troops of the *Reichsarmee* (15 battalions, 5 squadrons and 28 cannon). He had
the double bridge over the Saale set on fire, so as to secure his left flank, and continued in the
afternoon to the intended location of the first night's halt, which was at Eckartsberga. There, as
Brettlach senior confided in Colloredo, 'something happened which I'd better keep until I have
the honour of speaking to you in person!'[79]

'What happened was that a panic was occasioned towards four in the afternoon by a shout of
'The Prussians are coming!' This inspired our feet with new courage, so that our flight was speedier
and more ludicrous still than in the great battle.'[80] The enemy force consisted merely of Mayr's
free battalion and some of his hussars. The intruders made themselves scarce when Prince Georg
of Hesse-Darmstadt fired a few cannon shot in their direction, but the fright had been enough to
persuade most of the *Reichstruppen* to flee in the direction of Weimar.

The Prussians bothered to pursue only as far as Erfurt (Frederick now had other priorities),
but the retreat of the *Reichsarmee* had developed its own momentum, and Hildburghausen was
persuaded that it was impossible for the army to linger on the near side of the Thüringer Wald.[81]

The largest identifiable body of the *Reichsarmee* reached Erfurt on 7 November. 'Never in
my life have I seen such a speedy flight,' wrote Mollinger. 'It goes on and on, and we just keep
running.'[82] The troops came to Teichel on the 8th, and to Saalfeld on the 9th, having lost the first
of their comrades from cold overnight. They were still there on the 10th, devoid of any protection

against the snowstorms which were now setting in. On the 11th the men picked themselves up and trudged on to Gräfenthal, from where they set on the next day to begin the climb of the Thüringer Wald by way of Judenbach. The fourteenth of November saw the troops fleeing through Fürth on the far side of the Thüringer Wald, and on the 15th Hildburghausen assembled what forces he could in security around Lichtenfels, from where he dispersed the units in winter quarters behind the hills.

Many of the troops had already taken off as individuals or small groups without any intention of rejoining their parent regiments. The whereabouts of the regiment of Ferntheil were unknown for several weeks, and on the road Mollinger happened to encounter its colonel, Franz v. Hohenlohe-Ingelfingen, 'who had three colours of his regiment with him, one carried by himself, another by his huntsman, and the third by his runner, without a single armed man to accompany or escort them.'[83]

On 9 November Frederick had inspected the trophies and the prisoners of the late battle in the cathedral square in Merseburg, then travelled on to Leipzig, where he visited the wounded Seydlitz and Prince Henry. He could spare no further thoughts for what had just happened, because, writing of himself in the third person, 'strictly speaking the battle of Rossbach just released the King of Prussia to go in search of new dangers in Silesia.'[84] Two days later Frederick entrusted Field Marshal Keith with the command of the troops who were destined to stay in Thuringia, and on the 13th he began his march to the east with eighteen battalions and twenty-three squadrons to settle accounts with the Austrians.

Keith wrote to his brother, the Earl Marischal of Scotland: 'I swear to you that the members of this royal family will soon be extinct if this war lasts any longer. They take too many risks. There were occasions in the last battle when the king put himself in more danger than any of his generals. He got away with it that time, but on the next occasion he might not be so lucky. In that case we would be overtaken by a catastrophe which makes me shudder to think about it.'[85]

V

Austria Triumphant

The Austrian Army; the Bavarians, the Württembergers

Rossbach and Leuthen—to anyone with more than a passing interest in military history, at this distance of time, those two names run so easily together that it is natural to overlook how vastly different were the circumstances in which the battles were fought. At Rossbach Frederick eliminated an annoying diversion. The forces he defeated there did not have a single passage of arms to their credit, and were walking pathological specimens of every ill that is capable of infecting a military organism. At Leuthen the king was face-to-face with an enemy who had:

- got the better of him in open battle at Kolin (18 June 1757)
- defeated and killed one of his corps commanders (Winterfeldt, at Moys, 7 September)
- raided his capital (Hadik's expedition to Berlin, 11-23 October)
- stormed his newest fortress (Schweidnitz, 12 November)
- routed a respectable little army from its position and taken the capital of Silesia (Breslau, 23-24 November)

The last week of November therefore found the Austrians in possession of the greater part of the province of Silesia, which was one of the prime bones of contention in the Seven Years War. The timing of this conquest was as important as the fact, for the end of the conventional campaigning season was already past, and if the Austrians were allowed to remain in possession of Silesia until the spring they would deny Frederick the resources of this exceptionally valuable province, and be able to open the next campaign within a few easy marches of the heartland of the old Prussian monarchy. Only a stupendous blow would enable Frederick to get Silesia back, and he had to deliver that stroke in a matter of days rather than weeks.

In one way or another the formidable Austrian army of 1757 was the creation of the Empress-Queen Maria Theresa. Austrian military institutions had been at a low ebb when she came to claim her inheritance in 1740, for her father the late Emperor Charles VI had set no great store by military values, and a steep decline in Austrian martial prowess had set in during the declining years of Prince Eugene (died 1736). By 1743 Maria Theresa had won the defensive battle for the central territories of the Austrian dynasty, but the Austrian armies were unable to claw back the great northern province of Silesia, and at the Peace of Dresden (25 December 1745) Maria Theresa had to accept (with profound reservations) the signing-away of all but a small corner of her Silesian lands to Prussia.

There was still a great deal to be put right in the Austrian army, and Maria Theresa set about the task with the help of a small group of dedicated advisers—notably Leopold v. Daun in affairs concerning the infantry, and Prince Joseph Wenzel v. Liechtenstein in the reform of the artillery. In 1749 Daun codified the practice and drill of the infantry of the entire army, and corresponding regulations for the cavalry were published in the same year and in 1751, Prince Liechtenstein, largely at his own expense, not only created a corps of highly-professional gunners, but in the

System of 1753 introduced a range of standardised and thoroughly serviceable ordnance (which became in turn the inspiration for the artillery of the French Revolution and Napoleon).

In close association with Count Wenzel Anton v. Kaunitz, her foreign minister, the Empress also embarked on something more far-reaching, which was to create a new and distinctively Habsburg military ethos. To this end she founded the Military Academy at Wiener Neustadt in 1751 (another inspiration to the rest of Europe), ennobled deserving officers without regard to their birth, and in June 1757, immediately after the victory at Kolin, she founded the Military Order of Maria Theresa, a distinction which was accessible to all officers who had shown particular enterprise and courage, no matter how junior they might be in rank, or obscure in their ancestry.

The reforms were still far from complete when war with Prussia broke out in August 1756, which was much sooner than had been expected, and when many good officers were still disorientated by the recent changes. The operations in 1757 were too fast-moving to allow much more to be done, and indeed some of the most important reforms (like the establishment of the excellent General Staff) dated from later in the war. The Austrian army got much better as the contest went on, and the Prussian army much worse, but in 1757 the process had not begun.

In 1757, therefore, the Austrian military renewal was unfinished in terms of time. It was also incomplete in scope, for it concentrated in one direction on detailed matters of technique and equipment—drill, new muskets and cannon and the like—and in the other on a fundamental re-orientation of values. Whole areas remained untouched. There was no coordination between the light forces (the Hungarian hussars and the Croatian infantry) and the 'German' troops, and (shame of shames) the Prussians actually began to outclass the Austrians in *der kleine Krieg*. More importantly still, Maria Theresa had not dared to address the problem of the leadership of the active field army.

Maria Theresa's favourite commander, the charismatic Irishman Field Marshal Maximilian Ulysses v. Browne, had been beaten and mortally wounded at the battle of Prague on 6 May, and bottled up with his army inside Prague. The city, the army, and probably also the entire monarchy were saved when Field Marshal Daun put together a further army, and at Kolin on 18 June went on to prove to Europe something that was assumed to be impossible, namely that Frederick could be worsted in pitched battle. Daun broke through to the city of Prague, after which the re-united Austrian forces pushed the Prussians from Bohemia, and advanced beyond the Habsburg borders to Zittau, on the foothills just short of the north European plain. We shall take up their story shortly.

On merit alone Daun should by now have been installed as the overall commander of the Austrian field forces. He was the chief engine of military reform, a fine disciplinarian, and a professional soldier to his finger tips. His personal enemies taxed him with being over-cautious, but this charge loses much of its force when we consider that he had to try conclusions with Frederick of Prussia and the finest army in the world. Some of the élan which was undoubtedly lacking in Daun was supplied by Count Leopold Nádasdy-Fogaras, who was a level-headed but dashing commander in the Hungarian style, and who was loved even among the troops from the Austrian Netherlands as *papa moustache*. Many able officers (Loudon, Lacy, Hadik, Beck, Brentano and so on) were coming up fast, but they still had to make their names at the higher levels of command.

The team might have shaken down by the end of 1757 if it had not been for an undesirable consequence of the relief of Prague, which was to release Maria Theresa's brother-in-law Prince Charles of Lorraine, who had been Browne's nominal co-commander earlier in the campaign. Prince Charles was physically courageous, popular enough with the troops, and had done one or two good things on campaign, like crossing the Rhine into French Alsace in 1744. Without the support of his brother, the Emperor Francis Stephen, it is however doubtful whether he would have retained his post as long as he did. What was affability in the Emperor was transmuted in Charles into something altogether more coarse and indulgent. It was known that he was much under the influence of a notoriously loose-living set of cronies, though few people were aware that he had been overtaken by mental paralysis at a critical moment of the battle of Prague. Only after the campaign of 1757 did Maria Theresa detect another trait of his character, which was an underlying insouciance and irresponsibility.

In order to make up for Prince Charles's established shortcomings, Maria Theresa attached Daun to him at headquarters as an adviser and deputy—an ill-defined and unsatisfactory arrangement. It was also unfortunate that Nádasdy, who excelled as an independent commander, had his wings clipped when he and his troops were attached to the main army before the battle of Leuthen. Daun and Nádasdy did not get on particularly well, which had the effect of dividing the Austrian leadership still further.

When all of this has been said, the Austrian army was still robust enough to withstand a good deal of mismanagement. The officers and men admired and respected Maria Theresa, regardless of their national origins. The basic stock of the troops was sound, for the cuirassiers and dragoons were drawn predominantly from the Austrian and Moravian heartlands of the monarchy, just as the imperturbable and long-enduring Bohemians gave their character to the artillery and the 'German' infantry. The general sturdiness was complemented by the spark which was provided by the Hungarian and Netherlandish Walloon 'National' infantry. Men like these were going to take a lot of beating down.

That much the Austrians could rely on. They also had at their disposal two corps of German auxiliaries, to wit 4,000 Bavarians and 6,000 Württembergers (treaty strengths). These were very much an unknown quantity for they were not traditional associates of the Austrians, and they had been hired only through the good offices of France.

Bavaria was declining rapidly in the table of German states, and the fall was accelerated by the French subsidies, which had encouraged this south German electorate to commit itself beyond its native resources. With French support the late elector Charles had actually gained the Imperial throne of Germany in 1743 as 'Emperor Charles VII.' He died in 1745, and later in that year the Austrians overran his lands and regained the Imperial title for the Habsburgs. On 4 November 1756 Baron A.H. v. Wittgenstein warned the reigning elector Max Joseph how misguided it would be to throw Bavaria into a new war, and 'put at risk many millions of florins in return for a subsidy of a few thousand.'

Wittgenstein laid out in some detail how the Bavarian troops were 'never in a worse condition or less suited to face an enemy than they are now.' The officers would obey orders willingly enough, 'but not a single one of them will answer for the consequences if they have to face a mediocre enemy, let alone the Prussians, who are so formidable...' The cavalry (which was not hired by the Austrians) could be left out of the reckoning altogether, for it was to be mounted on peasant horses. Among the infantry, the long-service regulars formed an invaluable but diminishing element, now represented in some of the companies by no more than ten or a dozen men. The volunteers who signed up for four-year engagements were good men too, but both they and the regulars were demoralised by the poor conditions under which they served. Most of their pay vanished in deductions, and they had to wear their uniforms for three years on end, at the end of which their clothing was in rags. 'The consequence is that the Bavarian military service, which once stood so high in esteem, is now so demeaned, and has fallen into such disrepute, that nobody, or hardly anybody, wishes to sign up... also the existence of the cadet school has deprived the NCOs and the able ambitious private soldiers of the prospect of ever becoming officers, which makes them gloomy and recalcitrant.' (This objection did not apply in the Austrian service, where only a minority of would-be officers as yet went through Wiener Neustadt).

The men who were forcibly enlisted for three years were virtually useless, for experience showed that 'they throw away their muskets at the first sight of the enemy, and take to their heels without anybody being able to stop them.' The fourth and last category was that of the hastily-enlisted peasants' sons, who had been put through a few pointless drill sessions in their ordinary clothes. They were formed adults, who had their eye on marriage and their inheritances, and nothing was further from their thoughts than allowing themselves to get shot.[1]

Wittgenstein's advice counted for nothing, for on 1 March 1757 the Bavarians signed a new treaty with the French, and agreed to provide 6,800 troops to the alliance, 4,000 of whom were assigned to the Austrians.

Württemberg was a curious case, for Duke Carl Eugen, the ruler of this south-west German state, was a Catholic and genuinely attached to the alliance, whereas his people were Protestants, and removed by temperament from the easier-going Bavarians and Austrians. Stories are told about the gadgrind Württembergers even now: 'Grandfather is still at work: he is up there in the hour glass on the mantelpiece.'

The very appearance of the Württemberg troops awakened misgivings, for their blue coats and the metal-fronted caps of their grenadiers identified them at once with the military culture of Prussia. Landgraf Ludwig Egon v. Fürstenberg, who was sensitive to opinions in the Empire, warned that the Württembergers must be kept under close watch, and confined if possible to garrison duties. In the treaty with the French (30 March 1757) Carl Eugen bound himself to the over-ambitious target of providing 6,000 men, and the discontents in the gathering army, together with Prussian machinations, provoked a mass mutiny which ravaged Stuttgart on 21 June.

As finally constituted, the force destined to join the Austrians was made up of three grenadier battalions, the Leibgarde Regiment and four regiments of fusiliers, under the overall command of Lieutenant General von Spitznas. The corps set out from Ludwigsburg on 10 August, and marched south-east by way of Geislingen and Günzburg. There was much disorder and desertion on the way, and in a typical episode 'a number of men broke out of the camp by force, but the officers set after them immediately and drove them back. The ring-leaders were court-martialled and shot before the day was out.'[2] The troops reached Linz on the Danube on 30 August, and had thirteen days of rest and consolidation before they set off on the last stage of their journey. The attention of the officers was unflagging, and old military values and habits of obedience had re-asserted themselves by the time the corps reached the scene of operations on 17 October. The pity was that the Austrians did not appreciate the change which had overtaken the Württembergers, and they were going to hold them equally to blame with the Bavarians for the disaster which overtook them all on 5 December.

The End of Winterfeldt

Frederick and the main force of the Austrians parted company on 20 August 1757, and they did not see each other again for more than three months. The king had been trying in vain to resolve the confusion into which his affairs had been thrown by his defeat at Kolin on 18 June. He had been forced to abandon his siege of Prague, which was inevitable, but he had not expected the enemy to bundle the Prussians out of Bohemia as rapidly as they did. He had taken command of forces on the western side of the Bohemian Elbe, while the Austrians chose to make their main effort to the east, and chased the corps of his younger brother Prince August Wilhelm up the Iser valley and across the border hills into Lusatia, the easternmost province of Saxony. Frederick arrived there on 29 July, and subjected the mild and hapless August Wilhelm to a tongue-lashing that was severe even by Fritzian standards. The poor man never recovered, and sank into a decline which resulted in his death the next year.

The Austrians to the number of more than 100,000 were ensconced on the rolling plateau of Eckartsberg to the north of Zittau. Frederick, with only half that number, was determined to bring them to battle, or at least dislodge them from their position, for they were now emplaced within a few miles of the great east-west transverse route which ran along the edge of the north European plain. By 20 August he had exhausted his repertoire of feints and manoeuvres, without being able to persuade the Austrians to decamp, and he could no longer ignore how badly his interests were being threatened on other areas of operations. He had to trust that Field Marshal Lehwaldt would be able to hold the remote province of East Prussia against the Russians. He himself had to take measures against the French and *Reichstruppen* who were now advancing from the west. On the 20th he drew back closer to his magazine at Bautzen, and on the 25th he took off with a small body of troops. He gathered up forces on his way through Saxony, and by 15 September his hussars made their first contact with the outposts of Hildburghausen in Thuringia (p. 44).

Frederick had left two commanders of very different character to try to hold down the Austrians in Lusatia. Lieutenant General Hans Karl v. Winterfeldt was as tough an individual as any in the king's inner circle, and he was marked out by the shrewdness and discretion which had made him the royal spymaster, and given him access to Frederick's innermost secrets, not excluding the decision to open war in 1756. Winterfeldt was now put in charge of a corps of 13,000-odd troops, and was planted by the king on the right or eastern bank of the Lausitzer Neisse (the present German-Polish border).

Lieutenant General August Wilhelm of Brunswick-Bevern (not to be confused with Ferdinand of Brunswick) was a highly professional officer in the Prussian mould, but also a civilised man of the wider European world, and related on the female side to Maria Theresa of Austria. He now commanded a respectable corps of 45,000 men, and placed himself on the left or western bank of the Neisse in the neighbourhood of Görlitz, in a strong position which reached out to the isolated conical hill of the Landeskrone (420 m).

The Austrian main army had now built up to a massive strength of 112,000 troops, comprising 90,000 regular infantry and cavalry (84 battalions, 88 grenadier companies, 190 squadrons) and some 22,000 light troops (35 battalions and 14 grenadier companies of Croats, and 52 squadrons of hussars). It nevertheless took the co-commanders Prince Charles of Lorraine and Field Marshal Daun a long time to convince themselves that Frederick had removed himself from the scene, and longer still to decide what to do. The host finally descended from the Eckartsberg position on a rainy 2 September, but Charles and Daun found that they were still not free of the enemy, for Bevern and Winterfeldt were grouped on either side of the Neisse nearby. They blocked the way west into Saxony, and they would pose an intolerable threat to the Austrian rear if Charles and Daun turned east into Silesia.

Bevern's position on the far side of the Neisse was altogether too strong to be attacked, but the long dormant Austrian sense of enterprise was awakened by the prospect of being able to bring overwhelming forces to bear against Winterfeldt, who stood

Winterfeldt.

on the near side of the river. What was more, Winterfeldt had strung out his forces in a vulnerable way, with some of his troops being exposed to the south of his camp on the Jäckelsberg (Holtzberg) Hill. 'We were could not imagine how an intelligent and cautious commander like this could lay himself open to being surprised in such a way.'[3]

The Action at Moys, 7 September 1757

a) Austrians 32,549
Total losses; 1,577 killed, 1,358 wounded, 42 missing
b) Prussians c. 13,300
Total losses: 1,856, 7 colours, 5 pieces

Bevern rode out to the Landeskrone before daybreak on 7 September. The morning was misty, but when he looked east he saw that the rising sun was reflected from thousands of musket barrels on the far bank of the Neisse, confirming what he had long feared, that the Austrians had gone over to the offensive and were concentrating their effort on that side.

Even severe critics of the Austrian high command had to concede that on this occasion 'the arrangements were excellent,' and that 'the enterprise was carried out with truly admirable secrecy.'[4] The attack was to be spearheaded by an elite advance guard of 42 companies of grenadiers; six of the companies were in the lead, with the remaining 36 coming up behind, grouped in three brigades of 12 companies each. Finally Lieutenant General Arenberg brought up 21 fusilier battalions of the *corps de reserve*. They too were formed in battalion columns three battalions deep, making 7 columns in all. The two left-hand (western) columns were commanded by Lieutenant General Clerici, and came up in immediate support of the grenadiers, with the remaining five columns extending to the right. The orders explain something of how the system was to work: 'if a first-line battalion suffers heavy losses, or falls into disorder, we will file it off to the left or right, and replace it by the battalion behind.' This dictated a lateral interval of 100 paces between one battalion and the next, and 200 paces were to be left between the successive lines of battalions.[5]

The Austrians made use of their numerous light forces to cover the respective flanks. Major General Draskovich brought up the Banal Croats on the immediate left of the grenadiers. Out to the east of the attacking force Nádasdy deployed three further battalions of Croats and three regiments of hussars (Kayser, Dessewffy and Kálnoky) to deter the Prussians from threatening the right flank of the infantry from the direction of Leopoldshayn.

The combined force set out at one in the morning of 7 September. The approach came by way of the broken country which extended to the south of the narrow Jäckelsberg ridge, where the Austrians could exploit the cover afforded by the woods, hillocks, rocks, ravines, sunken paths and the willowy banks of the Rothwasser stream. The Prussians (unknown to the Austrians) had built a redoubt atop the Jäckelsberg, but the defenders had still seen nothing of the enemy by the time the Austrian grenadiers reached the foot of the hill at eleven in the morning, which was long after the conventional time for a surprise attack. No warning had come from the west bank, and the two Prussian grenadier battalions of Benckendorff and Dieringshofen were peaceably preparing their meals on the top of the Jäckelsberg, while the Prussian officers were already at table, or were accompanying Winterfeldt, who had ridden off to confer with the Duke of Bevern.

Taken completely off their guard, the Prussian grenadiers nevertheless sprang to arms and opened a heavy fire of musketry, supported before long by the six pieces in the redoubt. This spirited response won time for Winterfeldt to return from his encounter with Bevern, and for Prussian reinforcements to march to the threatened Jäckelsberg—first the grenadier battalion of Anhalt, then Major General Kannacher with the infantry regiments of Manteuffel and Tresckow.

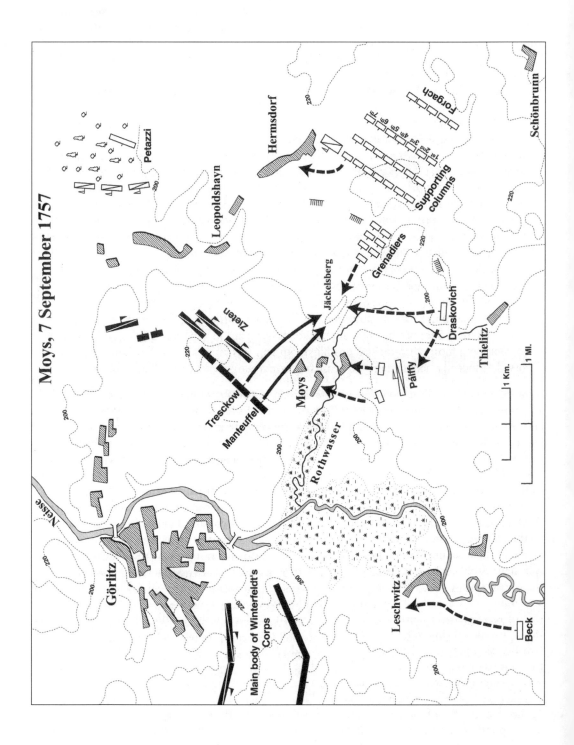

Moys, 7 September 1757

The first Austrian attack was checked when it had ascended only half-way up the Jäckelsberg; and the senior officers had to intervene to breathe fresh life into the assault. Major Franz De Piza had to use forcible means to prevent his men from lying flat on the ground or running away, and, at the urging of Nádasdy in person, he pushed to the crest of the hill, where he only now discovered the existence of the redoubt. He jumped into the ditch, followed by two of his grenadiers, and he seized the muzzles of their muskets and had himself propelled to the top. He reached back, hauled the grenadiers up after him, and, as soon as fifteen or sixteen of his men had collected at the top, they began to clear the work at bayonet point.[6]

To the left of the grenadiers, Major General Draskovich was storming up the hill at the head of his Croats. He lost 115 of his troops in the process, and his own sword hilt was shot away when he scrambled into the Prussian work on horseback. At this interesting juncture the Austrian grenadiers chose to disappear from the scene, almost certainly in search of plunder in the enemy camp. Winterfeldt and Kannacher were now well on their way with the Prussian reinforcements, and things would have gone badly astray if Lieutenant General Arenberg had not recognised the danger, and brought up the supporting Austrian fusiliers. Among these, the left-hand brigade (battalions of de Ligne, Königsegg, Sachsen-Gotha, Andlau and the two of Platz) was most directly on course for a collision at the top. Hand-to-hand combat was very rare at this period, but in this case the two forces were out of sight of one another until they ran together full tilt at the top. Captain the Prince de Ligne records in detail how 'for a few moments we ebbed to and fro, like the crowd in the pit at an opera house. I tried to put an end to it by consolidating and fixing our men by a barricade I improvised with my partisan and the halberds of my NCOs.' The troops disengaged, but 'the first ranks of the Prussians and our men were so close that the muzzles of their muskets almost touched, and now the action became truly horrific, for the hutments, field kitchens and tents were set alight by the discharges, and these blazing objects became a kind of barrier across which we exchanged fire at point blank range. For that reason the wounds gaped so widely that you would have sworn they were made by cannon shot.'

De Ligne finally broke the deadlock by gathering a small band of Netherlanders from his father's regiment and that of Sachsen-Gotha, and together they forced a mob of intermingled whitecoats and Prussians to fall back down the far side of the hill as far as the little village of Moys. 'When I was talking with the remnants of our men a cannon shot carried away four grenadiers of the Haller regiment who were standing between me and Prince Stolberg. A moment later another cannon ball covered me with earth, and a further one threw me to the ground.'[7] The Prussian major general Kannacher was taken prisoner during this desperate scramble of a battle, and he told his captors that Winterfeldt had been shot from his horse and that he was in a very bad way when he had last seen him (he died shortly afterwards).

Even now the Austrian victory was not secure, for the push of the infantry had exposed their right flank to a mass of 35 squadrons and 8 battalions commanded by Lieutenant General Zieten. However Nádasdy's command had been placed in reserve to meet such an eventuality, and the threat was countered by one battalion and two pieces of artillery which Lieutenant General Wied rushed to the village of Hermsdorf, and by a thousand Carlstädter Croats whom Colonel Velha threw into the woods behind Leopoldshayn. Luckily for the Austrians the Duke of Bevern did not dare to intervene from the west bank of the Neisse, for he was deterred by a little corps under Major General Beck which Daun had advanced to Leschwitz.

At one in the afternoon the acting Prussian commander Prince Karl v. Bevern withdrew his battered infantry from the fight. The Austrians themselves were badly shaken and in no state to pursue, and at midnight the regular infantry were withdrawn from the Jäckelsberg, and the guard handed over to the Croats, which, in an odd way, seemed to devalue what had been achieved there. A French officer walked the ground on the next day, and 'found large numbers of wounded and dying who had been on the battlefield for more than twenty hours without having received the slightest assistance. It is both inconceivable and appalling how such unfortunate men are treated in these parts.'[8]

Some observers identified the action at Moys as a turning point in the conflict, in spite of its tame conclusion. For the Prussians a chapter seemed to have closed with the death of Winterfeldt, the architect of what some of them regarded as an offensive war on their part. Winterfeldt had moreover been shot in the back, which opens the possibility that he had been brought down by one of his own men. For the Austrians, 7 September 1757 was the date from which they began truly offensive operations.[9]

The sinister Winterfeldt nevertheless died a hero. Prince Charles at once agreed to the Duke of Bevern's request to have the body conducted to his house at Pilgramsdorf in Silesia, and an Austrian guard of honour accompanied the coffin for one hour along the road.

But Bevern Wins the Race to Breslau

On the murky night of 10/11 September the Duke of Bevern abandoned his camp at Görlitz, and took a roundabout route which circumvented the Austrian army and set him on the way east to Silesia—the rich, fertile and heavily-fortified province which was the prize of the contest between Maria Theresa and Frederick. In a manner of speaking Prince Charles and Daun now had their minds made up for them by the Prussian move, and they determined to anticipate Bevern in the heart of Silesia, and establish themselves securely there before Frederick could return from his adventures in the west. By choosing a path around to the north Bevern had left the most direct avenue unguarded, and which enabled the Austrians to enter Silesia at Lauban on 12 September. They were at Löwenberg on the 14th, Pilgramsdorf on the 16th (possibly over-taking Winterfeldt's coffin on the road), and certainly gaining a lead over Bevern on the way to the key fortress of Schweidnitz.

Two further days of marching, the last of them in frightful rain, brought the Austrians to Jauer on 19 September. The 19th was devoted to celebrations in honour of the Russian victory at Gross-Jägersdorf (30 August), a delay which helped Bevern to reach the important road junction at Liegnitz undisturbed, and to take up a position to the east of the town beside the swollen Weidelache stream. Reconnaissance showed that Bevern was strongly emplaced, and on the 21st the Austrians entered a new camp on the opposite side of Jauer. 'It stood in a fine plain, and, now that the army was all together, the host appeared for the last time in all its brilliance.'[10]

The sight was indeed magnificent, but the delay in front of Liegnitz was the first check on the Austrian progress into Silesia, and it produced a new difference of opinion between Charles and Daun. The prince wished to attack and beat Bevern without more ado, and then get on with the siege of Schweidnitz undisturbed. Daun, on the other hand, believed that Bevern could prolong the campaign indefinitely by falling back from one strong position to another in the face of every new threat, and that the Austrians would do better to lay siege to Schweidnitz at once, and plant themselves snugly in Silesia for the winter.

Emperor Francis Stephen feared that further delay would compromise his brother's prestige in the eyes of the public, and under pressure from Vienna the commanders reached a compromise, whereby they would put together a force to besiege Schweidnitz, and meanwhile manoeuvre to threaten Bevern's communications, which ran east-south-east to Breslau, the capital of Silesia.

On 25 September the Austrians began to edge over to their right, a process which brought a series of collisions with the outposts in the villages in front of Bevern's camp. On that day the Austrians cannonaded and seized Koschwitz, and on the 26th they put into effect the tactic on a larger scale, when they planted a semi-circle of ten batteries to bring a concentric fire to bear against the Prussian positions around Barschdorf. They simultaneously formed heads of columns of grenadiers, fusiliers and cavalry as if in preparation for an assault, which induced Bevern to draw up his troops in line of battle. The Austrians fired 3,000 rounds of shot and shell, and inflicted 169 casualties, and the day ended with Barschdorf burnt to the ground and the Prussians heading back to their main position.

Daylight came dimly on 27 September, and 'those with the keenest sight among us believed that they could still make out the Prussian army in order of battle through the mist, which was very dense. But as soon as the fog lifted it was clear that the enemy had abandoned Liegnitz.'[11] Bevern had disengaged during the night, and was making down the Katzbach towards the Oder.

The Austrian army was constitutionally incapable of responding with the necessary speed. 'There is almost nobody to reconnoitre the terrain, stake out the camps or plan the marches, so that the best projects go to pieces because they are carried out so slowly.'[12] There was still a chance of getting to Breslau before the enemy, but on 30 September the Austrian guides confused the locality of two villages, both of which bore the name of 'Neu-Kretschman,' and the march stopped well short of the objective. Bevern had already crossed to the far side of the Oder, and he was now given the time to march upstream to the bank opposite Breslau, re-cross the river there by the bridge, and emerge on the southern side of the city, where he proceeded to entrench himself in the villages behind the little river Lohe. Prince Charles came within sight of the position on 2 October, and he is said to have thrown his telescope aside in his annoyance.

The news of the débâcle spread through Europe, and Count Henri de Callenberg wrote from Brussels to a friend how 'my heart bleeds when I think of the huge benefits which the capture of the provincial capital would have brought to Her Majesty and to the common cause, and how the same cause has been discredited by this blunder. The army's future will now be one of extraordinary toil and trouble.'[13]

This new check in the campaign endured a full seven weeks, until 22 November. Bevern's position—a Liegnitz writ large—was strong and getting stronger. The feud between Prince Charles and Daun continued unabated, the winter drew near, and the Austrians were losing their decisive edge of numerical superiority. There were more than 22,000 men lying sick and wounded in the army before Breslau, which by 22 October had been reduced to 38,000 infantry and 8,000 cavalry, chiefly by major diversions of force to the operational flanks, to wit:

- a corps of 24,000 troops under the aged General Marschall, left behind in Lusatia to observe the movements of Frederick, and reach out to the French and the *Reichsarmee*
- Nádasdy and a siege corps of 43,000 men, destined to attack the fortress of Schweidnitz

Some of these forces did great things, which must be recorded before we return to the confrontation at Breslau.

Hadik's Raid on Berlin, 11-23 October 1757

The genesis of one of the most celebrated episodes in the Seven Yeas War is to be found in a letter which Prince Charles sent to Lieutenant General Hadik on 15 September, asking him, as commander of Marschall's screening forces, whether it would be practicable and useful to send an expedition into the Prussian heartland of Brandenburg. It was known that the people there had been thrown into some panic at the news that the Russians had beaten Field Marshal Lehwaldt at Gross-Jägersdorf.

Andreas Hadik was an assemblage of paradoxes—an Hungarian of the Germanised kind; heavily built, and one of the fastest-moving of Maria Theresa's soldiers; a man of studious inclination, who seemed destined for a career in the Church, yet whose name was associated with dangerous enterprises, and who loved his wife to a near-comic distraction. Hadik replied to Prince Charles on the 17th that such a raid could be carried out by a mixed corps of 6,000 or so troops, and that the time was indeed propitious, for Brandenburg was covered only by hastily-trained militia, and Frederick's marches and counter-marches seemed to betray indecision. Charles approved the project on 21 September, and in the next month the foreign minister Kaunitz put the scheme in a wider context for the benefit of the French ambassador: 'We trust that this diversion, although only short-lived, will occasion considerable disorder to the civil and military economy of the King of Prussia, and, by forcing him to detach troops from Saxony to go to the help of his capital, will forward considerably our ambition of liberating that land.'[14]

The force assigned to the raid and the various supporting operations amounted to 5,100 men and 2,100 horses, comprising 1,100 hussars from the Baranyay, Hadik and Carlstädter regiments, 1,000 German cavalry from the Birkenfeld and Savoyen Dragoons, 2,100 Carlstädter Szluiner and Slavonian Gradiscaner Croats, 900 German infantry under Colonel Sulkowsky, and an artillery train of two 3-pounders and four 6-pounders.

While the main body was destined for Berlin, Major General Kleefeld was to be left at Elsterwerda with 1,400 of the Croats and German infantry, 160 of the German cavalry, and 310 of the hussars. His task was to line the Röder and the Schwarze-Elster and guard Hadik's western flank against interference from the corps of Prince Moritz of Anhalt-Dessau, who was charged with defending the inner Prussian provinces. This diversion of force was less damaging than it might seem, for the German infantry and Croats were drawn from men who were inadequately clothed for the main expedition. As a final touch, Hadik set out postal and courier stations to keep up the communications between the raiding force, Kleefeld at Elsterwerda, and the parent body under Marschall at Bautzen.

Hadik was meticulous in his paperwork, and he laid down guidelines for the conduct and routine of the expedition in a set of *Orders before we enter Enemy Territory*.[15] He warned that no kind of violence was to be offered to clergymen, old folk, women or other innocent and well-behaved people in Prussian lands, and that plundering and vandalism would be punished severely. In compensation 'I ask my troops to believe me when I say I will do everything in my power to provide for their necessities in enemy territory.' He told the advance guard to buy up meat and other commodities, while he sent the allied Saxon commissaries ahead to Doberlug and Sommerfeldt, in each of which places they were to requisition 8,000 rations of bread and 400 rations of fodder, ready to be sent by 14 October to wherever Hadik indicated.

The troops were to cook their rations of meat every evening, to save time on the next day. No tents were to be carried on the march, and the troops would bivouac in the woods and fields in all but the worst weather, when they could commandeer houses. The advance guard of hussars and Croats would scout several hours ahead, while the lead of the main force would alternate between the cavalry in open country, and the infantry in the woods. As for tactics

> if we encounter the enemy, the cavalry is to act with determination, and not allow itself to receive the charge. During the combat the cavalry will place small parties out on the flanks of the two lines, and, if circumstances allow, detach the third rank and get at the enemy flank and rear. The other two ranks continue to act in close order, and we must always retain a reserve. The infantry will advance boldly, and not open fire unless if finds itself in an advantageous position to do so, in which case it is to keep up a continuous fire at will. After the Croats have fired, their third rank will go over to the attack with drawn swords.

One of the objects of the expedition was to inflict economic damage, as Kaunitz had explained, and Hadik drew the attention of his force to the foundry at Alt-Schadow on the Spree, which cast thousands of shot, bombs and shells every year; the little walled town was garrisoned by a

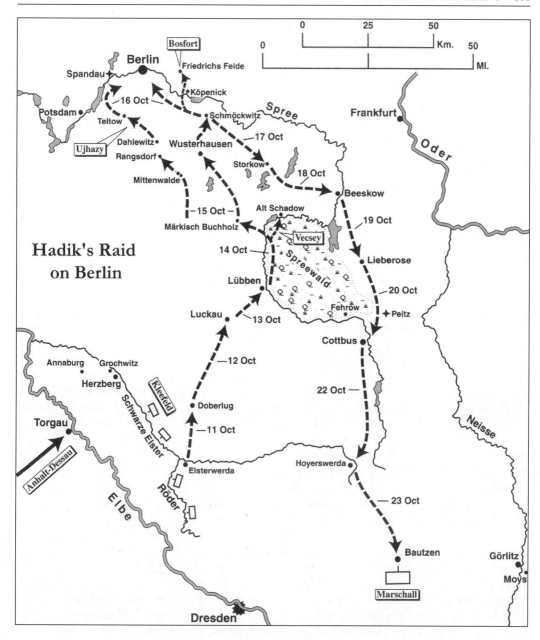

free company of one hundred soldiers, 'but they are mostly just children.' Hadik was in fact very well informed of conditions in Brandenburg, and he took with him a *Pro Memoria à observer en Berlin*—a shopping list of economic targets, embracing the Lagerhaus (the store of military textiles), the artillery depot, the flour magazine, the pontoon store, the gunpowder mills on the Spree, the cannon foundry in Berlin and its chief gunfounder, 'a famous Dutchman,' and the archives in the royal Schloss. He also specified the names of rich and influential individuals like the banker and contractor Splitgerber, the diplomats Podewils and Finckenstein, and the post-master-general Jordan. Finally it would be a good idea to 'burn all the boats on the canal, along with the store of timber to prevent them building new ones.'[16]

The start of the expedition was postponed for several days, because Hadik had fallen ill, but on 11 October he was able to write to the Hofkriegsrath from Elsterwerda that he was setting out on the same day. He had been forced to send further detachments to strengthen the cordon along the Elbe, which reduced his main corps to 3,400 men, of whom 700 were hussars, 'which means that the effect will not be as great as was at first conceived, but I will not fail to put forth my utmost efforts.'[17]

Conventional forces could approach Berlin only by taking roundabout (and heavily-defended) routes down the valleys of the Elbe or the Oder, and then striking across country. Hadik's avenue lay through the Spreewald, a tract of lakes, rivulets, and boggy or sandy woods, and he added to his chances of achieving surprise by making cunning changes of direction and throwing out diversionary forces. His first three marches lay within Saxon territory, and took the expedition to Doberlug (11 October), Luckau (12th) and then north-east to Lübben (13th), which was just short of the Brandenburg border.

The fourteenth of October was a day of complicated movements and diversions, for Hadik was now entering Brandenburg, and he wished to conceal the axis of his main advance. Colonel Ujhazy, who had been waiting at Luckau with 300 of the hussars, now set off towards Berlin by the most direct route, which ran north-north-west by way of Mittenwalde. At Lübben Hadik spread the word that he intended to continue his new direction of march north-east along the right bank of the Spree towards Frankfurt-an-der-Oder, and, so as to maintain the bluff, he ordered Major Bosfort to leave with a small detachment on the 15th and make for the Frankfurt-Berlin highway east of the capital.

Having devised the feints to his left and right flanks, Hadik turned once more towards Berlin, and marched the main body through the Unterspreewald to Märkisch-Buchholz in Brandenburg. The route took him close to the foundry at Alt-Schadow, and he ordered Lieutenant Colonel Vecsey to destroy or remove as many of the contents as he could. Vecsey took away 223 mortar bombs, 798 howitzer shells and 190 cannon shot, along with twenty-five brass moulds for casting shot. He chipped or broke up a further 4,000 cannon shot and up to 15,000 howitzer shells, though he had to leave 2,200 mortar bombs intact.[18]

By the evening of 15 October the Austrians were poised for the final move on Berlin. Hadik with the main force had reached Wusterhausen unopposed. Colonel Ujhazy out to the left was making for Berlin up the road from Potsdam from the south-west, while Major Bosfort had reached the Frankfurt highway and was approaching from the east.

The Austrians arrived before Berlin on 16 October. To have struck directly for the capital along the highway from Wusterhausen would have carried Hadik into open country where the puny size of his force would have been plain to see. He therefore turned to the right through the royal forests, and towards noon he arrived on the far side facing the Silesian Gate (Schlesisches-Tor). Even now he took care to arrange his force to make it seem as impressive as possible, forming the troops of his main body in two ranks in open ground, but in a single rank in the more broken terrain. Colonel Ujhazy simultaneously presented himself at the south-west approaches to the city.

Bold measures were needed if Hadik was to force Berlin into submission, for he had very little time at his disposal, he did not know what opposition he might encounter, and Berlin on the near (southern) side of the Spree was protected by a defensible excise wall. Although the Prussian governor, Lieutenant General v. Rochow, had been taken completely by surprise, he had a force of 4,000 assorted men at his disposal, and he sent Colonel v. Tesmar to confront the Austrians with a first instalment of troops, namely six companies of the reliable garrison regiment of Lange. The Silesian Gate of the excise wall was the entrance most immediately threatened, and here the defenders erected a barricade, and raised the drawbridge which spanned the outlying ditch.

When he had first arrived before the capital Hadik had sent a trumpeter with a summons to the town council (*Magistrat*), requiring the city fathers to send four deputies within the hour to

Lieutenant General Andreas v. Hadik. (Courtesy of the Austrian Military Academy, Wiener Neustadt)

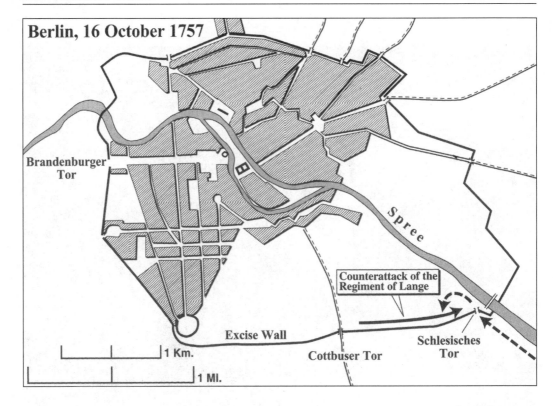

Berlin, 16 October 1757

Brandenburger Tor

Spree

Counterattack of the Regiment of Lange

Excise Wall

Schlesisches Tor

Cottbuser Tor

1 Km.

1 MI.

arrange the payment of a 'contribution' of 300,000 taler, and 'in the case of noncompliance we shall, after the elapse of one hour, and as we are entitled by the rules of war, take up torch and sword, and not hesitate to open a cannonade.'[19] One and a half hours passed without any sign of the trumpeter returning. Hadik was convinced that the Prussians were playing for time, and he proceeded with his attack.

The assault was led by Colonel v. Ried with an advance guard consisting of 150 volunteers, two Croatian grenadier companies (one each from the Szluiner and Gradiscaner regiments), and the two 3-pounders. Colonel Prince v. Sulkowsky gave immediate support with two small battalions of German infantry and two of the 6-pounders. To the left rear, Hadik formed the hussars under the major generals Baboczay and Mittrowsky, and the German cavalry led by Colonel Gourcy of the Savoyen Dragoons. This body of horse was formed in two lines, and was under orders to attack in the event of the infantry being repulsed. It would be difficult to improve on Hadik's account of the action:

> Upon this I sent the volunteers to occupy the nearest houses, while I advanced the two grenadier companies to the bridge and ordered them to open fire on the enemy. I had placed the two field pieces [the 3-pounders] on the bank, and ordered them to aim not only at the troops but also the chain of the drawbridge. The two falcons [the 6-pounders] fired at the gate. The gunner NCO Georg Joseph Thum here showed his expertise by severing the chain at the third shot, whereupon the bridge came down and the grenadiers attacked with the bayonet, inducing the enemy to abandon the bridge and the suburb on the far side—all in the greatest confusion, and with the loss of fourteen dead. Meanwhile the 6-pounders and the musketry had cleared the enemy from the Silesian Gate, and I advanced with 700 Croats, 300 hussars only (because all the others were assigned elsewhere) and 400 German cavalry through the

gate and towards the periphery of the town. I then ranged my forces in the little field which extends between the town and the gardens, leaving the German infantry and the rest of the cavalry in reserve by the gate, and placing one grenadier company and 200 Croatian fusiliers on and beyond the bridge over the Spree.

Hadik had now reached the extensive open ground inside the excise wall, and his next step was to advance on the Cottbus Gate. The Prussian commander responded by moving two incomplete battalions along the excise wall to meet him:

> I let them approach as close as I wanted, then sent the cavalry and hussars against them at an all-out gallop with their swords and sabres drawn, and at the same time advanced Colonel Baron v. Ried and his Croats to take them in the flank at bayonet point. The attacks came in simultaneously, and, in spite of coming under heavy fire, our troops did so well that not a single one of the enemy escaped—they were all shot dead, cut down, or made prisoners, and we took six colours in the process. The three to five hundred men standing in reserve behind the Cottbus Gate now took to their heels; they were overhauled by our cavalry, and, apart from a few who managed to escape, they were all captured or cut down.[20]

The survivors and a number of eminent Prussian civilians streamed away to the citadel of Spandau on the lower Spree, from where Rochow notified Hadik that the city was now empty of troops.

Twenty-eight of the 'Austrians' had been killed. The only officer to lose his life was Major General Baboczay, who was wounded by musketry and died in Berlin a few hours later. During the peace he had refused repeated invitations from Frederick to enter the Prussian service, and when he finally came to Berlin it was in a way of his own choosing.

Hadik had every reason to demand the formal submission of Berlin without delay. He had to keep this large and populous city under the impression that he had a full corps of 15,000 men under his orders; he must arrange an indemnity for his ragged and victorious troops, as an alternative to allowing them to run riot in the enemy capital; above all he had been informed by couriers that Prince Moritz of Anhalt-Dessau had crossed the Elbe at Torgau on the day before and was approaching by forced marches, and that Frederick was coming up behind him with the royal army. There was now no question of Hadik having the time to carry out his intended programme of demolitions and confiscations.

Captain Baron v. Walterskirchen now rode into the city with a trumpeter and demanded an augmented contribution of 500,000 taler as a penalty for its disobedience, and an additional 10,000 to placate the troops. The town fathers agreed to Hadik's terms, and the Austrians had Berlin at their disposal. Hadik had posted 300 hussars outside the various gates to maintain his bluff, but he was careful to keep all his troops outside the walls and free of temptation, and the only Austrians to enter the city itself were three of his officers who went to arrange practical details with the authorities.

Within eight hours Berlin had delivered an initial 200,000 taler, including a note of exchange to the value of 50,000 to be drawn in Vienna. 'After everything was agreed, General Hadik asked the council to deliver two dozen pairs of ladies' gloves, stamped with the city coat of arms, so that he could make a present of them to his Empress. The money and the gloves were duly brought to him, and he then beat a hasty retreat.'[21] By now the Prussians were so close to Hadik's path of escape that 'the aim of my expedition came down to extricating myself from the trap, and gaining a lead over the enemy, who were hastening to encounter me in greatly superior force.'[22]

At ten in the night the main body left the neighbourhood of Berlin, accompanied by fourteen carriages which were laden down with the cash and drawn by straining coach horses from the city.

Hadik remained to the last with the Croats, 'who march fast.'[23] Various legends tell that Berlin gained a kind of revenge by making sure that all of the Empress's gloves were for the left hand,[24] and that, out of deference for Imperial sensibilities, Austrian officers held their right-hand gloves in the left hand until the end of the monarchy in 1918.

Hadik chose an easterly route, which had the double advantage of putting the Spree between him and the approaching Prussians, and of opening up untouched areas of Brandenburg for his exactions. On 17 October he reached Storkau after an uninterrupted march of thirty miles from Berlin, 'on which occasion I cannot praise too highly the courage and good will with which all the troops faced their exertions.'[25] The men were exhausted, but they had held together without a single man deserting, and they found that Hadik had arranged to have two days' worth of provisions waiting for them. A Prussian advance guard arrived at Berlin on the same evening, and the corps of Moritz of Anhalt-Dessau followed on the next day.

On 18 October the Austrians reached Beeskow on the Spree, where with characteristic foresight Hadik had kept the crossing under guard since the 14th. On his right or western flank Colonel Ujhazy and a party of 300 men had the dangerous task of shadowing the Prussian movements, and Hadik learned that he had lost up to twenty of his troops in one of the inevitable encounters. Away to the north-east other parties exacted contributions in places as far distant as Frankfurt.

Having gained enough easting, Hadik made directly south for his rendezvous with Marschall at Bautzen. The Austrians reached Lieberose on 19 October, and then the Prussian enclave of Cottbus on the 20th—after a potentially risky march which compelled Hadik to post a detachment on the eastward bend of the Spree at Fehrow, and to throw a screening force around the little Prussian fortress of Peitz. The expedition rested on the 21st after ten days of continuous movement; it arrived at Hoyerswerda on 22 October, and reached the main body of Marschall's corps at Bautzen the next day.

Prussia's 'centre of gravity' was not its capital, but the king and his army. All the same Hadik's adventure deranged Frederick's plans in a way which the allied commanders might have put to better use. In its own right the enterprise had brought together boldness, trickery, accurate timing, good leadership and sound administration in an impressive way. Hadik had diverted altogether 25,000 florins'-worth of Berlin's contribution as a *douceur* for the soldiers, and on reading this section of his report Maria Theresa entered on the margin: 'this distribution is very moderate, and it speaks well of Hadik that he has taken nothing for himself. I have decided to give him 3,000 ducats.'[26] Hadik was delighted, for he was a poor man with six children, and he had set his heart on acquiring an estate in Hungary as a seat for his family. He was later rewarded with the extensive lands of Futak in the south of his native country.

The Siege and Storm of Schweidnitz, 26 October–12 November 1757

a)   Austrians: Siege corps of 43,000 (48 bns, 32 grenadier companies, 32 sq), including the Bavarian and Württemberg contingents and 10,000 Croats
Siege artillery: c. 50 heavy cannon and 10 mortars
Losses: Nearly 3,000, with sick and deserters, and 1,200 killed or wounded. Of these 31 officers and 417 men were lost in the storm.
b)   Prussians; c. 6,000 (9 bns, 11 sq of hussars), c. 180 pieces
Losses: 200 casualties and 911 deserters.

In the late autumn of 1757 we detect the first indications that the fortress of Schweidnitz, in southern Silesia, was to become the most keenly-contested strongpoint in the quarrel between Austria and Prussia (it changed hands four times between 1757 and 1762). The town itself was small and of little account, but long before the war Frederick had grasped the value of the site, located as it was hard under the border hills on the main axis of operations between Silesia and north-east Bohemia. Suitably fortified, Schweidnitz would provide the Prussians with an excellent base for offensives into the strategic heart of the Austrian monarchy, and a safeguard for the fat lands of Lower Silesia.

Work on Schweidnitz began in 1747. On Frederick's instructions Colonel Philipp Sers strengthened the well-preserved medieval enceinte of the town, and covered this inner defence with a ring of five detached forts which stood 500 metres into the country. When patriotic Prussian historians claimed so much for their hero, it is curious that they never gave Frederick the proper credit for this revolutionary plan. Vauban and other great engineers of earlier times had made use of detached forts to deny hilltops and other potentially dangerous sites to the enemy, but Frederick was the first to conceive the idea of employing a ring of detached forts in level country as a means of securing defence in depth, and holding besiegers at an unprecedented distance from the central core. The practice became standard in the nineteenth century, and culminated in the notion of the 'fortified region.'

The works at Schweidnitz consisted of five forts and five intermediate redoubts, which were capable of independent defence, as well as commanding the intervening open ground by fire. The forts were built on a characteristic star-shaped plan, and with a double rampart. The main, or inner rampart, had a scarp 12 feet high, and the earthen mass behind rose to another 24 to 30 feet. The outer ditch was swept by fire from low-lying flanking pillboxes (caponnières), and the rearward side (gorge) of the fort was closed by a wall. The wall, like all the masonry, was built from the light grey granite which was quarried in the nearby hills. The works were honeycombed with tunnels, and an elaborate system of countermines extended under the glacis (the slope leading to the open country). The garrison was appropriately strong, at about 6,000 troops, and it was commanded by Sers in person, who was now a major general.

For the Austrians, Schweidnitz would be a gain of the first order, for it would give them a bridgehead on the plain of Lower Silesia, and enable them to switch their line of communications—from the awkward dog-leg by way of Zittau to a new line which ran directly from north-eastern Bohemia.

Nádasdy's light corps first placed Schweidnitz under observation on 26 September. He then threw a loose blockade around the place on the 30th, and began to tighten the cordon on 14 October. On the 17th the Württemberg auxiliary corps of a nominal 4,000 men completed the final stage of its eventful march, namely from Würben to the Austrian encampment outside Schweidnitz. 'From then onwards the corps no longer marched with muskets slung muzzle-downwards, but loaded with ball, and shouldered smartly upright with fixed bayonets. Half and hour's distance from the camp we encountered His Excellency the Duke [he means Prince Charles] together with the field marshal [Daun] and a number of other Austrian generals and officers. We arranged the troops in divisions, and marched past and saluted to the accompaniment of sounding music.'[27]

By that time the Austrians had prepared 60,000 gabions and fascines for the intended siegeworks, and on 20 and 21 October the troops of Arenberg's *corps de reserve* marched from the main army to bring the siege force to a strength of more than 40,000 troops, which permitted Schweidnitz to be put under a full investment on the 24th. However the arrival of the heavy artillery was being delayed, not just because the roads were bad, but on account of an oversight on the part of Field Marshal Neipperg, who, in his capacity as acting governor of Vienna, had been entrusted with forwarding the siege train. After ten or twelve days, when everyone assumed that the pieces were well on their way, it transpired that they had never left the city. 'Count Kaunitz as the first minister had some strong words to say on the subject, but the damage was done…'[28]

Knowledge and expertise were also short. Schweidnitz was a ring fortress (the first of its kind, as must be emphasised), and was therefore designed on a novel concept as well as being

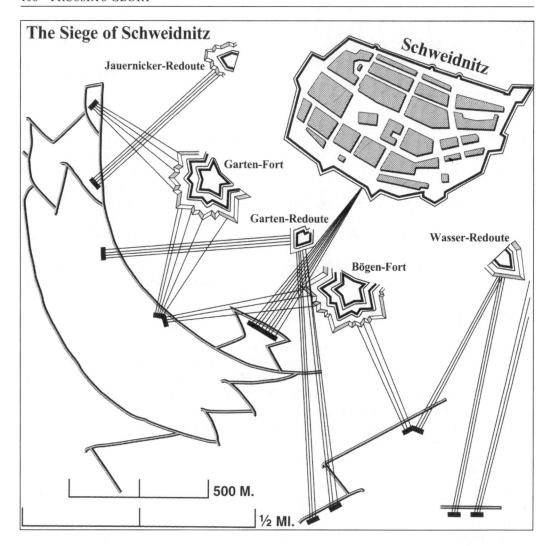

The Siege of Schweidnitz

Jauernicker-Redoute

Schweidnitz

Garten-Fort

Garten-Redoute

Wasser-Redoute

Bögen-Fort

500 M.

½ MI.

entirely new. The Austrian authorities were totally ignorant of the nature of the defences, and the Hofkriegsrath (Council of War) was reduced to applying to the regiment of Botta to ask after one of the captains who was said to have an accurate plan of the place in his possession. It was little encouragement to the Austrian engineering corps that on technical, as well as political grounds, Maria Theresa decided to hand over the direction of the siege to the French brigadier general Riverson.[29]

The first phase of the siege followed an entirely conventional course, whereby ground was won towards the fortress by successive parallels (support lines) and zigzags (approach trenches). At the same time batteries of heavy cannon were planted with the purpose of beating down the enemy artillery, and only at a later stage would it be possible to bring them much closer and smash open breaches in the ramparts. The first parallel was dug on the night of 26/27 October, and signified the formal opening of the siege, which was directed against the Bögen-Fort and the Garten-Redoute on the south-western sector of the defences. An additional parallel was opened on the following night under the protection of twelve companies of grenadiers. By 31 October the Austrian guns were gaining the upper hand in the artillery duel, though General Feuerstein commented that it was not thanks to Brigadier Riverson, who had not allocated enough ammunition. Prince Charles had to intervene to provide what was needed.[30]

In the first days of November the siege continued its course according to the near-scientific principles as established by Vauban in the last century. However the Austrians were now running out of time, because Prince Charles needed to have the siege corps and the heavy artillery with him to face the Duke of Bevern at Breslau. For this reason the Austrian high command (most probably Nádasdy in person) decided to curtail the proceedings by the very dangerous expedient of launching an outright storm across open ground.

Nádasdy commissioned the majors Johann Rhédy and Joseph De Vins to make the appropriate reconnaissances at night time, and he based his elaborate plan of assault on their findings. He targeted three works—the Bögen-Fort, the Garten-Fort, and the intermediate Garten-Redoute. Each of these works was to be assaulted by three companies of grenadiers, one or more of which

Nádasdy.

were assigned to attack the gorge. Supporting parties of three engineer officers and 800 fusiliers were to help in the donkey work of uprooting palisades and digging lodgements, and detachments of miners would cut the fuzes of any countermine charges that were detected. Separate battalions were told off to advance through the intervals between the works, and prevent the garrison of the town from coming up in support.

At nightfall on 11 November the cannonade was taken up with full violence, and the troops crowded into the trenches, laden down with ladders and other gear. The gunfire fell silent towards eleven, the hour when thirteen mortars were supposed to signal the start of the storm. Owing to misunderstandings the mortars were not fired simultaneously, with the results that the assaults were delivered one after the other—on the Garten-Redoute, the Garten-Fort and finally the Bögen-Fort.

The Assault on the Garten-Redoute

This little work was attacked first, and the Austrians, who were guided by a renegade Prussian miner, took the defenders by surprise and forced them to surrender after a short fight. The eight pieces in the redoubt were then turned around, and directed against the wall of Schweidnitz town.

The Assault on the Garten-Fort

Colonel v. Gablentz and his garrison of 350 men were fully on the alert by the time Major Rhédy led his three companies of grenadiers to the attack. The Prussians lured the Austrians by beating chamade, as the signal for a truce, but then exploded three fougasses (shallow directional mines, *Flattenminen*) which buried many of the grenadiers alive. The survivors pressed on through the spouting fougasses and a fire of cannon shot, canister, mortar bombs and howitzer shells. The ranks of the whitecoats began to break apart 'what with the murkiness of the night, the billowing clouds of dark sulphurous smoke, and the fact that many of the men were buried or thrown into the air by the mines,' but the Austrians managed to reach the crest of the glacis, cross the outer ditch (in spite of some desperate prodding by the half-pikes of the defenders) and reach the outer rampart. Here they tore aside whole rows of palisades and chevaux de frise, and seized the cannon on the terreplein and turned them about.[31]

Having thus won their way to the edge of the inner ditch, the Austrians found that it was too deep for their ladders, and they had to be content with lobbing grenades at the main rampart. Lieutenant General Arenberg ordered up reinforcements from the camp, with a battalion of the Italian regiment of Luzan in the lead. This time the attackers contrived to enter the main ditch, but their casualties were heavy, especially among the officers, and it proved impossible to climb the scarp of the rampart. Everything now hung on the progress of the attack on the Bögen-Fort.

The Assault on the Bögen-Fort

Out of all the works, the Bögen-Fort had been hit hardest by the Austrian artillery, and the garrison consisted of just 200 men, drawn mostly from the unreliable garrison regiment of Jung-Bevern. However the masonry was well-screened and intact, and anything more than a show of resistance would make the assault a perilous enterprise.

The details of the attack were concerted by Major De Vins, who knew something of the fort from his reconnaissances, and by Captain Joseph Baron Rummel v. Waldau. Two grenadier companies, one each from the regiments of Leopold Pálffy (under De Vins) and Heinrich Daun (under Rummel) were to work around to the rear of the fort, while a company of Württemberg grenadiers were continue on their way and attack the fort head-on.

The Württembergers were already at the tail of the column, and they arrived so late at the salient of the fort that the Prussians were on the alert and beat them off. The two companies of Austrian grenadiers meanwhile circumvented the fort, and arrived at the path which led from the town to the gorge. The passage was lined by palisades, and De Vins got eight of his men to sling their muskets and try to uproot the stakes without giving the alarm. They had hardly begun before a Prussian sentry barked two challenges in rapid succession and opened fire. There was no further need for silence, and the grenadiers now broke through or jumped the palisade, and made for the drawbridge which spanned the inner ditch of the fort.

The drawbridge was normally lowered every night, at least according to the unanimous reports of the Prussian deserters. This time it was raised. The Prussians opened fire from the loopholes on either side of the gateway, and in a few moments they killed four of Rummel's grenadiers and wounded another twelve. Rummel and De Vins had agreed that, in the event of being checked in one place, they would try their luck somewhere else. De Vins accordingly set off to the salient of the fort with his grenadiers and some of Rummel's, and left Rummel with the rest to keep up the fire against the defenders of the gate. De Vins and his men had only a few ladders at their disposal, but with the help of this diversion they were able to negotiate the outer rampart undetected. De Vins was in the process of scaling the inner rampart when the Prussians at last discovered what he was about, and shot dead two men at his side. There was nothing for it but to press on, and De Vins and the remaining twelve grenadiers with him sprang into the work. 'This so disconcerted the enemy that they retreated to the casemates, and opened fire from there.[32]

More and more grenadiers arrived in support, and De Vins summoned Rummel to make the ascent as well. 'When he reached the top he [Rummel] called out to the generals and the princely volunteers who had seen all this happening... It has been claimed that the defenders were taken by surprise, and even that they gave some help to the escalading troops. To look at the fort, and Rummel's huge belly, it is tempting to believe that they must also have helped him down from his ladder.'[33] De Vins now shouted to the Prussians to surrender, otherwise they would be cut down to the last man, and under this threat the enemy, or at least some of them, emerged from their lairs and gave themselves up.

In the confusions of the night Lieutenant Colonel Maximilian August Baron Zorn von Plobsheim arrived outside the fort with a supporting fusilier battalion of the regiment of Leopold Daun (not to be confused with the grenadiers of Heinrich Daun). He reached the foot of the main rampart, but found that the men who had been carrying the ladders had thrown them away when they came under fire. He told his troops to climb the scarp by digging their bayonets into the crevices, and clambering on one anothers' shoulders. 'This was going to take a long time, as you may easily imagine, and so I ran back 200 yards along the ditch and shouldered two ladders, only to engage in a struggle with Colonel Amadei who tried to take them from me—it was so dark that he did not know who I was until I enlightened him. I brought them back to the chosen spot, and I too was able to ascend the fort.[34] At the top he found that he could have spared himself the trouble, for the grenadiers of Heinrich Daun and Leopold Pálffy had got there before him. He therefore redeployed his battalion in the rear of the fort, to prevent any help coming from the town, and to enable the grenadiers to complete the mopping up inside. In this exposed position the battalion received heavy casualties.

When the fort was supposedly cleared, the gunner major Johann Wenzel Bärnkopp and a number of artillery and engineer officers climbed into the work. They intended to explore the casemates, but found themselves in total darkness. Bärnkopp ventured a few steps, and was encouraged to go further when he saw the light of a distant lantern, which he assumed was being carried by one of the miners he had ordered to investigate the enemy countermines. He called out to the supposed miner, but both the man and the light now disappeared. He then became aware of a file of troops who were creeping towards him in single file, holding their muskets at the trail. 'I could not discover their uniforms, and did not know whether they were friend or foe. "Who are you?" I called out. "Prussians!" they replied. At this I reached out with my right hand and grabbed the first man's musket. The man behind him tried to cock his hammer and fire, and so I seized the weapon with my left hand. "At them!" I shouted, in the hope of persuading the enemy that I had a support with me. At this the Prussians took fright and ran, while the two men asked to be spared.' The Austrian officers who were supposed to be with him had also fled at the noise, and Barnkopp, still clutching the muskets, hugged the two prisoners and staggered back until somebody could take them into safekeeping.[35]

By first light on 12 November the Austrians had advanced their communication trenches to the captured Garten-Redoute and Bögen-Fort, and were able to open a breaching fire against the town rampart. Emperor Francis Stephen had indicated that the garrison must be made prisoners of war, and Nádasdy sent word to the Prussians that he was willing to grant a surrender with military honours, but nothing more, and that in the case of a refusal he would resume hostilities at three in the afternoon. Major General Sers signed the capitulation, adding that he had hoped for better terms, but that he must bow to force of circumstances.

At Schweidnitz the Austrians captured 180 pieces of artillery, 48 colours, a war chest of 333,600 taler, rations to the value of 935,000 taler that would have fed 80,000 men for two months, along with 323 personnel of the field bakery, and 5,971 officers and men, including three major generals. One of their number was Johann Karl Rebentisch, who had left the Austrian service for the Prussian before the war. During the storm 'we could see his cheerful face peering through a palisade. He greeted a number of his acquaintances in a most courteous way. But then the command rang out: "Take aim!" At this he turned decidedly pale.'[36]

The frights in the tunnels were still not entirely over. The Württemberg colonel Friedrich Nicolai took the opportunity to tour the countermine galleries, guided by an NCO of the Prussian miners. He had not gone far before 'it dawned on me that the NCO had no authority to let me inspect the galleries, and that I was entirely at his mercy, since nobody had seen me crawl into the tunnels, or would know where I was. These thoughts curtailed my curiosity, and I extricated myself from the underground chambers.'

When the garrison marched out for its final parade Nicolai was glad to see his corps 'in its assigned place, spick and span, and complete with its white linen gaiters, even though the season was advanced. As the Prussians marched past their attention was caught by the sight of our corps, and they paid us the compliment of remarking that it was a pity to see such splendid men standing alongside such grubby ones [i.e. the Austrians]. The native Prussians threw aside their weapons with great reluctance; only the Saxons displayed any cheerfulness on this occasion.'[37]

The Final Reckoning with Bevern—Breslau, 22 November 1757

a) Austrians: 96 bns, 93 grenadier companies, 141 sq. About 73,000 regular troops (60,400 infantry, 12,000 horse), 10,000 light troops. Total c. 83,000. About 120 heavy pieces. Losses: 693 killed, 4,699 wounded, 459 missing. Total 5,851
b) Prussians: 20,700 infantry, 7,700 cavalry. Total 28,400. 80 pieces. Losses: c. 800 killed, 5,500 wounded. Total c. 6,350

Prince Charles was under increasing pressure to bring the confrontation with Bevern to a rapid and violent end. He was spurred on by his brother Francis Stephen, who had the prestige of the House of Habsburg-Lorraine at stake, and by Kaunitz and his own sister-in-law Maria Theresa, who told him that he ought to consult his generals about the best way to attack the entrenched camp at Breslau.[38]

Prince Charles put the question to his generals four times over (the last in a council of war on 18 October), but only the aggressive cavalry general Lucchesi consistently spoke in favour of an assault, and in any case the army was weakened by the departure of 10,000 troops to reinforce the siege corps in front of Schweidnitz. Maria Theresa was now struck by the thought that the Austrians might usefully adopt the tactics they had already employed to dislodge Bevern from Liegnitz—namely to rely on an accurate fire of artillery to drive the Prussians from their outlying villages and redoubts, after which little more than a show of force would be needed to persuade them to abandon the rest of their position.[39]

Prince Charles presented the case to his generals, but he was overborne by a mass of objections, and General Feuerstein as chief of the artillery dealt a technical coup de grace by explaining that only 24-pounder cannon had the range to hit the enemy entrenchments behind the Lohe, and 'the cannonade at Liegnitz was staged under totally different conditions. All our forces were ready to exploit, and so the enemy were induced to retreat from their positions. But that is unlikely to happen here, as we will be acting from a considerable distance.'[40]

For a time Maria Theresa toyed with the idea that the Austrians might usefully capture the little fortress of Brieg, in addition to Schweidnitz, for the two strongholds together would at least give the Austrians a foothold in Silesia for the winter. On 11 October, however, she wrote to Prince

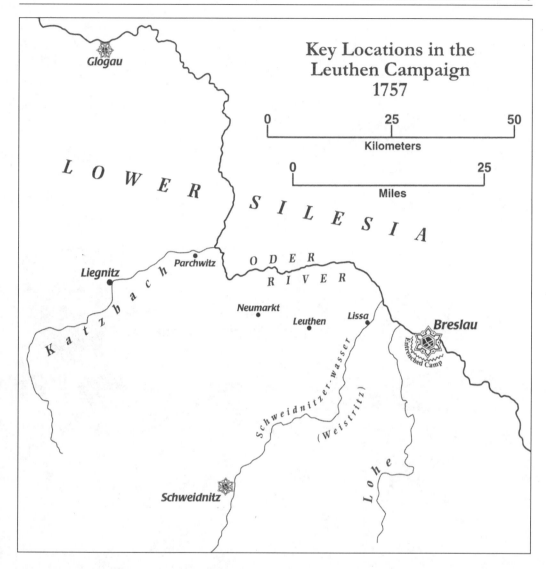

Key Locations in the
Leuthen Campaign
1757

Charles in much more forthright terms. It was important to show an example to the allies, and so the political circumstances as well as the military ones demanded something decisive.[41]

Prince Charles summoned a council of war for the morning of 18 November. The Austrians had to make some urgent decisions, and not just on account of Maria Theresa's letter—which came close to a prescriptive order—but because Frederick might arrive shortly in the neighbourhood with the Prussian royal army. News of the king's victory at Rossbach had reached headquarters on 12 November, and further reports from General Marschall indicated that the triumphant Frederick would either turn up the west bank of the Elbe and march south into Bohemia, or hold his eastward course by way of Lusatia. In the debate Charles was abandoned by Lucchesi, who maintained with Feuerstein that the Austrians should forsake the projected attack, and instead take up a strong position and await the king. However Kheul, Stampach and the French attaché Montazet all spoke out for assaulting Bevern, and Daun made a decisive contribution by arguing that there was nothing the Austrians could now do to prevent Frederick marching on Prague, if

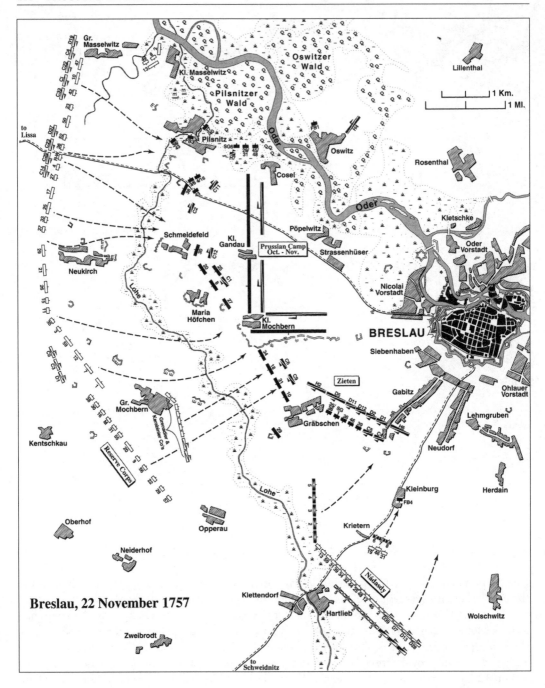

Breslau, 22 November 1757

he were so minded, whereas a blow against Bevern would at least end the campaign in Silesia in an energetic way.

This change of mind on the part of the normally cautious field marshal helped to bring the council to the unanimous decision to storm Bevern's camp. The siege corps from Schweidnitz returned on 19 November, and was followed on the 21st by the siege artillery, which gave Feuerstein the heavy pieces he needed.

The action at Breslau was certainly big enough to qualify as a respectable battle, but its character was somewhat unusual for the period, since it was essentially a set-piece attack on a prepared position. Moreover the happenings at Breslau on 22 November were going to be eclipsed altogether by the events that took place nearby on 5 December. For these reasons Breslau remains one of the least-known engagements of the Seven Years War.

Bevern was standing his ground just to the west and south-west of Breslau, and immediately behind the Lohe, a marshy-banked little river which was about ten metres wide, and which presented an awkward barrier to troops in formation, even if several weeks of unusually dry and warm weather had prevented the adjacent water meadows from flooding as they usually did at this time of year. In general terms Bevern's position was strong on its right or northern wing, but over-extended and weak on its left. He nevertheless had all the resources of the city of Breslau at his disposal, and in detail he had put them to good use.

We begin on the Prussian right wing. Here the marshy woods bordering the Oder had been cut down to form an abattis, and a group of four redoubts by Pilsnitz commanded the highway which came from the west by way of Lissa. The village of Schmiedefeld to the south had a redoubt to its right, and two outworks which bordered the marshes of the Lohe.

The entrenched villages of Maria-Höfchen and Klein-Mochbern to the south-east formed the cornerstone of the position. From there the left wing extended eastwards along a low but commanding ridge, which was lined with entrenchments and batteries.

In other words, the position as a whole consisted of a west-facing front that exploited the obstacle of the Lohe, and a south-facing front that took advantage of the ridge. The two fronts met at Maria-Höfchen and Klein-Mochbern, and the encampment therefore formed a compact and readily-defensible right angle, which gave the Prussians the benefit of interior lines. In one respect, however, the position was weaker than it ought to have been.

While the Austrians had a superiority in numbers, it fell short of the classic 3:1 ratio which is generally reckoned to give an attack a realistic chance against a well-prepared defender. However Prince Charles and Daun had done a great deal to redress the balance in their favour before the action began. In essence, they planned to lure Bevern's left wing out of its strong position along the ridge, and tease it as far as possible to the south-east. When Nádasdy arrived with 28,500 troops from Schweidnitz on 19 November he was therefore brought into position between the villages of Bettlern and Opperau, out to the right of the main Austrian army. Bevern responded on the 20th by ordering Lieutenant General Zieten to advance the Prussian left wing from the ridge and into the open country between Gräbschen and the upper Lohe.

On the 21st Nádasdy reinforced the threat by evicting the free battalion of Angelelli from the village of Krietem and constructing four bridges across the upper Lohe. The bluff worked so well that at first light on the 22nd Bevern betook himself to Zieten's wing, and further reinforced the far left, leaving only four battalions of infantry and two regiments of horse to cover the open ground between Gräbschen and the angle of the original position at Klein-Mochbern.

The Opening Cannonade and the Attack in the Centre

The plan of attack was devised by Major General Franz Moritz Lacy. An opening cannonade was to soften up the defence, after which the Austrians would put in their main assault against the centre of the new Prussian line between Klein-Mochbern and Grabschen, and deliver three subsidiary attacks:

- by their left wing against the Schmiedefeld and Pilsnitz sectors
- by Nádasdy's corps against Zieten's wing in the open country to the east

• by the corps of Major General Beck against the Prussian outposts on the far side of the Oder.

During the night of 21/22 November the Austrians built nine batteries. Eight of these were intended to open the way for the attack, and mounted a total of ten 24-pounders and thirty-six 12-pounders, giving a 'throw-weight' of 672 pounds of shot, which was heavy by the standards of land warfare. The signal for the assault was to be given by setting fire to three great pine trees, which were festooned with bundles of straw smeared with pitch. However 'the 22nd... dawned very foggy, which favoured the enemy, for we were unable to make out any features of the ground, let alone distinguish any detail.'[42] At last, towards 9.45 in the morning, the trees flared up, and the cannonade opened. The bombardment grew in intensity when more and more of the targets came into view. The flying shot show inflicted few casualties in the fortified villages, but within an hour they caused useful damage among the redoubts nearest the Lohe.

Major Franz Peter De Piza had stumped off on a reconnaissance in his curious woollen boots (he had been wounded in the feet at Moys). He found a place where the Lohe formed a single channel, and where the Austrians could make a crossing under the protection of their batteries. Colonel Spallard of the engineers fell in with the idea, and after the cannonade had lasted an hour he supervised the construction of seven pontoon bridges, together with a fascine crossing for cavalry just upstream. Colonel Peter Beaulieu de Marconnay had been dispatched by the high command to report on the progress of the work, and he discovered for himself that the rising ground on the far side would give enough space for several companies of grenadiers to establish a sheltered bridgehead.

The bridges were completed in forty-five minutes, and Lieutenant General Sprecher launched his corps of elite infantry and horse across the Lohe. Major General Reichlin was wounded almost at the outset, whereupon Colonel Carl Clemens Pellegrini took command, and wheeled a combined battalion of the second line of grenadiers to confront four regiments of Prussian cuirassiers (the wing of Lieutenant General Pennavaire) which threatened the open left flank of the Austrian bridgehead. The first attack was driven off by canister and a general volley of musketry. The Prussian heavy cavalry came on a second time, but by now Major General Prince Löwenstein had crossed the Lohe with the mounted component of the elite corps (twelve companies of carabiniers and dragoon grenadiers) and arrived on the scene.

A sceptical young captain of the Austrian infantry viewed the doings of the horsemen, and was much amused to see how the mass of elite Austrian cavalry came to a stand, apart from a few volunteers who broke away to attack some Prussian cavalry who were promenading by the villages nearer Breslau: 'as soon as they were close enough to get at one another with the sword, they trotted on parallel courses, lest they should actually come to grips. Then, to make absolutely sure of it, they made back to their respective friends at the gallop.'[43]

Some elucidation comes from one of the Scots in the Austrian service, the dragoon captain Franz Nangle, who had discovered a nasty-looking hollow in the path of the cavalry, and persuaded Löwenstein to halt on the near side. This (according to Nangle) was the ruin of the Prussian cuirassiers, for they tried to struggle across, got stuck in the marshy ground, and were shot up and finally put to flight by canister fire from some nearby Austrian cannon.[44] The bridgehead was now secure.

Early in the afternoon the main body of the Austrian centre crossed the Lohe in force. A lieutenant in the regiment of Andlau recalls that 'we were advancing to attack the enemy when, for the first time, I heard the Prussians sing—and sing very clearly—one of those famous songs in praise of their army. They were written by Gleim, the composer of all the Prussian military songs, and the one German poet who has managed to evoke the spirit of the classical odes.'[45]

The enemy were now bringing the passages under heavy fire, in spite of the counter-fire from a particularly large Austrian battery, and the Prussian musketry began to take is toll as well, as more and more Austrians formed up on the Breslau side of the Lohe. By about 1.30 in the afternoon, however, the Austrian infantry had got the better of the static fire-fight, and the depleted bluecoats were forced to abandon Gräbschen (rival claims for the credit were later entered by Major De Piza and the chief of staff Franz Guasco). The Netherlandish battalion of de Ligne was the first to enter the village, and found itself isolated under the converging fire of a nearby redoubt, and a battery which the Prussians had planted by a windmill. The aim of the enemy was getting better and better, and the battalion was saved only by the Bohemian lieutenant Przezina, who brought up eight cannon in support and opened fire on the windmill battery. The duel ended with the Prussians silenced, but all the Austrian gunners lying dead or wounded.[46]

The initiative was now taken by the restless General Lucchesi, who advanced his three regiments of cavalry and pushed the Prussians from Klein-Mochbern, where his Erzherzog Joseph Dragoons captured 7 officers, 100 men and two colours. Lucchesi then overran the neighbouring lines with the assistance of three cannon, and six companies of infantry helped him to consolidate his conquest. These gains came under a determined counterattack by a Prussian column, but the threat had drawn the attention of Prince Charles, who sent some timely support in the shape of the Hungarian infantry regiment of Erzherzog Carl, followed by Lieutenant General Sprecher in person with a further instalment of grenadiers. The Prussians were thrown back, and a great gap now yawned in the enemy position.

The Austrian Left Centre, and the Battle for Maria-Höfchen and Schmiedefeld

The lieutenant generals d'Arberg and Maguire brought a compact mass of eleven battalions to bear against the entrenched village of Schmiedefeld. Whereas the enemy defences at Klein-Mochbern had been sited well back from the Lohe, the Prussians at Schmiedefeld had built a work close to the river bank, and the houses in the village immediately behind were interconnected by ditches and breastworks. The Austrian crossing on this sector was therefore stalled by a heavy and effective fire until three in the afternoon, when the Hungarian regiments of Joseph Esterházy [37] and Nicolaus Esterházy [33] succeeded in getting across the stream. They fell into some disorder on the 'Prussian' side, and had to be rallied before they could attack the redoubt at Schmiedefeld, where they captured ten cannon and a 24-pounder howitzer. 'And now [according to Lieutenant Philipp de Souhay] my men of Nicolaus Esterházy took up a great cry of "Bring up the ammunition! Bring up the ammunition! We're out of cartridges!" The enemy must have heard something of it, for they now put up a most obstinate defence. I sent out a number of officers and NCOs to collect cartridges from the dead and wounded. I then launched an attack from all sides with the troops of the gallant Hungarian nation, and the enemy had to give way.'[47] Souhay did not mention that he owed much of his success to a battalion of Alt-Wolfenbüttel which had been sent by Major General Lacy to take the defenders in the rear.

The Prussian lieutenant general Lestwitz had ten battalions at his disposal on this sector, and he was still full of fight, but the entire defence of Schmiedefeld collapsed when Lieutenant General Wied swept up from the south with thirteen battalions of the Austrian centre, having evicted one battalion of the regiment of Prinz Heinrich from Klein-Mochbern.

Pilsnitz and the Austrian Far Left

If the Prussian defences had not been crumbling successively from the centre, in the way just described, it is doubtful whether the twenty-two battalions of the Austrian left or northern wing would have been able to achieve their final breakthrough at Pilsnitz. The Prussian positions along this sector were the strongest and most compact on the field, and not only did two of the component redoubts overlook the crossing points, but the Prussians held an abattis and a bridgehead fortification on the 'Austrian' bank of the Lohe.

The Austrians advanced in two lines of two divisions each, and took heavy casualties even before they reached the stream. The overall commander General Kheul had his arm shattered, the divisional commander Lieutenant General Clerici was wounded in the first exchange of musketry, while the excellent Major General Würben (leading the division of Angern) was killed outright. Major General O'Kelly took over the acting command of Clerici's division (then standing in the second line) and inserted the regiments one by one between the two leading divisions (Puebla and Haller).

Having thus formed a three-divisional front, O'Kelly fed the regiment of Ludwig Wolfenbüttel [10] across the bridges in the face of canister fire from two batteries. He brought up the regiments of Gaisrugg and Baden-Baden [42, 23] in turn, and he continued to direct the action on the far side of the Lohe until about one hour after nightfall, by when the loss of the Schmiedefeld at last forced the Prussians to give way at Pilsnitz as well. O'Kelly was led away with blood streaming from his face.

The Far Flank

Nádasdy on the Right

Nádasdy and his old opponent Lieutenant General Zieten (another hussar) confronted one another on the eastern flank of the field with wings of their respective armies, and grappled in no more than a half-hearted way. They had done just the same thing at Kolin on 18 June.

Nádasdy had thrown his first bridge across the Lohe on the 21st (see p. 115), and, unlike the rest of the army, he did not have to make a contested passage when he brought his corps across the river on the next day. He could oppose Zieten with an approximately equal force of cavalry (about 60 squadrons, including the attached cavalry division of Esterházy), and he had a clear superiority in units of infantry (40 battalions and 26 grenadier companies, versus 6 battalions of Prussians). However 23 of his battalions consisted of almost untried Württemberg and Bavarian auxiliaries, and he was all the less inclined to put them to the test because his objective was the limited one of drawing the Prussians over to their left, and so facilitating the intended Austrian breakthrough in the centre.

Having brought all his forces across the Lohe, Nádasdy deployed them in two lines between Krietern and Oltaschin. Both he and Zieten discovered that the ground was intersected by ditches, which impeded the movement of horse, and the action was therefore confined to lunges and short-lived charges.

This controlled confrontation was marred only by a shaming episode on Nádasdy's left flank, where he commissioned no less than sixteen grenadier companies and three battalions of fusiliers to clear the single Prussian free battalion of Angelelli from the village of Kleinburg. The responsibility was entrusted to Major General Wolffersdorf, who was 'not exactly the luckiest of our commanders.'[48]

The Prussian freebooters were duly driven out of Kleinburg, but they planted themselves in the ditches behind the village, and they threw the Austrians out again with the help of a battalion of Prussian regulars. The Austrians fought their way back into the village, or at least the part which was not already burnt down by the enemy, but they lost it a second time when they were assailed by two battalions of Prussian grenadiers. On this occasion the retreat of the Austrians amounted to a rout, and they abandoned thirteen of their cannon during their flight.

Major General Beck on the Right Bank of the Oder

Baron Beck had crossed to the far side of the Oder by a bridge of boats at Sandau, below Breslau, and on the day of the battle he advanced up the right bank with a force of 4,000 light troops and German infantry. His way was barred only by the Prussian colonel Krockow, who had posted a battalion by the river bank at Oswitz, and another in the two redoubts at Protsch. Beck subjected the positions to a two-pronged attack, and made a subsidiary assault on a post at Leipe.

In the face of these superior forces Krockow fell back to Breslau on the far side of the Oder. The battle was still in full swing on that side, and since Beck had won his way to the right rear of the main Prussian army, he was now able to post two 3-pounder cannon at Oswitz and open a harassing fire across the water. This so annoyed the enemy that they deployed two battalions and two 12-pounders along the river bank to face him. After nightfall Beck detected that the Prussians were in full retreat towards the Nicolai Gate of Breslau. What had been going on in the meantime?

The End of the Battle and the Fall of Breslau

The Prussian collapse had come suddenly. Outmanoeuvred by the Austrian breakthrough in the centre, the Prussian right wing at Pilsnitz had abandoned its defences late in the afternoon, and this move precipitated a general retreat on the city. The Austrians were unable to organise a pursuit in the darkness, but 'after the battle closed a general cry of *Vivat Maria Theresia!* was heard over the field, and the whole army gave a spontaneous feu de joie.'[49]

With a transposition of weapons and uniforms, the hard-fought little battle outside Breslau might have been an action from the First World War. Although Bevern had been pulled off balance by Nádasdy, which weakened the Prussian centre, the Austrians still had to cross the obstacle of the Lohe and assault the dug-in positions behind. The next day 'the field of battle remained until noon covered with the bodies of the dead, all of whom had been stripped naked.'[50] The successful storm had shown how 'good leadership enables our troops to draw on their full reserves of courage… The enemy had put up an obstinate defence, as is shown by the fact that many of their men had shot away seventy-five cartridges, and they were entrenched to the teeth. At last, however, everything had to give way to the bravery and valour of the Austrian soldiers.'[51]

The Austrians had lost 5,851 officers and men, which was not out of proportion to what had been achieved. But the price was more than Prince Charles could afford, when we consider that he would have to fight again two weeks later. 'At the recent affair at Breslau a number of able officers were killed, and others were too badly injured to be able to return to their regiments. The time was too short for us to be able to find replacements and sort things out.'[52]

Bevern left a garrison of 3,840 men in Breslau under the command of Lieutenant General Lestwitz, while he led the remaining troops across the bridge to the far side of the Oder. On the morning of 24 November Bevern set out unescorted for the river bank, ostensibly to reconnoitre the positions of the Austrian corps of Beck. According to his friends he had taken directions as to the best way to reach the village of Protsch, but he now mistook a party of Croats for an outpost of Prussian hussars, and was made prisoner. This distinguished captive was received with honour at the Austrian headquarters, and was taken under discreet escort to Vienna, where, as an Austrian officer records, 'the Empress loaded him with compliments and presents. I had seen the duke at our headquarters. I was taken aback by his huge size, though I have to say he was well proportioned.'[53]

Frederick took Bevern back into the Prussian service, after he had spent some time as an honoured house guest of Maria Theresa at the Schönbrunn palace. However the king did not believe for a moment that he had been captured by accident. The British envoy registered his surprise at hearing this, but Frederick answered that he knew it 'from the Austrians themselves, and that Bevern had sent a servant before him to know if there were Pandours [Croats] in that post, and then went and surrendered himself.'[54]

On the same day (24 November) that Bevern was taken prisoner, a Prussian major presented himself to the Austrians to negotiate the surrender of Breslau on behalf of Lieutenant General Lestwitz. 'He managed both to look shamefaced and speak with excessive arrogance. We threatened him with General Feuerstein and his artillery. We let him see our army, and we sent him back.'[55] Both parties were eager to conclude a settlement. Lestwitz believed that his situation was hopeless, and his judgement was further affected by painful wounds in the hip and knee. Prince Charles on his side knew that Frederick was on his way to Silesia, and that the essential thing was to gain Breslau as soon as possible.

As a sign of goodwill Lestwitz allowed the Austrians to take over the guard of two of the gates of Breslau at three in the morning of 25 November. While the negotiations were still in train a large number of Austrian officers took the opportunity to enter the city and inveigle the Prussian troops into deserting. They were seconded by monks and other pro-Austrian elements in the population, and soon whole knots of the Prussians were breaking away. They sold their muskets to the nearest bidder, or abandoned them in the streets along with their drums, to become playthings of the children.

The capitulation allowed the Prussians to leave for their own territory, on condition that they did not serve against the Austrians for the rest of the war. These terms proved to be meaningless, for when the garrison marched out on the 26th most of the remaining troops ran from their ranks to join the Austrians, or dispersed over the landscape. Only 120 officers, 151 NCOs and 328 men remained under command.

Inside the captured city, Prince Charles and his generals heard a solemn Mass of thanksgiving in the cathedral, after which the celebrant, the dissolute Bishop Schaffgotsch (an appointee of Frederick's) was led away to exile in a remote part of his diocese, and a reliable Generalvicar took his place. The power of civil administration was lodged with the Catholic *Obrist-Landes-Cornmissarius* Count Kollowrath, but the military authority in Breslau was shared between two Protestant generals, the Calvinist Lieutenant General Sprecher as overall governor, and the Lutheran Major General Wolffersdorf as commandant of the troops. Maria Theresa had guaranteed the Silesians religious freedom on 21 September, and in Breslau the Protestant clergy outdid even the Catholic in their effusions of loyalty, Pastor Weinisch comparing his city with the erring girl Hagar in the Bible, and with reference to the return of Austrian rule declaring: 'Blessed is he who comes in the name of the Lord.'[56]

There seemed every reason for the Austrians to believe that they had attained one of their prime objectives in the war, which was to return Silesia to the House of Habsburg. But the battle of Breslau had been a classic 'decision in suspense,' overtaken in a matter of days by something altogether greater, just as the Anglo-Saxon victory at Stamford Bridge was eclipsed in the eyes of posterity by Hastings.

'Hindsight handicaps historians. Perspective poses problems. Knowing that historical events developed in a certain way sometimes leads the student of history to assume that those events MUST HAVE developed in that way. Then, when those events result in something great and momentous, the student often focuses on that occurrence itself, paying little attention to its prelude, and even less to ways in which the situation might have developed differently.'[57]

Charles of Lorraine.

VI

Leuthen

To the Katzbach

For more than five months in the second half of 1757 King Frederick was forced to respond to allied initiatives, being pulled this way and that, and he was rarely able to bring affairs in any one direction to a satisfactory conclusion. It is easy to lose sight of him over this extended period, and here is probably a convenient place to present his comings and goings in summary form.

1. On 18 June Frederick was defeated at Kolin. He raised the siege of Prague two days later, but he hoped to be able to consolidate the Prussian forces in northern Bohemia on either side of the Elbe.
2. The Austrians concentrated unexpectedly to the east of the Elbe, pushed Frederick's brother August Wilhelm out of Bohemia, and on 25 July seized Zittau on the edge of the north German plain. Frederick arrived in the neighbourhood on the 29th, but in the course of a prolonged confrontation he was unable to force the Austrians from their position.
3. On 25 August Frederick had to take off to the west to face the armies of Soubise and Hildburghausen, which were now advancing through Thuringia. On 19 September an allied advance force fled from Gotha in panic, but on this theatre too the enemy evaded battle.
4. Berlin was now under threat from an Austrian raiding corps. Frederick broke contact in the west on 11 October, and hastened north-east towards his capital. The Austrians had already laid Berlin under ransom and escaped before the king could arrive on the scene, but in compensation he learned that the allies were advancing into Saxony and might give him the opportunity for a fight. He made back to the south-west.

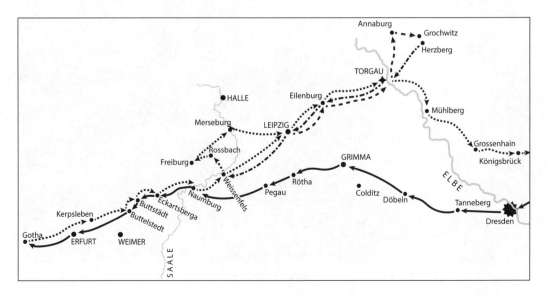

5. On 31 October Frederick's first attempt to cross the Saale was frustrated by the allies at Weissenfels, but he was able to cross unopposed two days later, and on 5 November he defeated the French and the *Reichsarmee* in a decisive battle at Rossbach. Meanwhile, over to the east, the Austrians had beaten the corps of Winterfeldt at Moys on 7 September, and turned with greatly superior force against the little army of the Duke of Bevern in Silesia. It was high time for Frederick to come to the rescue.

Frederick set out from Leipzig for Silesia on 13 November. He brought with him just 18 battalions and 23 squadrons, or about 13,000 troops of the 'Rossbach' army, but these men were buoyed up with confidence after their recent victory, and the king hoped that it would now be possible to take the Austrians in Silesia between two fires—the 'Rossbach' army approaching from the west, and Bevern's from the neighbourhood of Breslau. He at first envisaged marching along the fringes of the border hills, and he was confident of reaching Schweidnitz on about 28 November. He expected his troops to live mostly from whatever provisions they could exact along the way, but the area around Bautzen proved to be so thoroughly eaten out that he had to send a convoy of bread waggons ahead to that location.

The only obstacles in Frederick's path were the 1,200 troops of Loudon's flying corps at Freiberg in south-west Saxony (to be distinguished from the Freyburg in Thuringia), and the 12,000-strong corps of General Marschall—who had done nothing to help Hildburghausen, although assigned to his command, but who was now placed awkwardly from Frederick's point of view at Zittau in Lusatia. The king's solution was to detach Field Marshal Keith with 10 battalions and 10 squadrons from the left-behind troops on a foray into Bohemia, in hopes of drawing Marschall and Loudon out of the royal path to Silesia.

Frederick's first march from Leipzig brought him to Eilenburg. His force reached Torgau on the Elbe on 14 November, and stayed there the next day to receive the recovered sick and wounded from the hospitals, and fit itself out with its annual allowance of new uniforms—an impressive example of the workings of Prussian routine.

Having crossed the Elbe at Torgau, Frederick's corps reached Mühlberg on 16 November, Grossenhain on the 17th, and Königsbrück on the 18th. While he was resting there on the 19th Frederick learned that Schweidnitz had fallen to the Austrians, which represented the first check to his plans, and awakened serious fears as to the conduct of Bevern.

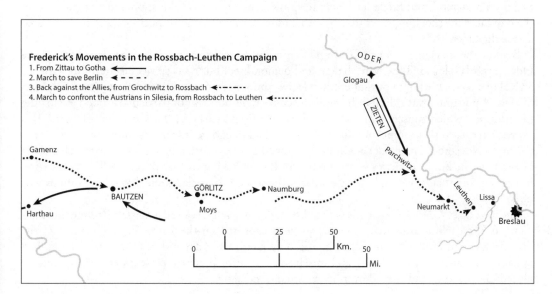

Frederick's Movements in the Rossbach-Leuthen Campaign
1. From Zittau to Gotha
2. March to save Berlin
3. Back against the Allies, from Grochwitz to Rossbach
4. March to confront the Austrians in Silesia, from Rossbach to Leuthen

On 20 November Frederick pushed on to Camnez, and from there to Bautzen on the 21st. He wrote to Bevern to tell him 'you will answer for it with your head, if you allow the enemy to push you any further back, or gain a single march on you.'[1] This kindly message never reached its destination.

Fortunately from the king's point of view, Marschall and Loudon were under discretionary orders to fall back from their blocking positions north of the border and cover Prague, if the city came under serious threat. That eventuality now seemed to arise, for Keith was assembling his diversionary corps at Chemnitz, and Marschall was told that Frederick was on the march from Thuringia with 40 battalions and 40 squadrons—a great force which might easily turn aside into Bohemia.

Even after it became clear that the royal army was making for Silesia after all, the Austrians still had to guard against Keith, who was capable of wreaking considerable damage in Bohemia with his corps, which they reckoned at anything between 8,000 and 18,000 men. On 26 November Keith was well inside Bohemia at Commotau, and an advance party under General Itzenplitz descended on Leitmeritz, where it set fire to the bridge over the Elbe, and the hay in the unprotected military magazine; the flour and oats could not be burnt so easily, and so they were thrown into the river or scattered over the ground. On the same day Loudon reached the panic-stricken city of Prague (which had never been under serious threat), Marschall arrived just to the north-east at Brandeis, and Lieutenant General Hadik marched from Hirschfeld in Lusatia for Bohemia with his mobile command of 1,500 Croats, 600 hussars and 200 German cavalry—thus removing the last obstacle of any kind from Frederick's path.

Keith took station at Postelberg on the Eger, from where he continued to sow alarm in Bohemia, by ordering the local authorities to repair the roads in the direction of Prague, and spreading reports that Frederick was on his way with a train of heavy artillery. His work done, he began a leisurely march back to Saxony on the 30th. Prince Charles wrote ruefully to congratulate Loudon on his 'far-sighted retreat on Prague… though in other circumstances I would have liked to have drawn you to the army here.'[2]

On 24 November, while the main force of the royal army rested, Frederick set off with an escort of dragoons, hussars and three battalions of infantry, and reached Naumburg-an-der-Queiss (not to be confused with the Naumburg on the Saale). Silesia extended on the far side of the river, and Frederick was told that the sound of heavy gunfire had been heard from the east two days before. A first message from Breslau explained that the Austrians had tried to storm Bevern's camp and had been beaten off, and Frederick began to spin schemes to exploit this supposed victory. Later in the day came the shocking news that Bevern had been routed from his position, and had retreated across the Oder.

By now the surviving troops of Bevern's command were retreating down the right bank of the Oder towards Glogau. They were shaken and demoralised, but their spirits began to lift with the arrival of a courier 'who, to our indescribable joy, announced the arrival of our glorious king from Saxony. A postillion was riding in front of the courier, but he was not particularly good at blowing his trumpet, which caused some of our Austrian prisoners to cry: 'He's run out of puff!' This expression caused them some amusement, and we had to endure it from them many times over.'[3]

On 26 November Frederick's main body reached Ludwigsdorf, still at least four marches short of Breslau. The king's anxieties were unrelieved, though he hoped that Bevern still had a garrison in Breslau, and that he would be able to co-operate when Frederick marched to relieve him by way of Jauer.

The next day Frederick was on his way to Lobendau when he received a message from Lieutenant General Kyau telling him that Bevern had been captured on the 24th. The true extent of the disaster was still hidden from the king, and only later in the day did he learn that Breslau had fallen to the Austrians, and that Kyau himself was retreating downriver. He ordered the man to be placed under arrest, and turned over his command to Zieten.

On 28 November Frederick and his army marched by way of Schönberg and Mühlraditz to approach the little town of Parchwitz on the Katzbach rivulet. So far Frederick had seen nothing of the Austrians except the parties of hussars who were falling back in the face of the advance guard, but it turned out that Parchwitz was in the possession of the enemy, which indicated that the main Austrian force must be close at hand.

Frederick's unopposed march from Saxony was at an end. His force had covered 308 kilometres in fifteen days, including the necessary rest days, which made an average daily progress of more than twenty kilometres, or nearly thirteen miles, which was a very creditable rate of sustained marching by the standards of the time. This feat had been made possible by the mild and dry weather (which had also facilitated the Austrians operations against Schweidnitz and Breslau), and by the high spirits of the Prussian troops, who were buoyed up by their victory at Rossbach, and were determined to make good what had been lost in Silesia.

On 18 November Prince Charles had been preoccupied with the preparations for his grand attack when the first disturbing reports reached him from Saxony and Lusatia. He had just heard from General Marschall that Frederick was marching east with a substantial force which might either swing aside into Bohemia, or continue towards Silesia by way of Torgau (p. 124). Charles had already heard that the allies had been defeated at Rossbach, but he was still unaware of extent of the disaster, and wrote to Maria Theresa that 'what happened to the French seems to me pretty bad, as is suggested by the fact that we still have no reliable account. But I hope that those gentlemen will do rather better if they choose to take their revenge.'[4] That was thirteen days after that battle had been fought and so irredeemably lost, which is a reminder of how slow and imperfect communications could be across a theatre of war. On 19 November Charles was able to confirm that Frederick had been at Torgau two days earlier, and on the 20th he learned from Marschall that the king was approaching Bautzen in Lusatia, which indicated that he was making for Silesia by the Lauban route under the border hills.

The margin of time available to the Austrians in Silesia was shrinking fast. On 22 November they beat Bevern's Prussians from their entrenched camp in front of Breslau. They took Bevern prisoner two days later, and received the surrender of Breslau town on the 25th. Charles ought now to have had his hands free to turn against Frederick, and the informed opinion of men at the time—and not just those who were wise after the event—held that he should now have marched his available forces the short distance to the west to deny the line of the Katzbach to the Prussians. It was scarcely a stone's throw from one side of this little river to the other, but the water ran swiftly, the banks were low but steep, and they were bordered by wide expanses of marshy meadows. The Katzbach therefore effectively divided Lower Silesia in two, as it traversed the plain by way of Liegnitz to reach the Oder just below Parchwitz. Major General Lacy records that 'after Breslau surrendered, the thoughts [of the high command] turned to taking up winter quarters, and allocating the cantonments and posts. I was consulted as to the necessary arrangements. I believed that we should not linger over-long at Breslau, but instead leave a suitable garrison there and march to Wahlstadt, where we would be closer at hand to the Katzbach and Liegnitz. The latter place had already been fortified, and we had a garrison in it.'[5] Lacy's advice was not followed.

On the 26th we find Prince Charles merely arranging his main force in a camp to the west of Breslau, and writing to Maria Theresa in terms that were less than decisive: 'My information is that the king arrived at Lauban on the 24th with 14 or 15,000 men. We will have to see what he has in mind… I will do everything I can to anticipate the king if he comes here, but I fancy that when he learns what has happened he will slow down his march, and that we will be able to do something to make him alter his plans. In two or three days from now we will know what will transpire.'[6]

The simplest explanation for Charles's posture is that he believed that he was managing the fag-end of a very long campaign, and that he did not grasp that Frederick would go to any lengths to recover Breslau and the rest of Silesia. However an official of Maria Theresa's household,

Count Khevenhüller-Metsch, claims that Charles was immobilised at Breslau by events that were beyond control. Count Franz Ludwig v. Salburg, the old, ugly but highly capable *General-Kriegs-Commissarius,* had aroused the hostility of the noble assemblies *(Stände)* of the Habsburg lands, and had just been forced to resign. The highly-specialised work of military logistics was handed over to the inexperienced *Directorium,* which was the chief organ of civil administration. 'The result was both immediate and inevitable, namely something of a crisis in the military system, and especially in the arrangements for supply, which caused much confusion and delay in our operations. Some people look on the changes as the reason why our army stayed so long as it did at Breslau after it had captured the town, and thereby allowed the enemy to come so near that we were virtually forced into battle.'[7]

With his main force fixed just outside Breslau, Prince Charles believed that he had no other course than to reinforce the detachments which were already scattered over Silesia, and to set out new ones. The little commands of Jahnus and Simbschen were in the deep rear, blockading respectively the fortress of Glatz and holding the line of the Silesian Neisse. Five hundred of the Württembergers were numbered among the garrison which was holding the newly-conquered fortress of Schweidnitz. Immediately behind the main army, Charles left the guard of Breslau town to a force which he described as ten or eleven battalions, and together with the weak dragoon regiment of Hesse-Darmstadt, making more than 6,000 troops.

Out on the far right flank, Major General Beck with 3,500 troops was still on the right or northern bank of the Oder, and was patrolling down river in the direction of Glogau. There was nothing for him to guard there, and his task was just to keep Charles informed of enemy movements.

It was a different story on the Austrian left or southern flank, for Frederick's initial axis of advance along the fringe of the border foothills seemed to threaten the communications with Bohemia, and more specifically the magazines just inside Bohemia at Braunau and Trautenau. The security of that part of the world depended on Lieutenant General Anton Kálnoky with 2,000 Croats and two regiments of hussars. On orders from Prince Charles, Kálnoky left one battalion of his Croats at Striegau, planted his main force at Jauer (an important road junction on the Landeshut route) and sent out detachments to Greiffenberg and Hirschberg.

The arrangements to hold the line of the Katzbach were complicated but ultimately inadequate. The one post of any strength was the walled town of Liegnitz, which had received the 2,000 troops of the former Austrian garrison of Görlitz. Charles reported to Vienna on 27 November that he was sending 1,000 men from Breslau to reinforce that place against the possibility of a surprise attack. On the 28th Frederick pounced on Parchwitz (below), on the uncovered main road to Breslau, which compelled the reinforcements to halt at Neumarkt. They were replaced there on the 29th by Major General Luzinsky with 2,000 Croats and two regiments of hussars, and were finally able to reach Liegnitz at five in the morning of 3 December. Colonel Bülow, the commandant of Liegnitz, was able to write to Charles that the reinforcements had arrived safely, and that he had spread the Katzbach inundations around the town. Bülow was a Lutheran, but also one of the best men of his rank in the army, and in fact Charles was soon to need all the insurance he could get for this important post.

The Austrian deployments in Silesia therefore consisted of a main body still encamped to the west of Breslau, and a scattering of detached corps and parties which were strong enough at best only to carry out patrols and guard little places against *coups de main.* The initiative was therefore left to the enemy. The Prussians had been approaching on a southerly axis, which had made Charles fear for his communications with Bohemia (above), but on the morning of 28 November he revised his ideas and wrote to his brother Emperor Francis Stephen that he suspected that Frederick would now turn north in the direction of Glogau, and perhaps with the intention of drawing the remaining regiments of Bevern's army to him. 'Whether this supposition is correct or not, Your Majesty may be certain that we will hold ourselves in constant readiness to counter the movements of the enemy. My only regret is that, until we have a better idea of what those movements might be, we will have to keep the army longer still under canvas, even though it has gone through a protracted and very hard campaign. Extremely cold weather has now arrived. This will bring further hardships, for there is a lack of firewood here. We cannot bring in enough wood from elsewhere, or indeed do anything to alleviate the sufferings of the troops.'[8]

By an oversight Charles and Daun had made very little provision to cover the Glogau-Breslau highway, which crossed the Katzbach by a little wooden bridge outside Parchwitz. This post was held by a Colonel Gersdorf and his force of 500 Croats, hussars and German cavalry, and on the same 28 November it was surprised and overthrown by Frederick's fighting advance guard of 4,000 troops, which enjoyed a superiority of eight to one. The Austrians were not given the time to burn the bridge, and Gersdorf's command was driven through the town and scattered, with a total loss of 43 Croats, 6 hussars and 76 German cavalry.

On 29 November Charles responded by placing Major General Luzinsky at Neumarkt with a small blocking force (above), but the main Austrian army still hung back outside Breslau, and the enemy still had a free hand. Charles merely wrote to Vienna that he hoped that 'the Prussian movements will declare themselves in two or three days' time, so that we can take such measures as are most advantageous to Your Majesty's service. In this we shall bear in mind the Kingdom of Bohemia.'[9] The last remark was significant, for it indicated that Charles was still worried about the security of his left or southern flank.

Frederick was therefore left undisturbed in his bridgehead at Parchwitz, and his 'Rossbach' army received a reinforcement from Glogau in the shape of three battalions (the grenadier battalion of Dieringshofen, the first battalion of the fusilier regiment of Kursell, and the first battalion of the garrison regiment of Mützschefahl). A convoy bearing ammunition and flour arrived with them, and Frederick was now able to set up a field bakery in the *Schloss* at Parchwitz.

The king knew that the Austrians would be at a decisive advantage if they were allowed to consolidate themselves in Lower Silesia for the winter, for they could reduce at leisure the isolated Prussian fortresses in the rear (Glatz, Neisse, Brieg, Cosel), command the resources of the best part of Silesia, and open the next campaign within striking distance of the Brandenburg-Prussian heartland (above p. 90). Frederick was aware of the odds against him, but 'I must attempt and achieve the impossible, for the salvation of the state is in the balance.'[10]

Frederick's immediate circle was under no illusion as to what was at stake. His secretary Eichel wrote to Berlin: 'Everything will be decided before the month is out. The king is absolutely determined, either to win, or not to survive his ruin. If the battle goes badly he will have nothing left, and all will be lost.'[11] If the king was killed, Eichel was to follow instructions to go to Berlin to present Prince Henry and his heir August Wilhelm with a copy of the *Testament Politique* of 1752, and a *Disposition de ce que doit se faire, en cas que je sois tué*, 28 November. It began: 'I have left instructions with my general concerning all that must be done after the battle, whether it goes well or badly. As for me, I just want to be buried at Sans Souci at night-time, and without pomp or ceremony.'[12]

The Opposing Forces

The Prussians

Total: c. 39,000, comprising 29,900 infantry, 9,800 cavalry (48 bns, the foot Jäger, 120 sq, 71 heavy pieces—namely 10 12-pounder *Brummers,* 39 ordinary 12-pounders, 13 light 24-pounders, 8 howitzers)

In the isolated bridgehead at Parchwitz the king forged the instrument of the coming battle. On 1 December thirty squadrons of hussars arrived from Glogau, as a further instalment from the forces which were being assembled there by Zieten. The newcomers included the Puttkamer (White) Hussars, who had not been involved in the defeat at Breslau, and logically speaking had nothing to be guilty about,

> and all the same we approached the king with sensations of the deepest shame. It is not too much to say that we shunned his first gaze as a condemned man evades the gaze of his executioner… We rode towards that dreaded encounter as silently and as seriously as if we had formed a particularly solemn funeral procession… It was a remarkably fine day of late autumn when we reached a hill, and became aware of the loud singing, the cries of jubilation and the resounding field music of our victorious comrades as they came nearer. Their columns were bathed with the golden sun, and they were the fitting escort of that man who was the saviour of our beloved fatherland, and the one who would avenge our honour. His expression was grim in the extreme, and even the most determined among us could not look him in the face. But scarcely had the king arrived before our regiment when his countenance relaxed into something more cheerful, and, quite contrary to his usual custom he raised his hat to us White Hussars, calling out: 'Good day to you, lads! You've had a lot to put up with, but everything will turn out well' We senior officers… were now treated to a splendid view as the victorious royal army filed past scarcely fifty paces to our front. Many of the units were bawling out hymns, while others preferred marching songs or soldier ballads. The men who were not inclined to sing could still not bear to remain silent, but chatted with their neighbours, raising their voices to make themselves heard.[13]

On 2 December Zieten arrived from Glogau with the main body of the 'Breslau' army, which brought the combined force to 48-and-a-half battalions, 133 squadrons, and the unusually large complement of 78 heavy pieces, including ten heavy fortress 12-pounders and seven mortars which Zieten had borrowed from the armament of Glogau. The Austrians had not bothered to keep the deserters from the 'Breslau' army under any kind of guard, and a large number of these men were now taking the opportunity to join the royal army, which accommodated them without asking awkward questions.

By this time Frederick calculated that he now had 39,000 troops at his disposal. This, he believed, was about the same as the enemy force (the Austrians actually had considerably more), though he expected that the Austrians would have the advantage of their strong position in Bevern's old entrenched camp outside Breslau. The king counted on being able to make up the difference by superior skill and superior morale.

Frederick never employed the positive side of his man-management to better effect than in these early days of December 1757. In terms of motivation, his army was the best he had ever led into the field. A veteran wrote that this little force was 'made up almost entirely of genuine native Prussians, for most of the foreigners had deserted, and those that remained had taken on our national character. Their guiding principle was an extraordinary attachment to their king and their fatherland, and if ever troops may be compared with the Spartans and Romans, it must have been the Prussians of that time.[14]

The units of Bevern's army had expected a typical tongue-lashing, but the king sensed that this was not appropriate. When he talked to the officers, his conversation turned on how well they had done in the past times. He walked among the soldiers, chatting with them in terms they understood. There were distributions of extra rations, and wine helped to revive flagging spirits. For the time being he kept these people in a separate encampment, but he encouraged the men of the

'Rossbach' army to come across to their lines and talk about the events of 5 November. All of this helped to turn discouragement into thoughts of revenge.

The campaigns of the Seven Years War show that it took most regiments a long time to recover from a bad experience in combat, and certainly a much longer interval than the one supervening between the battles of Rossbach and Leuthen. When Frederick drew up the common order of battle, he therefore took care to place as many as possible of the vulnerable 'Breslau' regiments in the second line, or at least between regiments of the 'Rossbach' army in the first line.

In the event, some of the 'Breslau' regiments were going to do well. However Frederick regarded them as inherently fragile, and for that reason they are listed here:

Grenadier Battalions:
Geist, Hacke, Kleist, Manteuffel, Ostenreich, Schenckendorff, Unruh

Standing Grenadier Battalions:
Kahlden, Platz

Musketeer Regiments:
Alt-Württemberg, Asseburg, Bornstedt, Prinz Ferdinand, Prinz von Preussen

Fusilier Regiments:
Jung-Braunschweig, Münchow

Cuirassier Regiments:
Gessler, Markgraf Friedrich, Krockow, Kyau, Leib-Carabiniers, Baron Schönaich, Prinz Schönaich

Dragoon Regiments:
Bayreuth (on the double establishment of ten squadrons), Krockow, Normann, Stechow, Württemberg

Hussar Regiments:
Werner (Brown), Zieten (Red)

Free Corps:
d'Angelelli, Kalben

Fussjäger (Foot Jäger)

N.B. the Puttkamer (White) Hussars and the Le Noble Free Corps were on the right (north) bank of the Oder on 22 November, and were not engaged in the battle of Breslau.

Frederick's solicitude extended to the generals. The king, unlike the Austrians, was notoriously stingy in dispensing praise and rewards, and something altogether out of the ordinary must have impelled him to proclaim a mass promotion on 1 December—Driesen and the princes Ferdinand of Prussia and Friedrich Eugen of Württemberg were advanced to lieutenant generals, and eleven of the colonels became major generals.

For the most important of the commands, Frederick selected men who, for all their differences in temperament, were guaranteed to work together as a team.

General Prince Moritz of Anhalt-Dessau (a son of the celebrated Leopold the 'Old Dessauer') was brutal, ignorant and hated by the troops, but he had the precious gift of being able to drive forward an attack against apparently insurmountable obstacles. At Leuthen he led the main force of infantry.

It was in the power of eighteenth-century cavalry wings to decide the course of an entire battle, particularly after the infantry were played out. Seydlitz was no longer in the reckoning, for he was still recovering from the wounds he had sustained at Rossbach. This put a heavy responsibility on the cavalry commanders at Leuthen.

Lieutenant General Hans Joachim v. Zieten was slight in stature, feeble of voice and of an amiable disposition. Before the war Frederick had berated him for the poor discipline he maintained his regiment, and other shortcomings, but he was now beginning to understand that Zieten was the kind of man who came to life in the presence of the enemy, even if he had performed below his best at Breslau. He was now entrusted with the command of the cavalry of the right wing.

The counterpart on the left wing, Lieutenant General Georg Wilhelm v. Driesen, was an ex-student of theology, a lover of books, advanced in years (at fifty-seven), and so fat that it was difficult to find a horse to carry him. He was also hot-tempered and demanding, and a shrewd judge of time and distance—a formidable combination.

Frederick still had at his disposal Colonel Karl Friedrich v. Moller who had commanded the artillery at Rossbach. He could be trusted to select the best battery sites—some obvious, and some much less so—and to move his pieces there with considerable speed.

The bringing-together of all elements of the army was consummated on 3 December. Frederick was convinced that the Austrians were going to stand and fight in Bevern's old entrenched camp behind the Lohe stream just outside Breslau. It would be the equivalent of the battle of 22 November but with the roles reversed, with the Austrians doing the defending and the Prussians on the attack. To overcome this redoubtable position would be the equivalent of storming a fortress, and he therefore assembled bridging materials, and called for volunteers, whom he formed into two battalions of four hundred men each to spearhead the assault. Extra weight was going to be given to the artillery by the train of heavy pieces which Zieten had brought from Glogau, and especially by the ten thick-barrelled 12-pounders that went by the name of *Brummers,* after their deep-throated boom.

Frederick summoned all his senior officers to wait on him at his headquarters at Parchwitz on the morning of the 3rd, so as to impress on then what was at stake. German artists have by tradition represented the scene as a snowy field, though Retzow suggests that the officers met at the king's table.[15] The king looked older than his years, he wore a shabby uniform, and his voice was weak— all of which was probably contrived to make an effect. His address had been transmitted with many variations, which indicates how widely it became known, but the most reliable version runs as follows:

Zieten.

The enemy hold the same entrenched camp at Breslau which my troops defended so honourably. I am marching to attack this position. I have no need to explain my conduct or why I am set on this measure. I recognise fully the dangers attached to this enterprise, but in my present situation I must conquer or die. If we go under, all is lost. Bear in mind, gentlemen, that we shall be fighting for our glory, the preservation of our homes, and for our wives and children. Those who think as I do can rest assured that, if they are killed, I will look after their families. If anybody prefers to take his leave, he can have it now, but he will cease to have any claim on my benevolence.[16]

Frederick was asking for the support of his army. He was an austere and unforgiving individual, and he allowed himself this display of emotion just once in his life, and when it mattered the most. The officers dispersed to their commands, and

> loud rejoicings resounded through the Prussian camp. The veterans, who had won so many victories under the king's leadership, now shook one another by the hand, and promised to stand by each other to the end. They made the young soldiers swear to go straight for the enemy, disregarding all opposition.[17]

The Austrians

At Breslau on 2 December the Austrian high command had held a meeting of a different kind. From the purely tactical point of view the Austrians would have done well to behave as Frederick expected, and wait for him to attack them in their entrenched position behind the Lohe. Instead, after they had spent several days sorting out the muddle in their supply arrangements, Prince Charles and his senior officers met in council and decided to leave the camp (and much of their heavy artillery), and march west towards the Katzbach.

All previous accounts of the campaign have put a great deal of weight on the only detailed description of the actual debate which has come down to us, the one given by Jakob Cogniazzo in his *Confessions of an Austrian Veteran*. Here Field Marshal Daun and General Serbelloni are represented as urging the assembly to wait in the position at Breslau, while General Lucchesi, supported by Charles's favourites, finally carried the day by persuading the prince that immortal glory was within his reach if he sallied forth to bring Frederick to battle.[18] Cogniazzo's writings provide us with some of our most valuable insights into the Austrian army, and his account of the debate seems all the more plausible because he was no particular admirer of Daun, and because the opinions as conveyed by him are so thoroughly in the character of the speakers.

Is Cogniazzo's account of the meeting correct? Almost certainly not. As a regimental officer he could have heard of the discussion at best only at second hand. Moreover the official documents and the letters of Prince Charles show clearly that the Austrians had no desire to rush into any kind of battle, and were responding slowly and unwillingly to the news that Frederick had reached the near side of the Katzbach, that a great quantity of artillery had reached his camp, and that peasants were preparing fascines, gabions and other engineering materials, 'from which it was easy to deduce that he would continue to advance, and seize Neumarkt and Liegnitz as his first objective. He would then either do battle with the Austrian army, which was then in the captured Prussian camp at Breslau, or cut the supply convoys from Bohemia and establish himself in the neighbourhood of Striegau and the Bohemian border.'[19]

This was the immediate occasion of the council of war, which concluded unanimously that the Austrians must reinforce Liegnitz (1,000 infantry being dispatched there immediately after the meeting), establish a mixed command of Croats, hussars, Saxon chevaulegers and Austrian cavalry at Neumarkt on the highway towards Parchwitz, and extend a cordon along the Katzbach as security for winter quarters.[20]

The charge of over-confidence may also be dismissed out of hand, for Charles knew that his army was in no condition to fight a pitched battle. He wrote to Maria Theresa that his cavalry was so weak that it was difficult to put together so much as three squadrons per regiment. The men had ridden off in various directions, whether on operational detachments, as escorts for prisoners, or just to collect remounts, 'all of which means they are scattered in ten different places, without my knowing exactly where; it is pretty much the same with the infantry, because most of the troops we send to the hospitals do not get better. The same applies to the hussars, so that on paper Your Majesty has plenty of troops, but of these hardly two-thirds are fit to fight.' He put the number at scarcely 50,000.[21] In a companion letter to Francis Stephen the prince counted the Croats, the Bavarians and the Württembergers in that number.

This evidence too is startling, for historians have estimated the army at between 65 and 90,000 strong. We must therefore pause a little to take more detailed stock of both the available forces and their quality.

It is certainly possible to arrive at the higher figures by multiplying the number of Austrian units in Silesia by their full establishments, by supposing the German auxiliaries at the full treaty number of 10,000 (6,000 Württembergers and 4,000 Bavarians), and throwing in Croats at will. It is a different matter entirely to determine the numbers actually present with the main army, and in a state to fight.

For a start, considerable forces had been left behind to garrison Schweidnitz (6,000, including 500 of the Württembergers), Breslau (another 6,000) and Liegnitz (recently reinforced to 3,000), and a number of detachments were out of reach—the force of Jahnus blockading Glatz, Simbschen's command on the Neisse, Kálnoky's 2,000 in the neighbourhood of Jauer, and that of Beck (up to 3,500) on the right bank of the Oder.

In detail the garrisoning of Schweidnitz and Breslau swallowed up:

- from the main army: the regiment of Alt-Colloredo, one battalion from each of the regiments of Mainz, Sprecher and Wied from its reserve corps, and the four squadrons of the Hesse-Darmstadt Dragoons from its first line;
- from Nádasdy's corps: one battalion each of the regiments of Botta, Leopold Daun, Erzherzog Carl, Moltke, and Thürheim.

Altogether the number of men on verifiable detachments must have come to at least 18,000.

There is no straightforward way of calculating the numbers which went forth to battle on 5 December, for the surviving lists enter the troops of the main army by different sets of standards, and exclude altogether the corps of Nádasdy, the hussars and the Croats.

The official Austrian returns of 30 November fix the average strength of a regiment of cuirassiers or dragoons at a feeble 377.

Two further documents[22] date respectively from 1 and 3 December, when the Austrians were working out the numbers of the serviceable infantry with the main army and the resulting lengths of frontage. The lists agree very closely, and produce an average total of 24,064 infantry, distributed as follows:

Left Wing	Right Wing	*Corps de Reserve*
9,121	11,869	3,074
Corresponding Frontages		
3,693.5 paces	5,016.5 paces	1,312 paces

The troops listed above are specified as 'being able to take to the field,' and exclude the sick, who are put at 3,312 men with the army, and 11,466 in the rearward hospitals, making a total of 14,778.

A third list[23] is dated 1 December, and sets out the infantry in a different form:

First Line:	1,757 grenadiers	14,373 fusiliers	Total: 16,130
Second Line:	1,840 grenadiers	11, 656 fusiliers	Total: 13,496
Corps de Reserve:	847 grenadiers	3,571 fusiliers	Total: 4,418
Totals:	4,444 grenadiers	29,600 fusiliers	
Grand Total:			**34,044**

The figures include the sick, who are specifically excluded in the previous documents.

The gunners are listed in neither the Prussian or the Austrian returns, but the number of pieces fielded by the Austrians at Leuthen probably amounted to 75 heavy cannon and 170 3-pounder battalion cannon.

The detached troops and the sick together amounted to at least 32,800 men. They were compensated only in part by the corps of Nádasdy, which may be estimated at:

- 10 battalions of German and Hungarian infantry: c. 5,000
- 4 regiments (21 sq) of dragoons: c. 1,600
- Croats and hussars: c. 5,000
- 3 regiments of Saxon chevaulegers: c. 1,200
- Württembergers and Bavarians: c. 8,000
  - Grand total: c. 20,800

With every effort it is difficult to push the number of combatants available to the Austrians at Leuthen beyond 55,000, and Prince Charles's lower estimate is probably nearer the mark.

Since the victory at Kolin the main Austrian army had enjoyed an unbroken run of successes. The troops were confused, certainly, by the muddle which had attended the river crossings and their overnight bivouac, and their ranks were thinned by the disease and casualties attending this very long-drawn out campaign, but they had the benefit of eleven days of comparative rest outside Breslau, and almost all of the 'German', Hungarian, Netherlands and Italian units could be counted as battle-worthy and effective.

The three regiments of Saxon light horse (Prinz Carl, Graf Brühl and Prinz Albrecht) had all escaped from Prussian captivity, and had helped to beat Frederick at Kolin. The battalion of Red Würzburg (maintained on the Austrian establishment) was a fine body, and probably the equivalent of a good Prussian grenadier battalion in combat effectiveness. It was a different story with the rest of the Germans. The Württembergers were holding together well, and their single company of grenadiers which had been in action at Schweidnitz had behaved respectably enough, but as Protestant bluecoats they were liable to take the blame if anything now turned out badly. The Bavarians were totally untried.

The Austrian leadership was fragmented to a dangerous degree. The nominal command was invested in Prince Charles of Lorraine. He was not without his qualities, as we have seen, but he lived on uneasy terms with Field Marshal Daun, who was level-headed and technically proficient, but was now relegated to the post of *ad latus* or adviser.

Cohesion was not helped by the fact that the sizeable corps of General Franz Leopold Nádasdy had so far functioned on campaign as a semi-independent entity, carrying out specific missions like the recent siege of Schweidnitz. Nádasdy himself was a fine leader—intelligent and active, a man who recalled in these respects his opponent Zieten—but he was accustomed to acting on 'recommendations' from the high command, rather than outright orders, or so Prince Charles reported after the battle.

General Giovanni Battista Serbelloni, the commander of the cavalry of the left wing at Leuthen, was unpopular to the point of infamy, having alienated almost every officer he encountered through his patrician hauteur, his coldness and his sluggishness. He had managed his division under fire at Kolin in a cool and efficient way, but he was a quirky individual, and he owed his position in at least part to his membership of one of the leading aristocratic houses of Austrian Lombardy.

The traditional cavalry virtues were more evident in Serbelloni's counterpart on the right wing, General Lucchesi d'Averna. He was a Sicilian, brought up in Spain, and his impatience, ambition and love of action had drawn him to the company of the turbulent Field Marshal Maximilian Ulysses Browne, who had been mortally wounded at Prague. Lucchesi had lost one patron, but he gained another in the Austrian chancellor Kaunitz, who recognised in him qualities that were rare among Austrian generals, and probably intended to groom him for high command.

Approach to Contact, 4 December 1757

The Austrian plans would have made sense against an enemy less determined, indeed less desperate than Frederick. There was nothing in the correspondence of Prince Charles to indicate that he intended to do anything more than secure advantageous quarters for his army for the winter. This would have been in keeping with the thought and practice of the time, and especially since the armies had been keeping the field long past the usual end of the campaigning season. To have remained in the entrenchments at Breslau would have yielded up the rich open country of Lower Silesia, and endangered the army's excellent new line of communication, which ran from south to north by way of Schweidnitz. A push to the Katzbach, on the other hand, might seal up the single Prussian bridgehead at Parchwitz, and gain the rest of the right bank as a screen for the Austrian winter quarters. The tactical advantages of such a position were by no means negligible, as Frederick was to going to experience in the campaign of Liegnitz in August 1760, when he was able to cross to the right bank of the stream only after repeated failures.

A number of incidental details confirm that nothing was further from Charles's mind than giving battle. He was marching into country which was largely unknown, and where nothing had been prepared in the way of fortifications. He was leaving his heavy artillery behind in the camp at Breslau, his field bakery was sited ahead of the army at Neumarkt, and his battalions of grenadiers had been split up and the companies re-integrated in their parent regiments to be ready for winter quarters, which deprived him of his most effective single striking-force.

At eight in the morning of 4 December the Austrian main army began to extricate itself from the encampment at Breslau in four great columns, namely, from right to left, the columns of the cavalry and infantry of the right wing (both assigned to march to the north of the highway), the infantry column of the left wing and the train of artillery (both along the axis of the highway), and the cavalry column of the left wing (to the south of the highway). The Austrians intended to reach the Katzbach in two days of marching, and the destination of the first day's march was on a line with the Pfaffendorder-Berg, a rounded hill just short of the little walled town of Neumarkt.

Fourteen or fifteen bridges had been built across the Lohe and its marshes, and another five across the further obstacle of the Schweidnitzer-Wasser to supplement the permanent wooden bridge at Lissa. Both the Lohe and the Schweidnitzer-Wasser were swollen by heavy rains, and the progress of the march soon began to drop behind schedule. The Württemberg staff officer Friedrich v. Nicolai did not know whether the confusion was general, 'but I can say, as regards the columns of the left wing, that they kept getting in each others' way and colliding... None of the columns would give way to the others, and every regiment or battalion, regardless of where it belonged or where it was assigned, just wanted to be the first to cross whatever bridge or passage it happened to encounter.'[24]

Overnight Frederick had learned that the Austrians were preparing to leave their encampment, and early the next morning he set his army in march westwards from Parchwitz in four columns. In the lead was the twenty-five year-old Lieutenant General Friedrich Eugen of Württemberg with an advance guard of fourteen-and-a-half battalions and sixty squadrons. A lieutenant Hohenstock had been posted close by the route that was being taken by the cavalry of the Austrian right wing (by way of Pilsnitz, Gross-Maschelwitz and Nippern). He saw enough standards being carried across the Lohe to convince him that the whole of the Austrian army must be passing the stream, and he galloped back to convey the news.[25] The report spread through the ranks of the army, and the cry of 'Now we've got them!' rang out from one platoon to another.[26]

Frederick had taken personal charge of the twelve squadrons of the White and the Zieten Hussars, and he was hurrying along the highway well ahead of the main body of the advance guard. The bells of the neighbouring villages were sounding across the fields, and on approaching Neumarkt columns of smoke could be seen rising from the town, which, as the peasants explained, were generated by the field bakery of the Austrians, which had been left in this exposed position. Although Neumarkt was the nearest defensible point to Parchwitz, it was guarded by Major General Luzinsky and Colonel Gersdorf with just two battalions of Croats and two regiments of hussars, and a body of reinforcements under Lieutenant General Nostitz (below) had not yet arrived.

Neumarkt and the bakery were incidental to Frederick's purpose, which was to anticipate the Austrian army on the Pfaffendorfer-Berg on the far side of the town. The king ordered Major Podgursky with five squadrons of the White Hussars to dismount and break in the gates *à la Pegau,* which they accomplished with the help of axes they took from the neighbouring farms. Inside Neumarkt the Croats tried to offer a defence from behind the shelter of houses, walls and fences, but they were soon driven out of the far end of the town. They re-grouped on the Pfaffendorfer-Berg, but were taken in a double envelopment which the Prussians launched across the Rohrwiesen-Graben on either side of the hill. The Austrian hussars had made themselves scarce, and so 'a frightful massacre ensued on the spot.'[27] Altogether 300 of the Croats were cut down or captured.[28] Lieutenant General Nostitz had been on his way, but all he could do now was to receive the survivors west of Borne.

On the captured hill Frederick saw the flagged posts which the Austrian staff officers and company clerks had planted to mark the lines of the intended Austrian camp, which reminded him how narrow the margin of time had been. While the Prussian advance guard pushed on to Kammendorf and Bischdorf, Frederick assigned the main force to bivouacs on either side of Neumarkt.

At noon the Austrian army was in the process of crossing the Schweidnitzer-Wasser when the first reports of the clash at Neumarkt reached Prince Charles at Lissa. The news was confirmed in graphic form by the sight of the Croats who were coming back with blood streaming from their heads. Charles and Daun could no longer doubt that something serious was afoot. They ordered the carts bearing the tents and the rest of the baggage to go back across the river, and tried to hurry the westward march of the army through the heavy rain which now began to fall. In the evening Charles penned hasty letters to Maria Theresa and Francis Stephen from Lissa. Writing to Maria Theresa he explained that 'a battle is more likely than otherwise, because the armies are now so close.' He trusted that the Austrian arms would once more be blessed with victory. Rather more of his thinking is betrayed in the companion letter to his brother: 'I believe that he [Frederick] intended to prevent us passing the Schweidnitzer-Wasser, so that he could take Liegnitz at his leisure, but we have arrived here in daylight and while there is still time to get our bearings a little... Tomorrow we shall see what will transpire, and I hope that God will finish his good work. The spirits of our men are high.'[29]

The regiments of the main army dumped themselves down wherever their march came to an end, on a rough north-south alignment to the rear of Nippern and Leuthen. Nádasdy's corps came up tardily to the left rear, and the Württembergers arrived only at eleven at night. There were no tents, and no straw to cover the ground, which was beginning to freeze, and 'before midnight half the army left the bivouacs for the woods, to cut firewood and drag it out. The din was so loud that it must have been heard for the distance of an hour's march or more.'[30]

Colonel Friedrich v. Nicolai was serving as adjutant to the Württemberg major general v. Romann, and 'in consequence of my duties I had to go to the headquarters of Prince Charles at Lissa to learn the password and receive the orders. However it was generally believed in the army that the Prince and Field Marshal Daun were still in the bivouacs over to the right, and that the password and the orders would be given there. I set off with the intention of making my way in that direction between the first and second lines. But it proved impossible. I would be riding along the front of such and such a regiment, believing that I could follow the line and arrive at the wing of the army, and then I would encounter the front or rear of another regiment which lay squarely across my path.' Nicolai went to Lissa, where he was told that Charles and Daun were with Nádasdy in the neighbourhood of Gohlau or Rathen. They were not to be found there either, and it was after midnight when he simply had to report to the Württemberg generals that 'nobody in the army is aware of any orders.'[31]

Frederick had meanwhile established his quarters in a house (No. 7) in the Market Place at Neumarkt. In this case there was no uncertainty as to where the chief was located, and in the evening of the 4th his generals assembled there to receive his instructions. He entered the room smiling, and he remarked 'the fox has crept from his den, and I shall punish him for his impudence.'[32]

The rain had cleared, but during the night showers of snow alternated with clear starlit intervals of intense cold.

The Battle of 5 December 1757

The Ground

The field of the coming battle belonged to the near-level plain of the Oder, with its vast horizons. It was arable country, now in the grip of winter, and the surface was hard frozen under a dusting of snow. The only obstacles to movement were presented by the marshes and the isolated Zettel-Busch wood up to the north-east by Nippern, by some copses, ditches and boggy ground to the south of Sagschütz, and by the contiguous Leuthener-Busch and Rathener-Busch to the north-east of Leuthen, which were part of the zone of mixed woodland extending towards Lissa. The Breslau highway traversed the field on an east-west axis, and the ground to either side was entirely clear.

The villages were isolated affairs, built (so far as it is possible to discover from the surviving older houses), of brick covered with plaster, and roofed with thatch or red tiles. In this largely open land-scape the eye was drawn to the spire of the Catholic church in Leuthen. This was the largest of the villages, and it appeared to be more extensive than it was, when seen from the north or south. Closer acquaintance showed that it consisted merely of houses and farm buildings strung out on either side of its dusty street—two rows to the north, and one to the south. A common feature Leuthen shared with Borne (to the west) was that their respective churchyards were each surrounded by a low but very strong wall of coarse-grained brown stone, formed into roundels at the corner.

The German word *Berg* can signify anything from a craggy mountain to a hillock, but it must have taken a leap of the imagination on the part of the Silesian peasants to attach this word to the elevations in this neighbourhood, which Carlyle describes more aptly as 'heavings of the ground.' The Pfaffendorfer-Berg to the east of Neumarkt was one such heaving, and so was the Schön-Berg south of Gross-Heidau, from where Frederick was to make his first reconnaissance. The tumulus-like Butter-Berg lay to the south-west of Leuthen, too distant from the Austrian lines to be incorporated in any scheme of defence. This feature was to acquire some importance as the battle wore on.

Highly relevant to the preliminaries and to the very end was the sequence of swellings which ran down the western side of the field from the neighbourhood of Borne to that of Lobetinz:

*   the adjoining Schön-Berg and Schmiede-Berg
*   the Schleier-Berg
*   the Wach-Berg

However the only feature of defensive potential on the whole field was the Kiefern-Berg ridge over to the east, which was crowned by the little settlement of Sagschütz and the tall pines that gave the hill its name.

Neither the Prussians nor the Austrians had expected to meet their enemies in the open field, let alone in the neighbourhood of Leuthen. The king had prepared his army materially and mentally to assault the Austrian positions in front of Breslau, while the Austrians had been moving tardily to shore up the threatened line of the Katzbach.

As things turned out, the terrain of the coming battle favoured the Prussians in two important respects. First it was almost entirely open, and therefore facilitated the rapid movement of all arms. The dusting of snow which had fallen overnight was no kind of obstacle, and even the heavy *Brummers* were unlikely to sink into the hard-frozen ground. Next, it was thoroughly familiar to Frederick and his commanders, for it was the setting of the major Lower Silesian manouvres which they staged every year before the war. Zieten, for example, happened to be acquainted with every tree and ditch to the east of Sagschütz, and knew how to extract every ounce of benefit from this otherwise unremarkable landscape.

Prince Charles and Daun knew nothing of the ground except what they had been able to glean before darkness fell on the 4th, and the lack of salient features told to their disadvantage. According to one story Daun had to ride up and down in front of his army on the morning of the day of battle, and ask the peasants to tell him the names of the villages and other objects. 'Amongst other things his eye was caught by the tower of a church which could be seen rising above a hill. "What is that?" he enquired of a peasant. The man assumed he was talking about the hill, and replied: "Your Excellency, that's the hill from where the our king drives the Austrians every year." Daun turned to his suite and remarked, "Gentlemen, I don't like the sound of that!"[33] Kolin in Bohemia had been the stamping ground of the big Austrian manoeuvres in the early 1750s, but here the tables were turned.

First Blood—The Clash at Borne

Frederick left his quarters in Neumarkt long before daybreak on the morning of 5 December. He toured the bivouacs of the right wing of his cavalry, then rode to the Gardes du Corps. The weather was fine but very cold. The riders were standing by their horses, and clapping their hands in an attempt to warm them. "'Good morning, Gardes du Corps!" called out the king. "The same to you, Your Majesty!" "How's it going?" asked Frederick. "Well enough, but it's bloody cold!" "Just wait, lads, it's going to be too hot before long!"'[34]

In fact Frederick was not confident that anything could be retrieved from the disaster if the Prussians were defeated, and, according to the gossipy Kalckreuth, he ordered Major Friedrich Wilhelm Kleist ('Green Kleist') to post himself with a squadron of his hussars well to the rear. 'What I am going to tell you,' writes Kalckreuth, 'I had from the major himself under the seal of the strictest secrecy. The king… told Kleist: "If it goes badly, I'll come to you, and you'll be my escort." After his brilliant victory the king never forgave Kleist for having been the recipient of his confidence.'[35]

The Prussians took up arms at five in the morning and formed themselves into their marching columns. Frederick was probing ahead through the mist with his fighting advance guard (the combined hussars, the three free battalions, the *Fussjäger,* the Württemberg Dragoons, nine battalions of infantry, with ten heavy 12-pounder *Brummers* close behind). The main force of infantry set off at six, marching in two columns 'by lines'. Between Neumarkt and Kammendorf the foot soldiers were joined by the cavalry, who closed in to form an outer column on either side.

The drums had not beaten the *Generalmarsch,* lest the sound should carry to the Austrians, but now the soldiers took up a Lutheran chorale to steel themselves for their holy task. They were accompanied by the regimental woodwind, for the tune was a familiar hymn by Johann Bermann, *O Gott, du frommer Gott.*

> Grant that I do whate' er I ought to do,
> What for my station is by Thee decreed;
> and cheerfully and promptly do it too,
> and when I do it, grant that it succeed!

A famous anecdote tells how Frederick halted, and an anxious adjutant rode up to ask him if the soldiers ought to be silenced. 'No, stay with me here.' The king recognised the value of religion, even if he had none himself, and he turned to the pious Zieten and commented: 'With men like these, how can I fail to win?'[36]

The advance guard must have been moving cautiously, or at least with frequent halts, for it was eight in the morning before Frederick had any sight of the enemy. The mist was beginning to lighten from the east, and the silhouette of what was taken to be an entire army stretched on the near side of Borne. Then, or not long afterwards, bodies of Croats were discerned in the Lampersdorfer-Busch and the thickets of the Borner-Berg, and Frederick ordered Major General Prince Karl of Bervern to take six of the battalions of the advance guard and post them to the right-front of the main army.

As the light strengthened and the distance closed, the Prussians could see that the force facing them was much smaller than had at first appeared—in fact a mixed corps of Croats, two regiments of Austrian hussars and the three regiments of Saxon chevaulegers—which had been posted to the west of Borne to serve as the eyes and ears of the Austrian army. The overall commander, the Saxon lieutenant general Nostitz, was a first-class officer who had been one of the heroes of Kolin, and now he gave discretionary orders to his troops to retreat by instalments, if they came under irresistible pressure.

Nostitz was unaware of the odds he was facing on the morning of 5 December, doubtless on account of the fog, and in the event he disengaged too late. The Prussians threw their first line of hussars into a frontal attack, while a body of the Székely Hussars closed in on the enemy right flank. The Austrian Nádasdy and Dessewffy Hussars made good their escape, but the horses of the Saxons were out of condition and heavily laden, and ran out of breath as they laboured after the fleeing Hungarians. The village of Borne was a further impediment to the retreat, and Nostitz lost a number of his men before he could win free. The Prussian hussars spurred on unchecked, and the French attaché de Marainville saw one of them split the skull of an Austrian cuirassier just thirty paces from the nearest house of Leuthen.

The clash outside Borne was typical of Frederick's methods, and just as typical of the Austrian high command in the way it failed to support its exposed detachments. 'Whenever he [Frederick] is on the move he is careful to screen his march by a large number of hussars… The Austrian hussars can never hold their own against them. The Prussian variety fights by squadrons, like the dragoons, and the king supports them with infantry backed up by cannon. In such a way he conceals his movements completely from the enemy, while being able to reconnoitre the enemy on their own ground.'[37]

The action at Borne had enabled Frederick to continue his advance, and take stock of the Austrian positions at his leisure. The psychological implications were also important. Nostitz and the surviving Saxons ultimately joined Nádasdy's corps on the far side of the field, but the fact remained that three of the best regiments of the army had received a severe mauling. Thus the Prussian gained a moral advantage at the outset of the battle, and Frederick took care to have the prisoners led past the advancing columns of his main army.

The Austrians Move into Position

The Austrians spent the rest of the morning in the business of advancing their troops from their chaotic bivouacs to their fighting positions which extended in a rough north-south axis athwart the highway. The main forces were arranged in a conventional style, in two lines, with the cavalry on the flanks and the infantry in the centre. The right flank was mostly tucked away behind the Zettel-Busch; Croats were stationed in the wood itself, and the grenadiers of the *corps de reserve* were detached to hold the outlying village of Nippern in a hollow to the right.

The Austrians were already heavily outgunned, and they did themselves no good by scattering most of their available heavy artillery in four batteries at approximately equal intervals along their main frontage. Two of the batteries were sited respectively to the north and south of Frobelwitz, and the other two to the west of Leuthen. A fifth battery was positioned in front of Nádasdy's corps, but for reasons unknown it scarcely figured in the coming action.

Some features of the Austrian deployment call for special attention. It was in the first place extraordinarily long, at more than seven kilometres (four-and-a-half miles) along its main axis, or nearer nine (five-and-a-half miles) if we take in the re-entrant which extended to the east in front of Sagschütz. By this stage of the war the Austrian commanders were well aware of Frederick's habit of concentrating his attack against one or other of his enemy's flanks, and the most obvious countermeasure was to form the infantry into three ranks instead of four, and extend the lines as far as was physically possible. Length was therefore obtained at the expense of depth,[38] and length itself could be damaging if driven to excess. At Leuthen it was going to take one-and-a-quarter hours to shift troops from one wing to the other, which hindered the various arms from lending mutual support, and actually added to the problems of dealing with a flank attack.

Daun has the credit for a further and more positive device, that of forming a mobile *corps de reserve*. This body had proved its worth at Kolin, where it had enabled him to check the first lunge of the Prussians, and the corresponding formation at Leuthen was commanded by the respected Lieutenant General Charles Leopold v. Arenberg, and consisted of three 'German' battalions, and five battalions of the liveliest troops of the army—one of Hungarians, and four of the French-Netherlandish Walloons, a people of ancient Gallic blood. Frederick would have to make all the more certain that he could trick the Austrians into sending their reserves in the wrong direction.

The far left flank of the Austrian army was formed of the semi-independent corps of Nádasdy, which was bent in a hook facing west and south. After the battle, Nádasdy was much criticised for the way he deployed his contingents of Bavarians and Württembergers, 'who certainly do not measure up to the Austrians, who are excellent troops.'[39] In detail, the ten battalions of Bavarian auxiliaries were positioned at the far end of the west-facing axis, and the thirteen battalions of Württembergers on a south-facing axis along the Kiefern-Berg. Prince Charles claimed to Maria Theresa that, according to one of his 'recommendations,' Nádasdy was to have constituted his first line entirely of Austrians, and relegated the untrustworthy auxiliaries to the second line, 'but when Field Marshal Daun inspected the left wing on the morning before the battle of the 5th, he found that the Bavarians had been placed at the extreme end of a salient, and the Württembergers on the [other] flank of that salient—a most dangerous deployment which corresponded with their seniority in the order of battle, but one which incurred great risks.'[40]

The charge does not make complete sense, for Nádasdy had only ten battalions of Austrians, as opposed to twenty-three battalions of auxiliaries, which meant that a number of sectors of the first line would have been allocated to the Germans anyway. With the advantage of hindsight we can see that Nádasdy should have shored up his extreme flank near Sagschütz with some of his Austrians, but the Württembergers had not disgraced themselves at Schweidnitz, and Nádasdy probably thought that they were up to holding this seemingly remote position.

One of the Württemberg staff officers, Colonel Friedrich v. Nicolai, knew this terrain from his experiences as an observer of the Prussian manoeuvres before the war, and pointed out that the ground which extended from the foot of the Kiefern-Berg to the little wood just behind Schriegwitz was not an impassable morass, as was supposed. 'On the contrary, it was dry and negotiable by all arms. A little after one in the afternoon General Nádasdy came to the Württembergers on the left wing, and Major General v. Romann reported this circumstance to him. It was now confirmed in Nádasdy's presence by several officers who were sent out to investigate, and he therefore knew for himself that the left wing was devoid of support. He... rode off at once, declaring that something must be done so that at least more artillery, and heavy guns at that, must be set in motion to the left wing.'[41]

The Württembergers were still awaiting these cannon when the Prussian attack arrived. The Kiefem-Berg ridge, along which the troops were arrayed, would have been a useful position if it had been supported adequately by heavy artillery, for it fell away sharply on its southern side, and was preceded by a field ditch which presented a nasty little obstacle to people attacking from that direction. However the ditch lay at the very limit of musket range from the ridge, and there was no other hindrance to an enemy advance except a number of Nádasdy's Croats, who were positioned in the belt of woodland behind Schriegwitz.

The Prussian Flank March and the Austrian Response

Frederick rode with Prince Moritz of Anhalt-Dessau and an escort of hussars to the gentle eminence of the Schön-Berg, just south of the highway near Gross-Heidau. The viewpoint was priceless, and he owed it to the successful little action outside Borne, otherwise 'on this day it would have been impossible for him to take in, as he did, all the elements of such a huge army as that of the Austrians. His own force was weak, and without a reconnaissance of this kind he would probably never have committed it to action.'[42]

The mist had cleared, giving way to a brilliant sunny day. The king was standing just two kilometres short of the nearest troops of the Austrian army. He knew that its right wing was positioned at Nippern, though hidden by trees, but he writes with some exaggeration in his history of the war that he could count the rest of the troops man for man, and that he could see that its left wing on the Kiefern-Berg was badly supported. In fact it would have been physically impossible for him to have distinguished so much detail in person from that distance, and we may suppose that he was weighing up in his mind the reports that were coming to him from scouting officers, and recalling what he knew of the ground—that the Kiefern-Berg was key terrain, and that the swells of ground extending to his south might help to screen a move around that vulnerable flank. Perhaps he made up his mind on the spot, or perhaps, as Colonel Nicolai suggests, he concluded that he must bring his main force nearer the Austrians so that he could assess their positions at closer range.

In any event Frederick deployed the cavalry of his advance guard about 600 metres to the east of Borne, and brought his main army onto the field by columns of wings (of which more later). The two left-hand columns marched to the left (north) of Borne; of the two remaining columns, one was directed through the village, and the other passed to the south.

By 10.30 in the morning at the latest Frederick had resolved on his plan. He would commit virtually all his force to a right-flanking movement that was designed to roll up the enemy from their left (southern) flank. This kind of march was a favourite ploy of the king's, but on the last two occasions he had attempted it, at Prague (6 May 1757) and Kolin (18 June 1757) it had gone astray because his troops were embroiled with the Austrians before they were properly in position. This time the initial move was to carry his forces southwards on a line of march parallel to the main line of the Austrians, but at a distance of three kilometres. It was probably the desire to maintain this separation, as much as the potential screening effect of the 'hills' which determined that the first march should be from Borne almost due south for the equivalent of five kilometres (three miles) to the ground behind Lobetinz. The line of march would then angle to the left (south-eastwards) and continue for another four kilometres until the army was in its final attacking position diagonally opposite the enemy southern flank.

The success of the enterprise depended on deception as well as speed, and so Frederick took measures to persuade the Austrians that the attack would arrive on their right wing, and not on their far left flank. According to Prince Charles, 'the Prussian army made various movements, sometimes to the left and sometimes to the right, but the central column remained in place until towards 11.30 in the morning. We could not assess what it was going to do, and we were unable to go to attack them, because they were on higher ground.'[43] It was useful for Frederick's purposes that the pursuit of Nostitz had been towards the Austrian right wing, and that the approach march around and through Borne had been in the crowded and (to the enemy most confusing) confor- mation of columns of wings, which according to Colonel Nicolai, made it difficult to judge the relative progress of the individual heads of columns.

General Lucchesi, as commander of the right (northern) wing of the Austrian cavalry, was convinced that he was about to come under attack, and he sent message after message to the high command to ask for help, and particularly by the precious *corps de reserve,* which was in any case earmarked to support his wing. Lucchesi's misconception was shared widely, and 'Field Marshal Daun himself... was inclined to accede to Lucchesi's demands... for he no longer had any doubt but that the Prussians were going to attack the right wing.'[44]

Towards noon Prince Charles and Daun consented to release the *corps de reserve.* Arenberg's command therefore hastened to the north from its first location behind the right wing, and took up a new position beyond the far right flank on either side of Nippern—three of the battalions in front of the hamlet, and the other four behind.

Daun rode off to the right to verify events for himself, and it could well have being during this temporary absence that Prince Charles was persuaded to send a second instalment of reinforce- ments, in this case a number of the regiments of Serbelloni's cavalry on the left wing. The troopers (most probably the brigade of Hohenzollern from his first line, and that of Ludwig Starhemberg from the second) swung eastwards at the trot to clear Leuthen, and then northwards to join Lucchesi on the right.

Between 11 and 11.30 in the morning the Prussian army, having halted in wings, began to wheel off to the right 'by lines.' The original formation 'by wings' was good for approach marches, as long as you had relatively open terrain available for the multiple columns, for it was much

The rolling country west-southwest of Leuthen, looking towards the scattered woodlands near the Sophien-Berg. The Prussians were marching from right to left.

shorter than the arrangement 'by lines,' and in the present case it enabled Frederick to cram the whole of his army into the space between Borne and Gross-Heidau.

As the first stage of shaking themselves into battle formation, the wings had to wheel processionally (usually to the right) into column 'by lines,' each of the new columns corresponding to a line of the order of battle. This involved each of the columns 'by wing' dividing itself in two, in the way explained in our diagram, with the first set of units wheeling to form one of the wings of the first line, and the units at the tail wheeling 2-300 paces further to the rear to form the matching column of the second line (there is no need for readers to understand any of this, as long as they feel as confused as the Austrian spectators).

The new formation 'by lines' continued on its way by column of platoons, two-platoon divisions or complete battalions, ready to deploy into line of battle upon command. As an additional complication, Frederick split the infantry of his advance guard into two unequal parts: six battalions had been told off to screen the right flank of the march of the main army, and they were now assigned to lead the march of Zieten's wing of cavalry; the remaining three battalions (the two of the regiment of Meyerinck and the second battalion of that of Itzenplitz) headed the march of the right wing of the main force of infantry, and they were assigned the privilege of opening the attack. The potentials for disaster were endless, but for the well-drilled Prussians it was 'a manoeuvre we had often rehearsed at our reviews, and which the army now carried out in its usual fine order.'[45]

The first leg of the march was aligned on the distant pyramid of the Zobten-Berg, which raises the question of whether or not the move was concealed from the Austrian positions by the intervening swells of ground—the Schmiede-Berg, the Schleier-Berg, the Sophien-Berg and the Wach-Berg. Field Marshal Helmut v. Moltke, the founder of the Prussian General Staff, maintained that the eminences were too low for this purpose. In 1904 the relevant volume[46] of the history of the Seven Years War by the German Great General Staff challenged the memory of Moltke in this

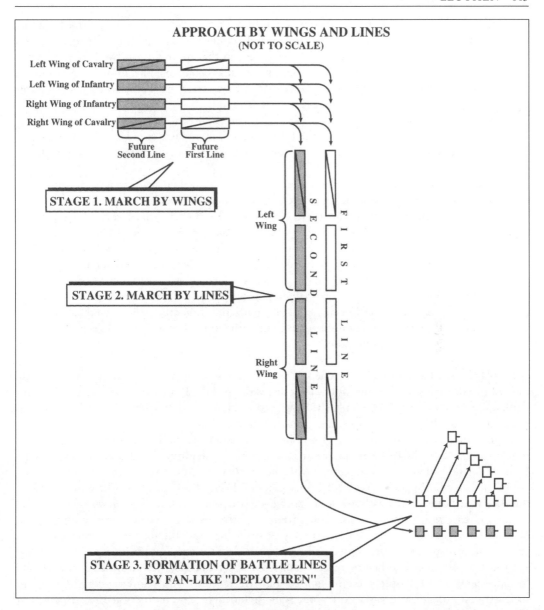

APPROACH BY WINGS AND LINES
(NOT TO SCALE)

Left Wing of Cavalry

Left Wing of Infantry

Right Wing of Infantry

Right Wing of Cavalry

Future
Second Line

Future
First Line

STAGE 1. MARCH BY WINGS

Left
Wing

SECOND LINE

FIRST LINE

STAGE 2. MARCH BY LINES

Right
Wing

STAGE 3. FORMATION OF BATTLE LINES
BY FAN-LIKE "DEPLOYIREN"

respect by stating (without specifying a date) that an experiment was staged afterwards, whereby a mounted corporal rode along the Prussian route with a raised white flag, and remained invisible the whole time to a pair of officers who were peering through good field glasses from the observation point of Prince Charles and Daun on the Breslauer-Berg near Frobelwitz. It is also significant that Driesen's cavalry command remained concealed from Lucchesi until the last stage of the battle, when it came pouring into the attack.

Erosion, digging for sand, and the planting of orchards have made the issue impossible to resolve from the state of the ground today, at least as far as the main force of the Prussians is concerned, but even the most myopic of the Austrians must have seen Frederick's escort of twenty-five squadrons of hussars, who were riding south between the two armies and along the tops of hillocks in question. Further evidence establishes that not just the royal escort, but the march of the Prussian army as a whole was visible to the Austrians for at least some of its duration. Prince Charles describes specifically that 'after various marches and countermarches he [the king] marched off to his right along the hills, and with incredible speed, so that for a moment we believed he was marching on Canth to cut us off from Schweidnitz.'[47] This is confirmed by an officer of his army, who states how Frederick's army came gradually into view. After that he marched sharply to his right, so that we all believed he was marching on Schweidnitz.'[48]

We may be sure that Jacob Cogniazzo would let slip no opportunity to deride his senior officers. He nevertheless took it for granted that the Prussian flank march was seen by the Austrians, and he turned instead to the central issue of what the commanders thought this move portended:

> If I am not mistaken it was about noon when Lieutenant General Puebla... came riding up to a body of officers who were standing by the windmill at Leuthen, and who for a considerable time had been observing the enemy movements in the direction of Radaxdorf and Lobetinz. 'Gentlemen,' asked Puebla, 'where do you think the Prussians are going to put in their main attack today? That is, if they mean to come to grips with us today at all, which I very much doubt.' The officers were of an altogether different opinion. They just smiled at one another and kept silent. There was one exception, an honest, elderly grenadier lieutenant of the old school, who had been through many battles, and had about as many scars to prove it. He alone made so bold as to say: 'General, I fear very much they've got the bit between their teeth. It's plain they're going to attack our left wing and turn our flank on that side—put any child here and he would tell you the same.'

Puebla was scornful: 'Ho! Ho!' he cried. 'You don't know what you are talking about!' 'Would to God I were wrong,' replied the officer. 'But just wait until the Prussians are killing us off in our flank and rear, and we will exclaim, as we always do: "How did that happen?!"' Puebla took this much amiss, and he and his Neapolitans turned around and made off.[49]

Cogniazzo dismisses as unworthy of serious consideration the notion that the Prussians were moving to threaten the Austrian communications with Schweidnitz. He did not know that the high command had long been concerned with the security of this flank.

On the late morning of 5 December Prince Charles, Daun, Puebla and the like were mistaken, but they were not necessarily obtuse, and here a little perspective is probably relevant. The kind of military history which moves without pause from one battle to the next can be misleading, in that it leaves out of account the everyday currency of campaigning—the marching, the encamping, and the near-bloodless confrontations which Paddy Griffith usefully describes as 'non-battles.' For every Rossbach or Leuthen there were half a dozen such non-battles, in which Frederick and his opponents were fully prepared for combat, but which ended with Old Fritz coming to a halt in frustration, or sidling away to carry out some manoeuvre. The business at Eckartsberg near Zittau had been a recent example, and on the day of Leuthen it was not illogical for the Austrian command to suppose that Frederick was acting according to type.

The misconceptions of Prince Charles and Daun were shared by some of the enemy. Major Podgursky with his White Hussars on the Prussian rear describes how his troopers had been fired up for battle, and how disillusioned they were when the column swung to the right as if to decline the encounter: 'Even some of our tried veterans, who were experienced in so many military strata-gems, were completely deceived as to what the king was up to. To begin with they grumbled in undertones, but soon they became altogether more violent, and directed their ill-humour against us officers. That made for a most uncomfortable hour.'[50]

The decisive moment came early in the afternoon, when the heads of columns veered sharply to the left over the Wach-Berg behind Lobetinz, and struck south-east across open and level country—that is, in the direction that would bring them into position facing the enemy left flank.

Among the waiting Württembergers on the Kiefern-Berg, Colonel Nicolai knew what was going to happen, and that the Prussians were going to strike far more quickly than the Austrian high command could imagine:

> The king and the heads of the infantry columns had scarcely reached the hill at Lobetinz when he saw the gap [i.e. to the far left of the Austrian army], and made the heads of columns execute a one-eighth turn to the left. To anybody who did not know how they formed their columns to deploy, or the technique of the deployment itself, it would have made no great impression. But we in the Württemberg corps were acquainted with this evolution, and from that moment onwards we could be in no doubt that the entire column (whose depth and breadth were concealed by the hill) would swing into the same direction as the head, and deploy in a matter of a few minutes. An imaginary prolongation of the head of the column would run about 200 paces… to the [eastern] side of the wood at Sagschütz. This meant that as soon as the Prussians deployed into line, they would form an acute angle with the first line of the Austrian left wing, and extend to a greater or lesser extent to its side, depending on the numbers of troops so deployed. The king spent only so much time as he needed to determine his points of view [i.e. choose the features of the ground on which the extremities of his line would be aligned], and position the column accordingly. As soon as this was done, we saw the army deploy by divisions, and something like forty cannon being brought into the intervals between the battalions. On our wing we could match them with no more than a few regimental pieces. This deployment was accomplished with the greatest proficiency, and so near to us that we could see and hear how the senior officers were busying themselves with positioning and aligning the heads of their respective battalions.[51]

This is important testimony, for it indicates that the Prussians were moving not in the conventional strung-out open columns, from which lines of battle were formed by 'processional' movements, but in compact closed columns, from which the component units formed line by fan-like or diagonal movements. The units in question could have been either the 'divisions' as normally understood at the time (namely units of two platoons each), or indeed building blocks of whole battalions at a time, as was certainly going to be executed by the Prussians at Torgau (3 November 1760), and makes more sense of the way the battle developed at Leuthen. In any case, by holding together as long as they did in compact marching formations, the Prussians would have encouraged the Austrian high command in its belief that they were not bent on giving battle that day.

A young Prussian officer describes the impact of such a manoeuvre: 'When a force is drawn up in this way, it takes up comparatively little space, and from a distance the mingling of uniforms and flags makes it look like a heap of troops who have been piled up in total disorder… But it only needs a nod from the commander of the army, and the whole human tangle deploys in the greatest order, and with a speed which resembles a racing torrent.'[52]

The arrangement of the army as a whole was intended to put the weight of the attack heavily on one of its wings, in this case, on the right. This was the grand tactic of the celebrated Frederician Oblique Order, which was the product of the army's peacetime manoeuvres, and its experience in the earlier battles of the Seven Years War. The king was aiming to form an immensely powerful concentration of infantry, cavalry and heavy artillery, while the weaker wing of the army was 'refused,'—that is, held back in reserve to fix the attention of the enemy, exploit success, or if necessary cover a retreat. The Oblique Order was given its fullest expression at Leuthen, and since the elements do not correspond exactly with the order of battle, it will probably be convenient to set out the components as they were grouped by Frederick for his purposes:

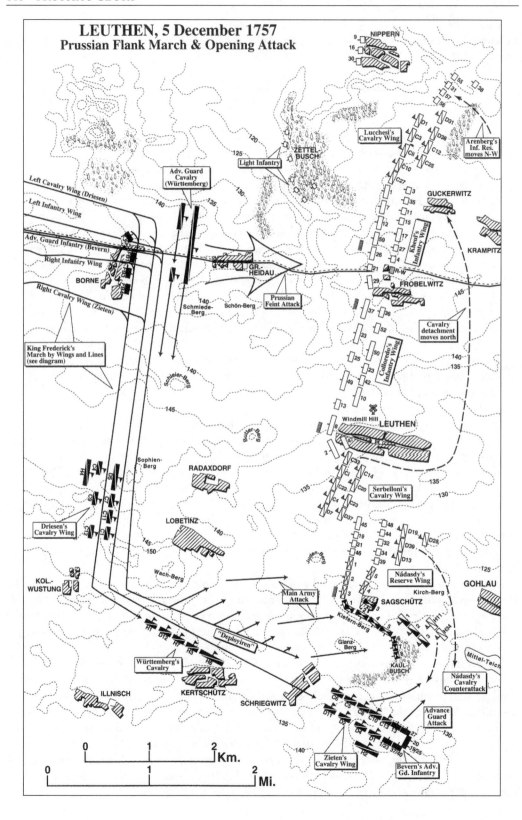

LEUTHEN, 5 December 1757
Prussian Flank March & Opening Attack

1. The Cavalry of the Right Wing
Lieutenant General Zieten with 53 squadrons, including the 10 squadrons of the Zieten Hussars which had been borrowed from the advance guard and composed the third line. This command, approaching through and around Schriegwitz, made up the right flank of the entire army, and its own potentially vulnerable right flank was covered by six battalions of the advance guard under the command of Major General Prince Karl of Bevern. This arrangement of infantry and horse recalls Frederick's first battle, at Mollwitz in 1741.

2. Three Battalions of the Advance Guard (Major General Wedell) and the Immediate Right Wing of the Infantry of the Main Army
The assault was to be spearheaded by the three remaining battalions of the advance guard (the two battalions of Meyerinck, and the second of Itzenplitz). This *Attaque* had close fire support to its right in the shape of ten *Brummers;* in its rear came up the right-hand regiments of the first line of infantry (Markgraf Karl, the Garde, the Grenadier-Garde Battalion, and Kannacher—all excellent units); to its right-rear there was a column comprising the stacked-up grenadier battalions of Kremzow, Unruh and Kleist, and a battalion of the Prinz von Preussen Musketeers (the right-hand battalion of the second line). There was an equivalent concentration of command assets, to make sure that this crucial attack was delivered with controlled force: in addition to Major General Wedell, who commanded the relevant battalions of the advance guard, Frederick in person determined the alignment for the attack, and Prince Moritz of Anhalt-Dessau, although he was the overall commander of the infantry, gave his particular attention to events on this part of the field.

3. The Main Body of the Infantry
The first line (20 battalions, including the Kremzow Grenadiers and the regiments of Markgraf Karl, the Garde, the Grenadier-Garde and Kannacher mentioned above) fell away to the left in a staggered line of battalions at vertical intervals of 50 paces, so that the left-hand battalion (Schenckendorff Grenadiers) marched relatively about 1,000 paces to the rear of the right-hand battalion (Kremzow Grenadiers) and would come into action a theoretical fifteen minutes later. This alignment was intended to prevent the 'refused' wing from engaging too soon, in the way which had led to the disintegration of the attack at Kolin. The Dieringshofen Grenadiers and the first battalion of the Kurssell Grenadiers closed up the interval between the first and second lines. The second line in question consisted of eleven battalions, which were spaced at wider intervals than those in the first, but marched in the same alignment. In addition to being arranged 'obliquely,' in the geometrical sense, the whole body inclined to the right as it marched, though the detailed mechanics of the thing have not been specified.

4. The Cavalry of the Left Wing
Lieutenant General Driesen with 50 squadrons, including the 10 squadrons of the Puttkamer (White) Hussars which had been borrowed from the advance guard and made up the third line. Driesen formed the tail of the army, and when the centre and the right wing inclined to the east, he remained along the original alignment of the flank march to the west of Radaxdorf and Lobetinz. Being part of the 'refused' wing, he did not take part in the opening attack. His brief must have been to wait, observe, and act as the opportunity presented itself.

5. The Light Horse of the Advance Guard
Lieutenant General Prince Friedrich Eugen of Württemberg with 30 squadrons (5 of dragoons, 25 of hussars, not including the Zieten Hussars detached to Zieten, or the Puttkamer Hussars, detached to Driesen). His station was an unconventional one, to the left-rear of the second line of infantry. His task was to exploit any success on the part of the main army.

6. Artillery

Apart from the *Brummers* mentioned above, the heavy artillery was deployed in four mixed batteries of howitzers and 12-pounder cannon: one each was assigned to the flanks of the infantry, and the remaining two were placed in front of the first line. From an Austrian account (below) it is possible that the Prussians also brought into action the siege mortars which Zieten had brought from Glogau, which would have been the only occasion formidable weapons of this kind were employed in a field action in the Seven Years War.

7. Free Battalions and Fussjäger

Colonel d'Angelelli with three battalions, together with the *Fussjäger* (the equivalent of a small battalion). These remained for the time being at Borne, to counter the Austrian right wing, but they took part in the closing stages of the battle behind Leuthen village.

The Attack on Nádasdy's Corps

The young officer candidate *(Freicorporal)* Barsewisch was carrying a colour of one of the two battalions of the regiment of Meyerinck, which was designated to lead the attack: 'In front of us we had the Austrian army, so vast that it was impossible to take in with the eye, and behind us all that of the Prussians was drawn up facing the enemy in battle array. Our army advanced in parade order to sounding music. The alignments were as exact as if at a review in Berlin, for the army was moving under the eyes of its great monarch.'[53] He noted that Frederick was taking great pains to ensure that the arrangements for the advance were correct (a lesson from Kolin), and overheard him telling his battalion commander, Lieutenant-General Bock, that he was to advance against the whitecoats who could be seen in the abattis in front, and that the other battalions would conform on him.

> When he was finished, His Majesty was gracious enough to come to me and my counterpart free corporal from the battalion of Unruh. We were in the lead and carrying the colours. 'Ensigns of the Life Company,' he said, 'be sure of what you are doing, you've got to advance on the abattis. But don't march too quickly, otherwise the army won't be able to keep up.' His Majesty in person then orientated our battalions on the position of the enemy line, and he told the soldiers: 'Lads, take a good look at those whitecoats over there. You've got to drive them from their defences. You must advance briskly and turn them out with the bayonet. Then I'll support you with five battalions of grenadiers and the whole army. It's do or die. The enemy are in front, and the whole army is behind you. You can't go back, and the only way to go forward is to win.'[54]

The target, as Frederick specified again and again, were Nádasdy's Croats (the 'whitecoats') holding the abattis which they had cut along the outer edge of the little wood behind Schriegwitz. Indeed the king was so attentive to the preliminaries that Prince Moritz had to come up watch in hand to tell him that he had only a few hours of daylight at his disposal.

The Prussian attack opened shortly after two in the afternoon. The two battalions of the Meyerinck regiment put the Croats to flight, broke through the belt of woodland, and advanced so rapidly across the open ground beyond that Frederick had to send them repeated orders to keep themselves in check. He wished to maintain the contact with the adjacent battalion of Itzenplitz, and probably also with the battery of ten *Brummers,* which was moving up to the broad swelling of the Glanz-Berg to the left. We have two accounts of what happened next.

As Barsewisch remembered it, seven cannon shot tore through the ranks of his regiment as the troops were crossing the ditch which lay across their axis of advance against the Kiefern-Berg.

However the musketry of the opposing Württembergers was ineffective, and once across the ditch the Prussians answered with a volley. 'Our artillery had wrecked two pieces with its first discharge. Now there was no holding our brave soldiers, who ran forward with levelled bayonets, so that at the second salvo we were already under their cannon. The grenadiers fought back bravely. They had formed up kneeling behind the fortification and the abattis, and had no intention of giving way. But our soldiers gave a mighty cry and fell on them with the bayonet, so that they had either to run or be killed.'[55] Barsewisch wrote his memoirs long after the war, and other evidence shows that he conflated some of the events. Colonel Nicolai insists that the Württembergers had made no kind of abattis, and the account of Barsewisch obviously combines elements of the fighting both against the Croats behind Schriegwitz, and the Württembergers on the Kiefern-Berg. Again Barsewisch calls the Württembergers 'grenadiers,' when they were in fact all fusiliers. In any event the Prussians chased the Württembergers as far as an opening in the sandy wood on the Kiefern-Berg, where they found ten or a dozen dead lying in a heap. They almost certainly belonged to the regiment of Röder, which suffered 219 casualties in the battle, and most of them probably in this first encounter.

The second account is from Colonel Nicolai, who describes how

> the Prussians stepped out smartly, as soon as they had formed up in lines. The first to take to their heels were the Croats and the other light troops whom Nádasdy had stationed in front of the little wood of Sagschütz. They put up no resistance, but fled through the Württembergers, and threw them too into disorder. We fired our first cannon shot at 12.30 [probably later]. It drew in return a hail of Prussian cannon shot and canister, which not only put both our regimental pieces out of action (we had nothing heavier), but demoralised our men totally. They had been standing motionless in position, awaiting the impact of greatly superior forces, and they saw themselves being taken in the rear by a whole enemy line... which included cavalry. You can imagine the result. There was a wavering among our troops. They then began to give way, and finally they executed a disorderly retreat—or, more accurately, they ran.[56]

Out on the distant left flank of the Prussian army the White Hussars had still been under the impression that their army was shying away from battle. They rode on for a good hour before a thick cloud of smoke could be seen rising from the far right wing, and immediately afterwards a thudding of artillery fire carried to their ears. A continuous chattering of musketry confirmed that the Prussian army was going into battle after all.[57]

Once the line of the Württembergers had been pierced on the sector of the regiment of Röder, all the other units of German auxiliaries—the three regiments and three battalions of Württembergers, and the five regiments of Bavarians—crumbled without even the show of putting up a fight. The regiment of Röder had been hit hard, as we have seen, but the dead and wounded among the rest of the Württembergers amounted to no more than 10 officers and 65 men by the end of the battle. Afterwards Prince Charles of Lorraine and his supporters found it convenient to fasten the immediate blame for the collapse on the left on the German auxiliaries, but, as Cogniazzo pointed out, even the Austrian grenadiers, the crack troops of the army, might have got off a few dozen rounds more, but they would still have succumbed before the Prussian effort on this flank.[58]

The larger responsibility was held to be that of Nádasdy, for the way he had deployed his forces on this exposed flank, and a French observer concluded that 'this general is good only to command detached corps of light troops.'[59] This charge too must be qualified, when we consider the diverse composition of his force, and the fact that he faced the principal effort of the Prussians—and not just the concentrated infantry and artillery in the neighbourhood of the Kiefern-Berg, but Zieten with the right wing of the Prussian cavalry, which was working around to the left rear—as the Württembergers had seen.

View east-northeast from Kertschiltz. The right wing of the Prussian infantry formed in the open ground to the left.

The low Kiefern-Berg ridge at Sagschütz as seen by the attacking Prussians.

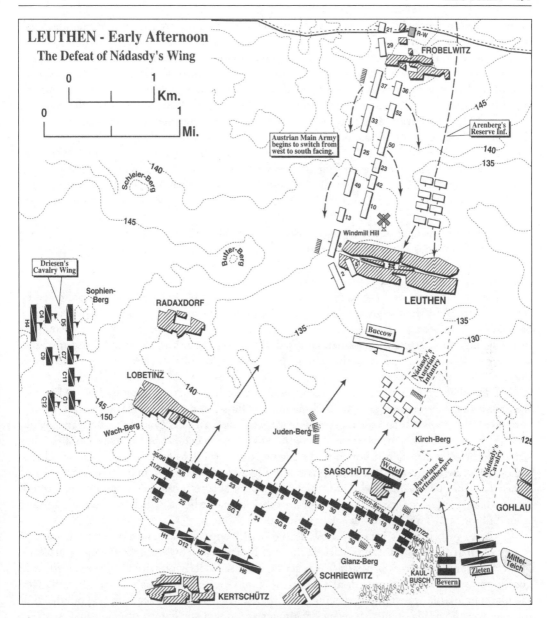

LEUTHEN - Early Afternoon
The Defeat of Nádasdy's Wing

0   1
└────┴────┴────┘ Km.

0   1
└────┴────┴────┘ Mi.

Austrian Main Army
begins to switch from
west to south facing.

R-W

FROBELWITZ

Arenberg's
Reserve Inf.

Windmill Hill

Schleier-Berg

Driesen's
Cavalry Wing

Sophien-
Berg

Butter-Berg

RADAXDORF

LEUTHEN

Buccow

Nádasdy's Austrian Infantry

LOBETINZ

Wach-Berg

Juden-Berg

Kirch-Berg

Nádasdy's Cavalry

SAGSCHÜTZ   Wedel

Bavarians & Württembergers

GOHLAU

Kiefern-Berg

H1   D12   H7   H3   H6

SG 6

Glanz-Berg   SCHRIEGWITZ

KAUL-
BUSCH   Bevern

Zieten

Mittel-
Teich

KERTSCHÜTZ

On his side Zieten had the advantage of superior numbers, and also (from the manoeuvres of 1754) his knowledge of this patch of ground, which was an exception to the generally open country of the rest of the battlefield, being obstructed by ponds, ditches and woods. Forces on this part of the field would have to be committed piecemeal, unlike the grand sweeps of entire lines of cavalry which we shall encounter on the other wing towards the end of the battle.

The Saxon lieutenant general Nostitz had brought his three regiments of chevaulegers from the scene of their clash at Borne, and, showing great determination, he united with the cavalry of Nádasdy's corps and joined them in a combined attack against Zieten's right (eastern) flank. The Prussians now reaped the benefit from Frederick's foresight when he sealed of this flank of his army with those six battalions of the advance guard under Prince Karl of Bevern. Instead of breaking into an exposed flank of cavalry, the allied horsemen therefore encountered an intact wall of infantry, who beat them off by fire.

This episode was succeeded by a series of ragged but violent clashes between the Austrian and Prussian horse, in which Nádasdy could pit only 5 or 6 squadrons of cuirassiers and between 16 and 18 of dragoons against Zieten's 12 squadrons of cuirassiers and 20 of dragoons. Nádasdy launched counter-attack after counter-attack, and a body of his hussars (probably the Nádasdy [H11] and Dessewffy regiments [H34]) contrived to work around the Prussian flank and attack the Stechow and Krockow Dragoons from the rear. This was unusually enterprising, for it was very rare to the Austrian hussars to intervene in a pitched battle. The Prussian dragoons were hard pressed for a time, and one of their brigade commanders, Major General Krockow the Younger, was wounded and taken prisoner, but the fighting turned to the advantage of the Prussians by the nearby dragoon regiments of Czettritz [D4] and Normann [D1], which came up from the right to help their comrades.

The initiative was now taken up by Lieutenant General Johann O'Donnell, who set his two regiments of dragoons (Jung-Modena [D13] and Sachsen-Gotha [D28]) against eight powerful squadrons of Prussian cuirassiers (the Gardes du Corps [C13] and the Gensd'armes [C10]) under Major General Lentulus. The consequences were murderous.

O'Donnell had been summoned by Nádasdy from the left to help to fill the void presented by the flight of the Württembergers and Bavarians. The Saxon chevaulegers and the Austrian hussars had likewise dispersed by the time the dragoons arrived, and Nostitz was lying mortally wounded in the hands of the enemy. O'Donnell attacked vigorously enough to drive the Prussians back, and give the German auxiliaries a breathing space, but he found that these folk were no longer interested in making a stand.

Field Marshal Daun arrived on the scene, which must have further impressed on O'Donnell the urgency of the situation, and the Irishman ordered his troopers into a counter-attack against two squadrons of Gensd'armes who were at their heels. The Austrians gained a first advantage, but their regiments were very much under-strength, and after the contest had ebbed to and fro they were overborne by the superior forces of the enemy. 'I was trying to force my way through them,' writes O'Donnell, 'and was in the process of aiming a blow at the first man in my path when I received a sword cut in the head. I still might have been able to break free if the wound had not rendered me so weak and feeble that I could scarcely stay on my horse, which had received another wound of the same kind.'[60] He was taken prisoner.

We return to Nádasdy's infantry, now devoid of all support when the concentrated force of the Prussian artillery and infantry carried the enemy attack northwards into the open left flank of the Austrians. The *Brummer* battery was acting in close association with the Prussian advance guard, and was pushed to an initial site on the Glanz-Berg, from where it could cannonade the German auxiliaries who were fleeing from the Kiefern-Berg, and send its 12-pounder shot roaring over the heads of the Meyerinck regiment and down the length of Nádasdy's Austrian infantry behind. As Barsewisch put it, 'as soon as His Majesty the King saw the excellent progress that was being made, he established a battery of ten heavy cannon on a hill to our rear. From this we received the most powerful support, so that the effect of the heavy artillery was felt as far as the second line, and the enemy were unable to rally out of its reach even there.'[61] With this help, and that of the right wing of the Prussian infantry coming up behind, the advance guard under Wedell pressed on so rapidly that Frederick had to send a succession of adjutants to tell it to slow down.

Over to the left, as the Prussians saw it, Colonel Moller was bringing together an immense concentration of firepower on the open Juden-Berg, which was the lowest of all the low *Berge* on the field of battle, but which commanded an unobstructed view as far as the woods on the right and the distant village of Leuthen to the front. The Prussians were making use of their unmounted cavalry recruits to help to serve and manhandle the pieces, which were moving with surprising speed across the frozen ground: 'Fifty or sixty cannon were being brought forward with the leading infantry, and as soon as they were within range they invariably brought a superior fire against the point which had been selected for the attack. These pieces maintained their fire during the advance, and moved as fast as the infantry.'[62] In all probability this mass of ordnance comprised the battery of 15 cannon and 2 howitzers which had been assigned to the right wing of the infantry of the main army, together with the 2 batteries each of 12 cannon and 2 howitzers from the centre of the first line of infantry.

The nearest three battalions of Nádasdy's first line of Austrian infantry (Maguire, Haller and Leopold Pálffy) now found themselves exposed both to the main Prussian army coming up on their left flank, and the pounding from the Prussian ordnance on the Juden-Berg. The troops gave way under this ordeal, and they carried Nádasdy's second line with them.

The Austrian artillery was unable to reply in kind, for too many of their heavy pieces were out of reach on their right wing, 'and so, because it was deployed so badly, it did little service that day, and contributed much to our defeat.'[63] All that the Austrian command could do was to withdraw the only two available batteries (sited respectively to the west and north-west of Sagschütz) and place them on the gentle Kirch-Berg behind the hamlet. It seemed for a time that Nádasdy's shaken infantry would be able to rally on this feature, but the only effect of the crowds of troops was to mask the fire of the batteries which had just been established there. A new storm of shot, canister and howitzer shells from the Prussian pieces was the prelude to a new combined attack on the part of Wedell's troops and by the Kremzow grenadier battalion, which was brought up by Prince Moritz of Anhalt-Dessau in person.

Nádasdy's infantry broke, whereupon the Prussians captured all the Austrian heavy guns, and were able to assemble a mass of more than 50 of their own heavy pieces on the Kirch-Berg, namely the three batteries which had just been in action on the Juden-Berg, and the ten *Brummers* of the advance guard. These thick-barrelled pieces on their massive carriages could take heavy charges which would have wrecked the ordinary 12-pounders, and the Prussian gunner captain v. Holtzendorff testifies that 'this was the first time that the Austrians had been exposed to the shot of the *Brummers*. They were inclined to regard us as barbarians who had broken international law, and the prisoners directed the most bitter reproaches against the Prussian gunners for having employed these pieces, which devoured everything in their path, and shot them up without a Prussian being in sight.'[64]

The New Austrian Line, and the Storm of Leuthen Village

The essential problem now facing the Austrians was that they were still mostly facing west, whereas Frederick with the main force of his army was working his way up from the south. The whitecoats were therefore faced with the prospect of being destroyed systematically from left to right, unless they could manage to form a new south-facing front in the neighbourhood of Leuthen.

The only intact body in the immediate path of the Prussians was the left wing of the cavalry of the main army, which had been depleted by the dispatch of two of its brigades to support the Austrian right (p. 141). The wing commander, General Serbelloni, had faced a similar crisis at Kolin less than six months before, and on that occasion he had held his ground so doggedly that he had helped to save the army. He was disinclined to repeat the experience on 5 December, and now he withdrew his second line to safety through the village of Leuthen, which left Lieutenant General Adolph Buccow to face the Prussians with the Kalckreuth and Erzherzog Ferdinand Cuirassiers [C22, C4], five companies of elite carabiniers and mounted grenadiers, and the Batthyány Dragoons [D7].[65]

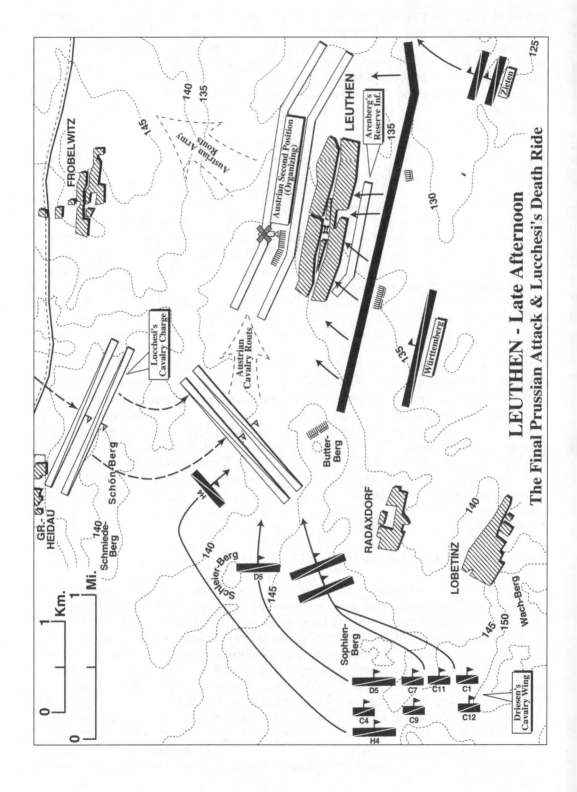

LEUTHEN - Late Afternoon
The Final Prussian Attack & Lucchesi's Death Ride

According to Buccow's circumstantial account, he was left with his division to confront what seemed to be a column of 6,000 Prussian infantry which was advancing across a zone of boggy ground, and accompanied by a numerous and heavy artillery which was firing in their support:

> I believed that the moment had come when it was possible to turn the battle completely around, and cancel out everything that the enemy had so far gained. I therefore decided to attack this column with the five companies of carabiniers and mounted grenadiers. As soon as they had broken in, I would ride into the breach with the Batthyány Regiment, and spread out to right and left; Major General Hedwiger was to support this attack with the two regiments of Erzherzog Ferdinand and Kalckreuth. The cavalry duly charged, but was unable to effect the break-in. The Batthyány Regiment had meanwhile approached to within a very close distance of the enemy. I now had to pull it back, and reassemble my force somewhere out of reach of the fire of the enemy musketry and canister, which was very intense.

A body of ten Prussian squadrons now came up, but did not dare to attack. The nearby Austrian infantry was able to fall back unmolested, and, having faced the enemy out, Buccow re-formed 500 paces to the rear.[66]

Through its self-sacrifice Buccow's brigade had meanwhile helped most if not all of the eight battalions of the Austrian *corps de reserve* to arrive at Leuthen village ahead of the Prussians. This too was a remarkable achievement, when we consider that this body had been rushed north to Nippern on the far right when the Austrians were wrong-footed by Frederick's manoeuvre in the morning.

The *corps de reserve* had to double back south, and not just to its original position, but all the way on to Leuthen, which amounted to a distance of about seven kilometres (one German *Meile*, or about four-and-a-half English miles). Although the timings cannot be established with any certainty, it is reasonable to suppose that the message of recall cannot have reached Lieutenant General Arenberg until after one in the afternoon, which means that his men had to cover this distance in a little over an hour. Captain Prince Charles de Ligne describes his battalion of the same name [38] as making south at a run. The troops passed Leuthen to their right, and began to form to the south of the village under a hail of roundshot and canister which killed his superior officers and left him in command of the battalion. To the front he faced the Third Battalion of the Garde, drawn up less than eighty paces (fifty yards) away, as if on parade. The battalion of Andlau should have been forming to his right, but the nearby houses did not allow enough space, and so it piled up thirty deep behind his battalion—and began to shoot into its back. Over to the left the battalion of Mercy [56] fell back fifty paces with heavy casualties. De Ligne's own men were breathless and scattered, but 'an ensign of d'Arberg helped me for some time to form a line out of the wreckage of his battalion and mine. He was killed. Two officers of grenadiers… brought up their men. Finally I had 200 men at the most with me, including what was left of my battalion, and some Hungarians whom I managed to rally as well.'[67]

Finally the battered *corps de reserve* was withdrawn to the windmill hill on the northern side of Leuthen, by which time Prince Charles and Daun had set altogether more substantial forces in motion. At their command Lieutenant General Puebla galloped to the right wing with an order for the regiments to execute a right turn in their ranks and make for Leuthen as fast as humanly possible. The infantry brigades of Maguire and Angern (from the right wing of the first line) were the first formations to appear on the scene, and they were followed by the whole of the infantry of the second line. An officer recalls

> When we got there we found dire confusion reigning not only among the Bavarians and Württembergers, but the Austrian regiments who had gone over to the attack before us.

Things were made worse because the heavy cannon and the ammunition carts to our front came under strong fire from howitzer shells and mortar bombs as well as cannon shot, and they fell back at great speed, reducing our regiment to chaos. I myself was jammed between two ammunition carts, and carried back—or rather dragged—for more than forty paces.[68]

By about three in the afternoon the Austrian infantry had consolidated in Leuthen and across the country on either side to a total length of three kilometres (two miles). The ranks and files had been lost in the process, and in some places the troops were piled one hundred deep, but at least the Austrians were now facing south and in very considerable force. Colonel Nicolai explains that Daun was trying to anchor the new line on the two supports of Leuthen and the Schweidnitzer-Wasser, as a short but potentially strong position where the arms could offer better support, and enable the Austrians to assemble a powerful reserve in the rear. 'And now, under the force of necessity, and in great haste, we were striving to do what we should have done before the battle opened.'[69]

With the Austrian *corps de reserve* beaten out of the way, the defence of Leuthen village rested upon the Austrian battalions of the left wing of the second line, and on the German battalion of Red Würzburg [RW]. Men were told off with entrenching tools to throw up a kind of parapet, but they had to abandon the work almost immediately on account of the enemy fire. However the east-west alignment of the village now turned to the advantage of the Austrians and their friends, for it extended for nearly two kilometres (one mile) athwart the axis of the Prussian advance. It was only three rows of buildings deep (p. 136), but it was cluttered with walls, stables and yards, and the defenders had a ready-made fortress in the enclosure of the Catholic church.

The low wall of the church had been built in the last century by the local landowner Christoph von Hohberg as an architectural folly, matching the similar wall at Borne (p. 136), but its corner roundels and strong masonry made it an admirable redoubt for a hard-fighting battalion like that of the Red Würzburgers. When the Austrians executed their general left wheel, the first grenadier company of Würzburg remained in Frobelwitz, while the second company and the whole of the fusilier battalion took over the defence of the churchyard under the acting command of Captain v. Adelsheim, and had time to make loopholes in the walls and the corner roundels. The position was strong in itself, and gave the defenders a clear shot at attackers coming up from the south.

The entire body of Prussian infantry assembled against the Austrians in two lines, and at 3.30 in the afternoon the bluecoats threw themselves into the assault. They made a number of penetrations into the village at their first onrush, but soon found themselves engaged in costly hand-to-hand fighting. Particular mention is made of the part played by the Second and Third Battalions of the Garde, the Retzow Garde-Grenadier-Bataillon, and the regiments of Pannwitz, Münchow and Markgraf Karl, which indicates that the forces engaged were mostly from the Prussian right wing. Significantly, perhaps, three of these regiments sustained the highest Prussian unit losses in the battle, namely Pannwitz with 709, Markgraf Karl (688) and the two Garde battalions (total 501). It is curious that one of the young Garde officers to die was First Lieutenant von Warkotsch, who was the current proprietor of Leuthen village, and who was shot down in front of the churchyard wall.

An important breakthrough was finally made by Captain Wichard Joachim Möllendorf with the Third Battalion of the Garde, which came at the eastern gateway of the churchyard:

> Its commander came to a halt, and so did all his troops. It was now a question of breaking in or falling back—and we would have to retreat if we did not break in at once. The senior captain [Möllendorf] called out to him: 'We can't stand around wondering what to do!' But he still could not make up his mind… Möllendorf sprang forward with the words: 'We need someone else! Men, follow me!' They crashed into a barricaded gateway. They battered at it

Leuthen Church. The wall shows the original stonework, and one of the low corner roundels is in the centre of the picture.

The Prussian infantry advance on Leuthen.

and tore the leaves of the door aside. Twelve muskets were levelled at them, but the leader and his gallant band plunged on. The battalion pressed through the captured gateway in column, and made to right and left.[70]

Prussian field artillery simultaneously effected a breach in the southern wall of the churchyard, and so there was desperate fighting among the crosses and gravestones as the Red Würzburgers came under attack from two directions. The odds were too great, and the garrison had to make its escape over the northern wall.

The capture of the churchyard broke the back of the resistance in Leuthen village, and put an end to a bloody contest which a number of observers believed had been unnecessary. Cogniazzo maintained that the Austrians would have done better to disengage and re-form to the rear between Frobelwitz and Saara, instead of heaping themselves up as a target for the enemy artillery.[71] The Prussian major Warnery noted that Frederick's army suffered more in the assault on Leuthen village than in the rest of the battle put together. 'The Prussians would have been better advised to wait for their heavy artillery, instead of taking the place by storm. But the Second and Third Battalions of the Garde, and other elite troops, were bent on showing just how brave they were.'[72]

All of this smacks of wisdom after the event. In those days of linear tactics the Prussians could not have ignored the existence of Leuthen village without breaking up their array. The fighting there was of use to the Austrians, in that it imposed a check on the hitherto undiminished momentum of the enemy advance. The Prussians who had been engaged there were now putting themselves back in order and waiting for the ammunition carts to arrive with fresh supplies of cartridges, while the nine battalions of the advance guard (Wedell) and the far right wing (Karl of Bevern) were extending the line to the east of the village in the direction of Saara.

This interlude helped the Austrians to pull free of Leuthen, and gather their forces along the low ridge of the windmill hill to the north-west. They were joined there by the largely intact units of the right wing, and the powerful if disordered forces of the Austrian infantry were now able to take advantage of the ditches and sandpits north of Leuthen, and garrison the round, masonry-built bases of the two windmills on the hill.

The Prussians renewed their advance in the fading light, and at once ran into trouble. The attack from Leuthen village was disrupted by a continuous ditch which ran along the northern edge of the gardens. Over to the west, the Austrian heavy artillery had for the first time been brought together in a mass, and enjoyed an excellent field of fire from its site on the windmill hill, from where it wrought execution among the regiments of the Prussian left wing.

Frederick had moved from his first standpoint, on the Wach-Berg behind Lobetinz, to the Radaxdorfer Goy—a little wood of old trees (since disappeared) much closer to Leuthen, so close, indeed that he was caught in the cross-fire between the Austrian artillery and a number of pieces which his younger brother Prince Ferdinand brought up to the Prussian centre. The king had to send word to Ferdinand to desist until he could find another viewpoint.

There was no escape for the six battalions of the Prussian left. As they had been designated the 'refused' wing, these troops had been held back from the action, but now that they were trying to come into line to the west of Leuthen they received the almost undivided attention of the Austrian artillery. The casualties began to rival those sustained by the right wing in the original assault on Leuthen village, as witness the experience of the second battalion of the regiment of Forcade. The regiment's first battalion had been detached to support the centre and right, and lost almost nobody, whereas the second battalion, striving to reach the Austrian guns, had 260 of its men killed or wounded in less than half an hour. The Prussians fell back in some disorder, and rallied in a shamefaced way only when Lieutenant Retzow brought up the last remaining regiment of the second line to support them.

Möllendorf's gateway at Leuthen Church.

The southern wall of Leuthen Church. The lighter stonework behind the cross shows the location of the breach, and the hole in the wall to the right is possibly one of the loopholes made during the battle.

Frederick recognised the danger, and he summoned up the *Brummers* to join the heavy battery of the left wing, which was already thundering from the Butter-Berg. This was an excellent site from which to take the densely-packed Austrians in partial enfilade, but the time was already after four in the afternoon, the enemy were standing their ground, and Frederick had committed every last unit of his line infantry. He had routed the Austrians from more than half of their original position, but he still had to win his battle.

Lucchesi's Throw

Now that the opposing infantry was deadlocked at Leuthen, the only intact forces immediately available to the armies were two wings of their cavalry:

- that of the Prussian lieutenant general Driesen (55 squadrons) biding its time behind the mound of the Sophien-Berg,
- and that of the reinforced right wing of the cavalry of the Austrians (about 65 squadrons) which General Lucchesi had advanced to the low ground south-east of Gross-Heidau

In all probability Lucchesi was unable to see Driesen's wing from this position. However the combined Prussian batteries on the Butter-Berg would have been clearly visible, as would the unsupported and battered left wing of the Prussian infantry, extending to the west of Leuthen.

An officer of the Austrian infantry caught sight of Lucchesi, and records that as he rode up and down the line his magnificent bearing, his gestures and his voice made him seem like a man

The trees in the centre crown the Butter-Berg mound, the site of the great Prussian battery west of Leuthen, as seen from the edge of the village.

inspired.[73] At Piacenza (16 June 1746) he had contributed mightily to the victory which gave the Austrians the mastery of northern Italy, and now at Leuthen he had the opportunity to overrun the unprotected Prussian guns on the Butter-Berg and roll up the line of the Prussian infantry from its shaken left.

At about 4.30 in the afternoon Lucchesi set his cavalry in motion in a counter-clockwise sweep which, if it had run its course, would have brought the Austrians up to these magnificent targets. Lucchesi's cavalry extended across a frontage of about two kilometres, and when taking account of the times and distances we may presume that he was holding his squadrons to a walking pace.

Professionalism rather than charisma was evident among the Prussian cavalry of the left wing, which was the sole body capable of countering the deadly stroke that was now at Lucchesi's command. Major General Krockow Senior had been wounded rather badly in the foot at Breslau only fourteen days before, but he was so determined to lead his brigade (the Krockow Cuirassiers [C1] and the Leib-Carabiniers [C3]) that he overcame his fever and pain to force the affected limb into the thick and heavy cuirassier boot, and have himself hoisted into the saddle. The wing commander, the fat and ageing Lieutenant General Driesen, had stationed himself out ahead on the Sophien-Berg, and, as soon as he detected that the Austrian cavalry was in motion, he sent orders to his squadrons to make north at a fast trot, so as to bring themselves into a position from where he could attack the enemy in flank. In order to orientate his regimental and squadron commanders (who had seen nothing of what was going on), he summoned them to his viewpoint, and they could take in the sight of the mass of the Austrian horse moving from left to right in front of them. The officers returned to their units, and the Austrians were still well short of the Butter-Berg when the Prussians came crashing into their right flank.

Lucchesi's wing was taken completely off its guard. A number of the left-hand regiments were able to veer sharply to the east and get behind the protection of their own infantry, but the rest were caught in the open. Lucchesi was beheaded by a flying cannon shot, which deprived the Austrians of their inspirational leader, while the Kollowrat Dragoons were taken in the rear by the Puttkamer (White) Hussars [H4], who were delighted to get into the fight at long last: 'My men [writes Major Podgursky] attacked like raging tigers. There was no possibility of putting up any organised resistance against them. The enemy were cut down one by one. Occasionally a particularly determined officer would bring together a few files, but it was never long before they were broken apart, or lay bleeding or dying under the hooves of our horses.'[74] However three of the four regiments of the Austrian second line (the Serbelloni [C12] and Anhalt-Zerbst Cuirassiers [C25], and the Benedict Daun Dragoons [D31]) turned to the right as best they could, and threatened to gain the upper hand over the leading Prussian brigade, that of Normann (the Bayreuth Dragoons [D5] and the Driesen Cuirassiers [C7]).

The Bayreuth Dragoons had been present at the battle of Breslau, but they continued to hold a high opinion of themselves, which derived partly from their inordinately large numbers (ten squadrons), and partly from the memory of their battle-winning charge at Hohenfriedberg (4 June 1745). They therefore escaped the opprobrium which was now attached to the five cuirassier regiments of the brigades of Krockow and Bredow. These people too had been involved in the defeat at Breslau, and were very conscious that they had not only been relegated to the left wing, but were now being held back from the mêlée now raging to their front, where the Bayreuth Dragoons were being mauled. 'The cuirassiers in the second line were in a position to give them immediate support, but their finest officers said: "Let the King's favourite dragoons suffer a little!" Finally, when the danger became altogether too great, they came up and saved them.'[75]

The numerical advantage turned decisively in favour of the Prussians when Lieutenant General Prince Friedrich Eugen of Württemberg brought the light cavalry of the Prussian advance guard (30 squadrons) up from behind the infantry to join in the combat. An intermingled mass of victorious Prussians and recoiling Austrians bore down on the Austrian foot soldiers to the north of

Leuthen, and in the gathering darkness hundreds of Austrian infantry at a time cast away their muskets and ran. The right wing of the Prussian infantry was now able to resume its advance, striking out with the bayonet and musket butt, and the Prussian free battalions and *Jäger* came up from Borne to help to complete the success.

The windmill hill now became a scene of massacre. The Austrian fusilier regiments of Wallis [11] and Baden-Durlach [27] stood their ground, and were ridden down by the Leib-Carabiniers [C11] and the Bayreuth Dragoons [D5], while the gunners of the great Austrian battery were bayoneted or clubbed down by the Schenckendorff Grenadiers [35/36].

The Close of the Battle

Frederick writes in his history of the war that 'if the Prussians had not run out of daylight, this battle would have been the most decisive of the century.'[76] It would be wrong to take Frederick to task for exaggeration, for he was one of the least boastful of the great captains, but it must be pointed out that many episodes in the last stages of the battle were hidden from him by the murk, and by the drastic changes in the alignment of the two armies. The losses among the Austrian colours and standards was disproportionately low (below), and a number of incidents confirm that the retreat did not correspond with the mass flight of Prussian legend.

Driesen's left wing, seeking to work around to the rear of the apparently defenceless Austrians, was thrown back behind the Prussian infantry by an unexpected counter-attack. This was the work of Colonel Ludwig Caracciolo di S. Eramo, who had been shot clean through the body, but who managed to retrieve three squadrons of the Stampach Cuirassiers [C10] and Benedict Daun Dragoons [D31] from Lucchesi's battle, and now put them to good use.[77]

The regiment of Thürheim had been thrown into the fight in the disintegrating centre, but it now began to break up when knots of fugitives began to break through its ranks. The Prussian cavalry would have completed the process if Captain Alexander v. Humbracht had not ordered the rearward rank of his company of grenadiers to turn about, and was able to deliver an orderly fire to front and rear until the parent regiment could re-form.[78]

The battle was already lost by the time Prince Charles ordered Colonel Carl Baron Amadei, as commander of the Hungarian infantry regiment of Nicolaus Esterházy [33], to venture out to the left to take the advancing Prussians in their right flank. This was a hopeless task in itself, but Amadei was fortunate enough to encounter General Stampach and five regiments of horse (probably from Serbelloni's second line) who were floundering through a bog. After a prolonged argument, during which Amadei had to call up two of his officers as witnesses, Stampach agreed that they must stay together and take the pressure off the main army, which was in danger of being overwhelmed before it could reach the bridges at Lissa. Stampach's troopers finally crossed the Schweidnitzer-Wasser by the so called 'Müller-Brücke,' where Amadei stood guard until he received orders to burn it.[79]

A glance at the map will show how well Zieten ought to have been placed to cut up from the south, and get between the Austrians and their bridges, which would have rendered all the work of Caracciolo and Amadei in vain. This disaster was prevented by Nádasdy, who had rallied his corps on the woodlands of the Leuthener-Busch and Rathener-Busch. Nádasdy now ensconced five or six of his battalions with their regimental artillery just outside the woods, while he deployed the main force of his cavalry in front, and sent two squadrons out to skirmish with the enemy. According to a Prussian account

the dragoons were affronted to an extraordinary degree by this display of bravado, and they charged with amazing fury. But the enemy, instead of awaiting the shock, at once dispersed, and made way for a hail of musket balls from their infantry, which had been concealed from view in the dense woods. Our dragoons recoiled at some speed, realising that they should have observed better order. General Nádasdy then proceeded to send 12-pounder cannon shot after them. We did not dare to leave the battlefield, and we had no infantry cover with us, and so we had the uncomfortable experience of letting ourselves be cannonaded until darkness fell, and Nádasdy was able to retreat without fear of being disturbed.[80]

By about five in the afternoon, and in complete darkness, the victorious Prussian infantry had come to a halt, well short of the main crossing of the Schweidnitzer-Wasser at Lissa. Frederick was determined not to allow the Austrians to consolidate themselves there, and he rode along the front of the troops and asked if any of them were willing to follow him in one last effort. The Manteuffel, Wedell and Ramin grenadiers responded, and the king set off with these three battalions and the Seydlitz Cuirassiers [C8].

Riding ahead, Frederick and his suite encountered a regiment of Prussian dragoons. The commander knew nothing of the whereabouts of any of the other regiments, though some of his troopers reported that a whole line of Austrians was eight hundred paces in front of them. Frederick had the two battalion pieces of Wedell brought forward to open fire on the alleged enemy location, and sent out a number of officers to investigate. While waiting for them to return, a large fire flared up in the distance. Frederick assumed that Lissa must be ablaze, but he was told (correctly) that the Austrians must be setting fire to the hutments they had built during November's campaign against Bevern.

The reconnaissance parties returned to say that they had ventured as far as an isolated farm-stead, but had seen nothing of the enemy. Frederick grasped at once that the building must be the inn at Saara, and that they must therefore be very close to the highway. Zieten's attention had been attracted by the sound of the cannon shots, and he now caught up with the royal party, accompanied by twelve of his hussars. Frederick impressed on him how important it was to secure the bridge at Lissa, and he asked the battalion gunners how many rounds they had left. He learned that the number was thirty, and said 'That will do—come with me. Now, Zieten, stick with me as well, and send some of your hussars ahead—about thirty paces. We'll talk loudly, so they won't lose contact with us.'[81]

On reaching Saara, Frederick wished to commandeer the inn's lantern, for the night was darker than ever, and the snow was falling heavily. Hans the innkeeper did not recognise the king, and was anxious not to lose sight of his treasured lamp (an oblong object, surmounted by a little funnel), and he therefore offered to light him on his way. Hans chatted in his Silesian dialect as he kept pace with the unknown rider, and Zieten's hussars reined back so as to be able to catch what was being said. The lamp hung close to the ground from its loop, which was a happy circumstance when, just short of Lissa, the light drew a blast of fifty or sixty Austrian musket shots from a range of scarcely fifty paces. The party scattered to right and left through the lines of willows to the lower ground on either side of the highway. Frederick was the first to give voice: 'Good God, Zieten! That wouldn't have happened if the hussars had done what they were told, and kept thirty paces in front.'[82]

Frederick summoned up the three battalions of grenadiers. They arrived half an hour later, towards seven in the evening, and advanced unopposed through Lissa to where the street opened into a little square. In front stretched the two hundred feet of the wooden bridge which spanned the two arms of the Schweidnitzer-Wasser. The elegant *Schloss* of Baron Mudrach stood in its little park to the left, but the workaday houses of the burghers were discharging Austrian troops who carried bundles of straw on their backs. They stumbled into the arms of the Prussian grenadiers, and explained that they belonged to a party of 150 men who had been told to set fire to the bridge. A bed of straw had already been spread over the planks, but the snow had been falling heavily, and the fugitives had trampled the layer into a deep mud. Their captain had therefore had the mess thrown into the river, and told his men to gather fresh straw from the houses.

Frederick was still talking with the prisoners when the enemy opened fire from the far side of the river in a last gesture of defiance. The grenadiers replied, and the king ordered the battalion guns to keep up their fire until they ran out of ammunition. Meanwhile the bridge remained intact and at his disposal. Frederick turned aside to the *Schloss,* and called out to the proprietor, Baron Mudrach, to ask if his mansion were free of the enemy. Mudrach was in some confusion, and answered in the affirmative, but once Frederick had passed the bridge and entered the building he found himself in the company of a large number of wounded Austrian officers. The king was furious, 'but his anger soon subsided, because Mudrach was a loyal subject, and some important men among the Prussian generals spoke out on his behalf.'[83]

The generals had been drawn to Lissa by the sound of the action at the bridge, and they now crowded into a chamber of the *Schloss* to receive the royal *Parole,* which on this occasion was certain to be more than the standard sequence of orders and rebukes. The king entered, and, after receiving the felicitations of his officers, he remarked 'We have worked hard, and I think we have deserved a little rest.' He thanked the commanders for the courage and dedication they had shown, and declared 'This day will enshrine the glory of your name and the nation until the furthest posterity.'[84] Turning to Prince Moritz of Anhalt-Dessau, he said, 'I congratulate you on the victory, field marshal!' The brutish Moritz did not take in the fact that he had just been promoted, and Frederick had to repeat with new emphasis: 'Don't you hear what I am saying? Field marshal, I congratulate you!'[85]

Baron Mudrach's Schloss at Lissa.

Frederick entering Baron Mudrach's Schloss at Lissa.

Frederick dined on the scraps of a meal which Mudrach's cooks had prepared for the Austrian officers, and he passed the rest of the night in a larger corner room on the first floor. He knew nothing at the time of a happening among the troops of the main army, out in the shelterless countryside, where an unknown soldier began to sing a familiar hymn of Martin Rinkert, dating from the end of the Thirty Years War. Exhaustion was forgotten when the words were taken up by 25,000 voices:

Nun danket Alle Gott!
Mit Herzen, Mund und Handen…
[Now thank we all our God
with heart and hands and voices
who wondrous things has done
in whom the world rejoices…]

'You would have had to be a witness of this battle to experience all that was meant by that extraordinarily charged moment… They kept up their singing for a good hour, to the accompaniment of a perpetual firing of cannon.'[86]

The Reckoning

The Immediate Cost

A captain of the White Hussars found that the Prussians, still in the euphoria of victory, had thrown themselves down on the site of the Austrian bivouacs. 'The commotion was indescribable. Thousands of our men were drawn by the light and comforting warmth of the fires. They lay around them singing, drinking, gambling, smoking or just sleeping. There were unlimited provisions of every kind... hundreds of enemy prisoners shared our open table, and they no longer counted as our foes... Admittedly this wild, splendid and cheerful vision had a hideous, darker side. You just had to go a few steps to encounter bloody bodies which had been torn by cannon shot or mangled by the sword.'[87]

The next morning countless little mounds of snow revealed the location of the dead. One of the Austrian captives, Prince Joseph Lobkowitz, was released on parole to take stock of the casualties, and 'the spectacle which presented itself to his view, was such as no language could well describe; great numbers of the men and horses which had fallen on the previous day, remained hard frozen, and their limbs fixed in the attitudes of pain or distortion in which they had expired.'[88]

Altogether the Austrians and their associates lost approximately 23,190 men in the battle of Leuthen. The figure is made up of about 19,831 Austrians (including Red Würzburg), 479 Saxons, 630 Bavarians and 2,250 Württembergers. The number of 19,831 Austrians[89] includes educated guesses as to the losses in the Hungarian infantry regiment of Haller and Dessewffy Hussars. When these are omitted, the established losses of the Austrians stand at 19,248. The official list groups the Austrians together with the 479 Saxons to yield a total of 19,917, broken down as follows:

Killed	Wounded	Missing or Prisoners
1,983	4,591	13,343
9.95 per cent	23.05 per cent	66.99 per cent

The very high proportion of missing and prisoners (which included the many unreported dead and wounded) is explained in large part by what happened in the hours immediately following the battle. At ten on the night in question Prince Charles, Daun and their surviving generals had met in council at Neukirch, and decided to withdraw the whole army at once behind the Lohe. The order was transmitted in a haphazard way by whatever cavalry troopers or civilian horse-handlers were available, and the phrasing was disastrously vague, for it referred merely to the rendezvous as being the 'former camp' in front of Breslau. 'Nobody knew whether this meant the camp which had been made before the battle of Breslau, or the one afterwards, and so many troops remained between the Lohe and the Schweidnitzer-Wasser and were rounded up the next morning as prisoners.[90] Cogniazzo noted that a number of men had hidden themselves in villages and thickets, just waiting to give themselves up to the first Prussian hussars that came by.[91]

The losses among the Saxon chevaulegers amounted to 479, namely 214 in the regiment of Prinz Carl, 154 in that of Prinz Albrecht, and 111 in that of Graf Brühl. These units had been in action twice over—in the initial clash at Borne, and then after they had joined the corps of Nádasdy.

Red Würzburg had defended the churchyard at Leuthen valiantly, and had then been hit very hard by the Prussian cavalry north of the villages. The price was correspondingly high, at 517. Three of its four cannon were lost, and afterwards the survivors numbered just four officers, one ensign and thirty-three men.

The historians of the German Great General Staff put the losses among the German auxiliaries as:

- Bavarians: 1 officer and 161 men killed; 37 officers and 164 men wounded; 11 officers and 256 men missing. Total: 49 officers, 581 men
- Württembergers: 4 officers and 130 men killed; 14 officers and 146 men wounded; 43 officers, 1,913 men missing. Total: 2,250.[92]

Colonel Nicolai specifies that to his knowledge four of the Württemberg officers had been killed or mortally wounded, which corresponds to the figure just given, and that 41 more were being held prisoner at Neumarkt on 13 December, including three colonels, two lieutenant colonels, and nine captains.[93]

The trophies gathered up by the Prussians comprised 46 colours, nine standards and 131 pieces of artillery, which contemporaries believed was less than might have been expected after a victory of this magnitude. One explanation was that the Austrians had preserved a surprising measure of cohesion, and the other, advanced by a French observer, was that 'all the Austrian regiments all came into action successively, so that when the regiments first engaged were beaten, they were replaced by others which covered their retreat.'[94]

We do not know the strengths of the Austrian units on the day of battle, or the numbers of casualties listed with the missing and prisoners. However a number of generalities are possible. Battalion for battalion, the Austrian infantry of Nádasdy's corps suffered only about three-quarters of the losses among their counterparts in the main army, which lost about 72 per cent of its infantry effectives. Here the regiment that was hit the hardest was Baden-Durlach at 1,016 from all causes. Carl Lothringen and Neipperg stood at 872 each, Kayser at 792 and Wallis at 789.

More telling is the proportion of the missing and prisoners within each unit, for this points to the degree of general disintegration. This accounts for 100 per cent of the losses in Wallis, 99.61 in Baden-Durlach, 97.95 in Nicolaus Esterházy, 97.01 in Deutschmeister, 96.89 in Joseph Esterházy, 96.49 in Hildburghausen and 94.87 in Gaisrugg.

The picture which emerges is that of a battle which grew markedly in intensity, with Nádasdy's corps breaking away early, and the main army, and especially its right wing, suffering very heavily indeed towards the end of the action.

Figures can tell us nothing about the impact of the losses within the society of a regiment. An officer in the Netherlandish regiment of Los Rios, who happened to be on garrison duty in the Netherlands, was told that 'your regiment has suffered badly in the battle. Nearly all the officers have been wounded, and two of them killed.'[95] In fact just two had been killed and five wounded, but the regiment, like most of the Netherlandish infantry, had been knocked about earlier in the war, and had still to recover. The officer losses in the companion regiment of de Ligne were not much greater, at two killed, five wounded and two missing. However Captain the Prince de Ligne was chagrined to learn that they were all people who owed him gambling debts, and who had staggered into the line of fire: 'the battle of Leuthen could not have turned out worse for me. My officer friends were none of them drunkards, but they had had nothing to eat for two days, and were poleaxed by a little keg of spirits. They went into battle dead drunk, and ended up dead in the literal sense, for they were killed or wounded.'[96]

The losses among the Austrian generals were heavy, but not unduly so. General Lucchesi had been killed outright, and the Prussians had taken prisoner the lieutenant generals Haller and Maguire, and the major generals Joseph Lobkowitz, Johann O'Donnell, Otterwolff and Preysach.

The Prussians losses were light, according to the standards by which such horrors were reckoned, and amounted to:

- 59 officers and 1,116 men killed
- 164 officers and 5,043 men wounded
- Total: 223 officers and 6,159 men, excluding a small number of prisoners

The casualties among the generals were nevertheless heavy in proportion. Major General Lorenz Ernst v. Münchow was killed, and the giant major general Daniel Caspar v. Rohr ('the Long Tube' [*Rohr*]) was mortally wounded by a canister shot. Major General Krockow the Younger was captured (an embarrassing fate in this overwhelming victory), and the most spectacular wound was sustained by Major General Johann Sigismund v. Lattorff, who had his left eye plucked out by a bullet, but carried on in command of a battalion of grenadiers.

The Battle Lost; The Battle Won

For the Austrians, the process of defeat had begun on 28 November, when their overlong stay at Breslau allowed Frederick to seize his bridgehead across the Katzbach at Parchwitz. Much that happened thereafter may be explained by a difference of perceptions. The king was bent on forcing a decisive battle at the very end of this unusually protracted campaign. The Austrians believed that they were engaged in nothing more than a juggling for a line of suitable winter quarters, for which they must have a secure communication from Bohemia. That was why they left most of their heavy artillery behind when they finally marched from Breslau on 4 December, and why, even on the morning of the battle, it was not unreasonable for them to think that Frederick was just manoeuvring to gain the line of the upper Katzbach.

With hindsight we can see that the Austrian economy of forces was very poor. Their overwhelming numerical advantage was whittled down drastically at Leuthen by the way they scattered their troops over the landscape of Silesia. Again, the Austrian high command failed to exploit its advanced troops at crucial places and times—at Parchwitz on 28 November, and at Borne early on 5 December, when the Prussians swept aside the chevaulegers of Nostitz.

The Austrians were thereby forced into accepting battle without any of the benefits that would normally accrue to the defensive. They were standing on unfamiliar and unreconnoitred ground, they had no time to make entrenchments, and most of their heavy guns were out of reach. The regiments had been positioned as they happened to arrive on the scene piecemeal in the darkness, and the one guiding principle was to prolong the line of battle to such an extent that the enemy would be unable to march around one or the other flanks—an impossible ambition. The Austrian lieutenant colonel Rebain (a prisoner of the Prussians) could write with authority that 'we could have won that battle if the army had not been so strung out. When you are fighting the Prussians you have to arrange your order of battle as if you are facing the Turks. You must provide support everywhere—on the wings, between the two lines—and post the *corps de reserve* in the middle behind the second line. In a battle of this kind long lines are no use, because a long line is unable to hold if one of the wings is overthrown.'[97]

Even after the encounter at Borne a judicious deployment of observers would have enabled the Austrians to make better sense of what the Prussians were doing. After Frederick had recaptured Breslau he asked the captive Austrian major general Beck how the Austrians could have been so completely deceived. Beck replied: 'it all goes back to our first mistake. We expected the main attack to arrive on our right wing, and we made our arrangements accordingly. 'How was that possible?' asked the king. 'If you had sent a good patrol against my right wing you would have discovered straight away what I had in mind.'[98]

As the battle actually developed, the respective arms of the Austrian army—the infantry, cavalry and artillery—were so strung out as to be incapable of offering mutual support, except when they were thrown together north of Leuthen towards the end. The combined battalions of grenadiers had been broken up, and the *corps de reserve,* which had made a signal contribution to the Austrian victory at Kolin, was here committed in the wrong direction, and it had to be retrieved in literally breathless haste in the attempt to fill the gap left by the collapse of the Württembergers and Bavarians.

The evidence is too fragmentary and too biased to enable us to apportion the blame to individuals among the Austrian senior officers, though the relations between these people were obviously unhappy. It was inherently wrong to go on campaign with a divided command, and the arrangements became unworkable when the men in question had so little in common as the showy Prince Charles of Lorraine, and the dour Field Marshal Daun. General Lucchesi did not survive the battle, and was therefore in no position to offer any defence against the two accusations that were laid to his charge—the first, and the least credible, that he had spurred on Prince Charles to unwise action on the council of 2 December, and second that he had been deceived by Frederick's feints on the morning of the battle. His final attack—which promised so well and ended so badly—was nevertheless true to what we know of his temperament, and was strikingly reminiscent of the last deed of his friend Field Marshal Browne, who had been mortally wounded when he led the Austrian grenadiers in a counterstroke at the battle of Prague on 6 May of the same year.

The silence of Nádasdy was imposed not by the grave, but by his loyalty as a public servant. He shouldered the ultimate blame for the collapse of the left flank of the army, when he could have pointed out in his own defence that he had made as good a choice of the ground as was possible, and that the Württembergers and Bavarians were inevitably going to be placed in an exposed position, for they made up a significant proportion of his command, and they had to be put somewhere. Oddly enough, Nádasdy has been acclaimed by posterity on no firm evidence for having sent repeated warnings that his wing was going to come under attack, when Colonel Nicolai of the Württemberg staff states so clearly that he showed an almost irresponsible lack of concern (p. 140). In the subsequent cavalry battle on this wing the Austrians nevertheless did well, considering they were facing heavy odds, and in the final moments Nádasdy was able to keep Zieten at a distance from the bridges of the Schweidnitzer-Wasser while the other troops were making good their escape.

The record concerning Nádasdy is therefore full of contradictions, and it will perhaps be helpful to refer to a wider context. The basic problem at Leuthen was that of integrating Nádasdy's command with the rest of the main army. Large roving corps were typical of Austrian operations, and proved very useful for laying siege to isolated fortresses, or carrying out major raids, but they were not easy to re-integrate with the parent armies for a field action. Just as Nádasdy fought his battle on the left wing at Leuthen almost independently of the main army, so the corps of Lacy, recently returned from another of the raids on Berlin, was going to remain a largely passive spectator of the defeat of Daun's army at Torgau (3 November 1760).

Scapegoats like these lay all too conveniently at hand when Prince Charles sent his reports to Vienna. The Württembergers and Bavarians made another easy target, and on the basis of the first detailed relation Maria Theresa was ready to believe that the blame rested entirely on those people, and she consoled herself with the thought that 'my troops were in no way disconcerted by this bad example... but fought on with heroic valour, and by their blood have earned the praise of all right-thinking military men.'[99] Elector Max Joseph of Bavaria was himself disturbed by the contradictory and unsettling reports that were coming to him, and he could only exclaim that 'we must suspend our judgement, because we are not sufficiently informed of the circumstances of the case and about what really happened.'[100]

Critical attention focussed soon eventually on the role of Prince Charles (p. 184), but the favourable verdict on the performance of the Austrian troops stood the test of time. 'The Austrian infantry could not have fought better,' wrote Warnery, 'but it was badly placed.'[101] The Austrians in general had fought well, indeed, probably too well for their own good. It made the Prussian victory a worthy one, as Frederick was aware,[102] and it afforded Maria Theresa her sole crumb of comfort. She told Prince Charles to thank the troops in her name for the effort and dedication they displayed, and which in due time, 'and with the help of God, will unfailingly give our unjust enemy cause to regret ever having broken the public peace.'[103]

The Prussian assault on the Austrian left flank on 5 December 1757 was the culmination of the 'oblique order,' which had been perfected by the lessons learned at Prague and Kolin, and which at Leuthen brought a 'clean' concentration of overwhelming forces to bear against an overextended enemy. It was an irresistible instrument when, as in 1757, it was wielded by a king and his army that were at the height of their powers, and when the enemy had not yet learned how to respond.

Among the Prussian infantry, the tactics of firepower had replaced those of trying to frighten the enemy out of their position by the advance with cold steel—a procedure which had cost Frederick dearly at Prague and Kolin. Plenty of ammunition was now at hand, and carts to transport it to the fighting lines, and at Leuthen the men of some of the battalions fired more than 180 rounds each, which means that they must have replenished some of their cartridge pouches more than twice over. The Prussian superiority did not end there. According to the Lieutenant Colonel Rebain 'the Prussian troops have the advantage over ours not just in the quantity of the powder, but the quantity in each cartridge. It is believed that in the battle of Leuthen the Austrian musketry inflicted many contusions, but few actual wounds.'[104]

Zieten's cavalry on the right wing performed no more than respectably, but over on the left Driesen's timing and use of the ground were worthy of Seydlitz, who was still nursing the wounds he had sustained at Rossbach a month before, and was absent on 5 December.

Frederick's artillery was never employed to greater effect than at those two battles, and the credit on both occasions was due largely to Colonel Moller's eye for a good battery site, and the speed with which he rushed his pieces from one location to the next. In his instruction of 20 June 1758 Frederick urged that 'we must keep pushing the batteries forward in the same way as at Leuthen.'[105]

At Leuthen the complement of artillery was particularly heavy, both in numbers and calibre, because Frederick had borrowed a number of heavy pieces from fortress of Glogau, in the expectation that he would have to storm the entrenched camp at Breslau. This mighty ordnance was thrown around the battlefield with remarkable facility. The ground was frozen and generally hard, and the mobility was further enhanced by that the fact that prisoners of war and deserters had returned in great quantities, and, being without weapons, they were now employed to help to serve and move the artillery. The authentic *Brummers* were drawn by teams of twelve horses each, and (having no permanently assigned field gunners) they were served by dismounted cavalry recruits. The remaining 12-pounders were thin-barrelled pieces with conical chambers, which were relics of an otherwise unsuccessful attempt by Frederick to lighten his artillery before the war; they were no direct match for the excellent Austrian 12-pounders, but they proved ideal for giving close support to the Prussian infantry.

The core of the Prussian army was formed of the troops who had marched from Rossbach to Leuthen, and it was 'an unparalleled elite, since the cowards and malcontents had had all the time they needed to desert.'[106] These men and their achievements under their king were the best possible example to entice the lost sheep—the escaped prisoners, the deserters and the other remnants of Bevern's army—to return to the ranks. Never was Frederick more attentive to the spirit of his troops than during this campaign and battle, and he reaped an ample reward.

The secrets of the Prussian success resided not just in the immediate circumstances of the battle. Much of what we have witnessed was the working-through of a military culture which had settled in over generations, and also the intense schooling which Frederick had given his army before the war, and the relationships he had established with his generals, officers and troops. This depth of resources was expressed at Leuthen in the speed and control of the Prussian movements, and the concentration of troops, heavy firepower and command at the decisive points on the battlefield.

Frederick had little to say about his personal contribution. The British envoy Mitchell found him 'pleased and happy, but not elated, with the great and almost incredible success of his arms. He talks of the action of the 5th December, and what has followed since, with the modesty becoming a hero, whose magnanimity is not affected with the smiles, nor with the frowns of fortune.' Mitchell enquired into the matter more closely, and discovered that 'the disposition was entirely the king's own, and his orders were punctually obeyed; some officers of the greatest experience assure me that it was impossible to mend [i.e. improve on] it, the troops say they marched up to the enemy with a countenance, as if they had been going to a review, and the success was answerable.'[107]

VII

Reaping the Harvest

The Flight to Bohemia

The campaign of Rossbach had ended three days after the battle of that name, when Frederick turned back east to confront the Austrians in Silesia. In contrast, the work of exploiting the victory at Leuthen extended until April 1758, when the Prussians reduced the last enemy-held strongpoint in Silesia, and by when the Austrian losses far exceeded those they had suffered in the battle on 5 December.

The awakening of the Austrians on the 6th was as horrid as it is possible to imagine. Lieutenant Giuseppe Gorani of the regiment of Andlau had lived through the first defeat of his career, and 'in the hurry of our retreat we spent the first night among fields covered with snow and sheets of ice. When I came to, I still could not believe what I had seen on the day before… Soon enough I heard our drums beating, we formed up in haste and continued our flight as far as Schmiedeberg.'[1] Captain the Prince de Ligne was hauled from his resting place by the Duke of Arenberg, who told him to come along with him to Gräbischen, and 'there I saw the prince and the field marshal sunk in a state of total despair. One seemed to be saying, "I just can't believe it!" and the other, "I told you so!"… every report indicated that the enemy battalions were passing the Lohe, and that we were going to come under a new attack… Nobody knew what to do. Banalist Croats were shooting at the pigeons in the courtyard of the farm where we were staying. Total confusion reigned until, at last, people came gradually together, and the least battered regiments began to take on a recognisable shape.'[2]

Prince Charles and Daun assembled what they could of their army between Gräbischen and the Ohlau suburb of Breslau. They had abandoned all hope of disputing the open country of Silesia, and now their plan was just to throw reinforcements into Breslau, disengage from the enemy, and gain such a lead on the way to Schweidnitz as to be able to cover their communications with Bohemia, and the magazines at Landeshut and Trautenau.

The sheer numbers of troops crowding through Breslau made it secure for the immediate future. A citizen records that 'every street was a human stream, and every alley a living torrent.'[3] The fugitives from the battle were joined in the city by Major General Beck's command of 3,500 light troops from the right bank of the Oder, and together with the original garrison they made a total force of more than 11,000 men who were fit to serve, as well as 6,000 sick and wounded. The commandant, Lieutenant General Sprecher, sought in vain for some guidance from headquarters before he lost contact with the main army on 7 December.

Prince Charles and Daun were too busy organising the escape of their own troops. It was a matter of some urgency, for the enemy were hard on their heels. In the darkness of the early morning of the 6th the victorious Prussian army was called into battle order, and the regimental commanders read out the royal message of thanks to every officer and man. At the end 'a joyful "long live the king!"… resounded in powerful unison over that wide, white field.'[4] At five in the morning the army crossed the undefended Schweidnitzer-Wasser in four columns, and continued in the direction of Breslau, preceded by an advance guard of nine and half battalions, sixty-three squadrons, and a battery of twelve 12-pounders, forming a total of some 8,000 troops under the orders of Zieten.

Five kilometres further on Zieten made some tentative crossings of the Lohe (which gave rise to the alarms mentioned by de Ligne), but he was checked by a force of eight regiments of infantry and nine of cavalry. The commander was General Serbelloni, who was a singularly awkward individual on most occasions, but suited by temperament for his present obstructive task. The reassembled Austrian army was drawn up behind him, ready to do battle, and the confrontation degenerated into a prolonged cannonade. In the afternoon the main Austrian force broke contact under the protection of Serbelloni's screen, and marched slowly through the rain of a sudden thaw to Rothfürben and Weignitz. The tents and the rest of the heavy baggage were sent ahead by way of Grossburg and Landeshut under the protection of the surviving Saxon chevaulegers, which suggests a strange order of priorities, for the Austrians would now have no cover against the elements. Zieten had failed in his main purpose, but he succeeded in snapping up a convoy of 400 carts carrying bread, for which Serbelloni had neglected to provide adequate cover. Now the troops lacked both food and shelter.

On 7 December the Austrian field army was already out of touch with Breslau, which was now blockaded by the Prussians. Frederick himself remained close by to supervise the siege, and for a time he was content to leave the pursuit entirely to Zieten. On that day Zieten made further rich pickings in the shape of 1,500 prisoners, and a massive convoy of 2,000 wagons laden with provisions, ammunition and cash. He was nevertheless unable to overhaul the Austrian main force, and on the 8th he was checked on the Klein-Lohe by Serbelloni's rearguard, which had sunk to six battalions and five regiments of cavalry, but was standing firm on the heights to the east of Klein-Breslau and Bohrau.[5]

Behind this screen the Austrian army marched all day to reach a comfortless bivouac site on the steep Zobten-Berg. Colonel Nicolai returned there after a vain expedition to find suitable quarters for the Württemberg generals, 'and the only thing I had to show was a piece of bread which I discovered after having searched through an entire village. I found it in one of the houses, where the entire family begged me to spare the loaf, which they saw as their last hope of survival. I cut it in two, left one of the halves for the poor family, and divided the other between myself and my commander.'[6]

Frederick was becoming exasperated. He wrote to Zieten to urge him not to allow the Austrians to come to their senses. He knew that Zieten's troops were tired, but it could not be otherwise, and in the present circumstances one day of exhausting effort would be rewarded a hundred-fold.[7] Zieten could not be persuaded to move any faster, and on 9 December the Austrians reached their immediate objective, and bivouacked to the south west of Schweidnitz, between Polnisch-Weistritz and Kroischwitz. For the last three days Prince Charles had been 'in a state of frantic anxiety' lest the Prussians should cut him off from Bohemia, but he was now relieved on that score.[8]

The halt outside Schweidnitz was amongst other things a physical necessity. Prince Charles reported to Francis Stephen that a number of regiments had no more than four surviving officers, and that fifteen of the generals had been killed or wounded. 'The field marshal can hardly drag himself along. He does what he can, but the loss of the battle weighs on his spirits. I must admit to Your Majesty that the troops are at the end of their resources, and I cannot imagine how the King of Prussia can get his men to do what they are doing.'[9]

There was no alleviation for the sufferings of the defeated army, for it was still not possible to distribute proper rations, many of the troops lacked coats and shoes, and the open bivouacs were in a squalid condition. 'The rain has made the fields and roads so sodden that the men can scarcely extract their feet from the ground. The troops lie in the mud along with their knapsacks and equipment, and even their muskets are half-buried in the mire.' Nerves were on edge after the shattering defeat, and an order of the day in Nádasdy's corps read that 'the Saxons, Bavarians and Württembergers must desist from their plundering, and return to their former state of discipline... The army was overtaken by a spirit of contention, and as a result the ill-feeling between the Austrians and the auxiliaries deepened every day. Fights broke out every time we took up quarters, or even when we went to draw water at the streams.'[10]

On his side the Bavarian commissary M. Mayer complained to Elector Max Joseph how 'our men are scattered over a distance of two or three hours of marching time, like a herd of sheep without its shepherd, which in itself makes it impossible to furnish them with uniforms, tents, cooking pots or water bottles. All the troops of the army are badly off in these respects, but ours worse than all the others. At Breslau our regiments had just been assigned 2,055 shirts, 815 pairs of stockings and 1,459 pairs of shoes, but the trouble was that instead of being worn, most of these items were put in away in the knapsacks, which were lost, together with the pots and water bottles, in the battle on the 5th... I must also report to Your Princely Highness that since the last battle the Austrians have behaved very badly towards our troops, swearing at them in the most scandalous and contemptuous terms... all you hear from them is how we deserve to be shot or hacked in pieces... these are not idle threats, as is shown by the fact that the Austrians beat a private in the regiment of Minucci to death, and cut off the fingers of a man in Duke Clemens.'[11]

On 11 December a tremendous commotion was caused when a sutler announced that the enemy were in full march to attack, and Field Marshal Daun rode up to put the troops in battle order. It was a good thing that the alarm was without foundation, 'for if we had really come under attack, less than one-third of the army would have been able to move, or have its weapons in a usable condition.'[12]

On 13 December the 25-26,000 surviving troops began the march towards the border hills with Bohemia. The heavy snow and the compacted ice made the going so difficult that even the senior officers had to dismount and pick their way on foot. On the 16th the army reached Landeshut undisturbed, and for the first time some of the soldiers were able to rest under cover, though most still had to bivouac in the woods. The Prince de Ligne looked about him, and discovered that two Netherlandish regiments of de Ligne and Sachsen-Gotha and the nearest four regiments of Hungarians could muster scarcely six hundred men together.

On 20 December the main army reached the military security of Bohemia. The border at Schwarzwasser was marked by the gallows hill, which was not calculated to raise spirits, and when the Netherlanders reached Bernstadt the place seemed to be under the spell of the gloomy Jesuit house which stood on the rock above. Worse things awaited the troops deeper into Bohemia, as we shall see.

Down in Silesia the enemy had come to life, for the tough and fanatical Lieutenant General Fouqué had taken over command of the advance guard from Zieten on the 16th, and reinforced it to a strength which the Austrians put at 17,000 troops. The responsibility of holding the Prussians at bay now rested with Lieutenant General Adolph Buccow. Buccow arrayed the rearguard along the low ridge at Kunzendorf, and bought enough time to be able to send two convoys of flour and cattle to the fortress of Schweidnitz, retrieve eleven cannon, eight mortars and a considerable quantity of ammunition which had been abandoned during the retreat, gather up more than 1,000 sick and wounded soldiers, and evacuate some of the contents of the magazine at Landeshut.

Having retired to the hills above Landeshut, Buccow beat off a first attack by Fouqué on 21 December. At ten in the morning of the following day the Prussians came on again in three columns. Buccow was confident that he would be able to hold his position, but his arrangements began to unravel when his Croats abandoned the Buch-Berg without waiting for the earmarked reinforcements to reach them. The Prince de Ligne commented that 'never in my life have I seen such confusion in the transmission of orders.'[13] Buccow fell back to the Kirch-Berg, then broke contact at four in the afternoon and made good his escape in the direction of Liebau, having lost 185 of his men as prisoners.

Behind this screen the defeated army streamed over the border into north-east Bohemia. An Austrian officer wrote on his way there on 19 December: 'I put on my shirt two days before the battle, on 3 December. After that I was constantly on the march and unable to take it off, so that a tribe of monster lice gathered therein. Yesterday I was finally able to remove it, and went about just in my cloak while it was being washed. Today I am get up like a prince, except for my stockings, which lie in rags about my feet. On my head I wear a little Prussian hat which I bought on the march for two groschen.'[14]

The Württemberg corps reached Arnau on the upper Elbe, where an epidemic very soon carried off many more of the men than had been struck down by the Prussians at Leuthen, leaving some of the peasant houses full of nothing but corpses, and others with just an individual alive. Colonel Nicolai was assailed by a high temperature and raging headaches, and when his troops left Arnau on the snowy 22 December he wondered whether he was in any condition to accompany them. His mind was made up for him by the news that 1,600 of the crude Austrians were about to arrive in the place. He clambered onto his horse more dead than alive, and collapsed several times on his subsequent ride with heavy nose bleeds.

Mopping Up in Silesia

Back in Silesia some 27,000 men had been left stranded in the three fortresses, namely:

- Breslau: about 17,700
- Liegnitz: 3,700
- Schweidnitz: nearly 5,000

Prince Charles explained to Vienna that the fortresses were 'well provided with all that they need, and they cannot be taken without a siege, and for that the season is too advanced. I am therefore confident that these three places will be able to hold out for the winter.'[15] Maria Theresa and her advisers knew how important it was to hang on to Schweidnitz, for both offensive and defensive purposes. They were not much concerned for the garrison in Liegnitz, for it was likely to gain good terms from the Prussians, who would be anxious to be rid of this minor nuisance. However there seemed to be no good reason for Prince Charles and Daun to have cast so many troops into Breslau after the disastrous battle, leaving 20,000 men (as it was calculated) stranded in the middle of Silesia. Maria Theresa conceded that it would be difficult for the Prussians to mount a formal siege of a city which held a virtual army, 'all the same it is not impossible that the King of Prussia will again be tempted to trust to his effrontery and streak of luck, and decide on something quite extraordinary. If he succeeds, it is easy to imagine the dire consequences if he manages to seize not just the town, but the large garrison, along with all the wounded and sick, the artillery, the ammunition and baggage and so on.'[16]

Just two days after the battle the Prussians threw a cordon of investment about Breslau and cut off the city from the outside world. Frederick himself could not afford to stay long in the neighbourhood, but chose a house in the outlying village of Rothkretschan for his temporary quarters. The place was built of wood, and the officer of the watch was unable to prevent a party of dragoons from assailing the timbers for their fires. '"Now look here, you dragoons," said the king. "If you carry on like that the snow will be falling on my bed, and you don't want that, do you?" The penitent dragoons beat a retreat, and the house was spared.'[17]

The Prussians opened a bombardment of Breslau on 13 December. They were not very good at sieges, but in the circumstances they hardly needed to be. On the 26th a mortar bomb touched off a magazine and wrecked the Taschenbastion on the south-western sector of the ramparts. Two days later they opened their trenches, which was a deadly threat, for the wet ditches around the city were frozen, and the rampart behind consisted merely of an earthen bank with palisades. On 20 December Lieutenant General Sprecher surrendered his garrison as prisoners of war. The troops, a miniature army, filed out of the Schweidnitzer Tor on the next day. Frederick and a few officers were standing by to take in the spectacle, and the procession of troops seemed to have no end. 'Fully armed and equipped, they wound out of Breslau, and laid down their muskets only after they had filed past their conqueror. How easy it would have been for somebody in that throng to have murdered the king, whether from religious fanaticism, national hatred or desperation!'[18] It took four days just to make out the list of the captured officers, and the final total of the prisoners came to thirteen generals, 670 other officers, 17,000 rank and file, along with the fortress guns, 81 field pieces, 1,000 horses and a war chest of 144,000 florins.

What transpired at Liegnitz shortly afterwards could not have been more different. The defences were weaker still than at Breslau, for the town was surrounded only by medieval walls, and the defenders were only about one-fifth the number, being 3,700 men under the command of old Colonel Friedrich v. Bülow. 'He was not at all like most of our generals, being friendly, obliging, even-handed and generous. He had the gift for inspiring obedience and affection at the same time, and just because we hated the thought of displeasing him.'[19]

Bülow did what he could to put the place in a state of defence, by burning down the suburbs and spreading the inundation of the Katzbach. He came under investment on 18 December, and on Christmas Day Moritz v. Anhalt-Dessau arrived on the scene, breathing fire and fury. Bülow replied by insisting 'once and for all on a free evacuation with every possible mark of honour, failing which I am determined to hold out to the last man.'[20] As a sign of his resolution he put Lieutenant Gorani in command of a redoubt outside the Breslauer Tor with a forty-two Croats, eighteen gunners and eight cannon, under strict orders to have himself cut in pieces rather than surrender.

The frost was so severe that not only did the inundation of the Katzbach freeze over, but the picks of the besiegers could make no impression on the ground. The Prussians were already exhausted by weeks of marching, and now that the season was so advanced Frederick's priority was to spare the troops. He authorised Moritz to offer favourable terms, and this monster's second summons came in the form of a disconcertingly polite letter, inviting Bülow to surrender his fortress with the honours of war, after which he and his garrison would be free to rejoin their army. Bülow capitulated on these conditions on 28 December, and a French attaché noted that 'if the governor of Breslau had shown the same resolution, he would unfailingly have obtained the honours of war from the king. The contrast is striking—it means that he is going to be court-martialled, and that his disgrace is all the worse in comparison.'[21]

There were no other grounds for consolation. The Austrians had been between 80,000 and 90,000 strong when they had crossed the Queiss from Lusatia into Silesia on 19 September. Now there were none of them left except the marooned garrison of Schweidnitz (surrendered 18 April 1758), and corpses and captives. Frederick commented that his great difficulty was simply to feed the vast quantities of prisoners. Out of the survivors in Bohemia probably only about 20,000 were fit for action.

That was not all. A 'spotted Hungarian fever' broke out among the captives: 'it was one of those burning fevers which are accompanied by all the symptoms of the plague... the infection was so virulent, speedy and lethal that it consigned a man to the grave in three days.'[22] The pestilence spread through all the armies, and did not spare the Württemberg auxiliaries, who dragged themselves to the quarters assigned to them in north-western Bohemia. They set up hospital in Saaz, 'but there the number of sick piled up to such an extent that it was difficult to find space to lay them down, and more difficult still to care for them, since... most of the men assigned to that task died, or at least fell ill themselves. Nobody would volunteer for an office that had to be carried out under disgusting conditions, and with the prospect of almost certain death... every day eleven or twelve men were piled into a cart and buried in a common grave, and the hospital was full of the dead or dying.'[23] Lieutenant General Spitznas was one of those who perished. Stricken Austrians meanwhile jammed the makeshift infirmaries in northern-eastern Bohemia and in Olmütz in Moravia, where the Jesuit fathers demanded that these offending objects must be removed from their house.

In terms of men killed, captured, died of disease or permanently disabled, the cost to the Austrians of what happened at Leuthen stood at between 40,000 and 45,000 souls,[24] or up to 50,000 if we include the surrendered garrison at Schweidnitz. Austrian officials put together a most curious and interesting document which sets out the financial penalty, calculated on the extra costs that were needed to put the army to take to the field in 1758.[25] The total came to a staggering 7,426,024 florins, which was the equivalent of one quarter of the state income for that year. The largest single items comprised 2,400,000 florins for replacing uniforms and regimental equipment, 1,878,222 for cavalry remounts, 1,439,706 for recruits (not including those for the Netherlands and Hungarian regiments), and 1,281,622 to make good the artillery.

The Austrians march out of Breslau, 21 December 1757. They are piling their muskets in the left of centre.

VIII

Prussia's Glory

The Consequences

In the strategic dimension the impact of the staggering defeats of the Allies at Rossbach and Leuthen fell most severely on the French, who never again ventured so far eastwards in this war. To Cardinal Bernis, as the principal supporter of the Austrian connection, it seemed that nobody was left on the military stage now that the Austrians had lost three-quarters of their field army in ten or twelve days, and that no trust could be placed either in the Russians, or in the indisciplined and poorly-commanded French army in Germany. Over the following years the effort of the French in continental Europe was concentrated on what had been their interest all along, which was to conquer and hold the German lands of George, Elector of Hanover and King of Britain.

The first news of the catastrophe at Leuthen was brought to Vienna towards eleven in the morning of 9 December. Maria Theresa spent the whole of the rest of the day in seclusion. 'The Empress wept incessantly and was almost inconsolable. She went straight to the chapel, where she prayed amid her streaming tears, and, in spite of her extreme distress, she spent the remainder of the time working with the ministers of the various departments.'[1] She was also suffering from the progress of her last pregnancy, and for a number of days thereafter she was not always equal to signing the orders which were being issued in her name.[2]

Frederick believed that he would have no better opportunity of wresting favourable terms of peace, and he sent the captured Colonel Joseph Lobkowitz to Vienna under parole to put out the necessary feelers. The king had underestimated the temper of Maria Theresa, who now came to herself and authorised the Vienna press to publish conditions that were certain to be unacceptable to Frederick.

> The defeat at Leuthen had spread consternation throughout our states and armies, but Maria Theresa was almost the only person not to lose heart. She bore the weight of this crushing blow with all the dignity of her character—never did she show herself greater. Her ministers advised her to change her place of residence to Hungary; she would not hear of it, and stayed put. She displayed an amazing energy throughout that winter. You would see her every-where—at the councils of war, in the arsenals, in the artillery park, in all the departments. She was determined that we would be in a state to stand up to the King of Prussia in the next campaign. She had issued the appropriate orders, and she tolerated no delay in putting them into effect.[3]

Although Maria Theresa committed herself to continue the war, the ability of her army to sustain that struggle had been compromised in a number of ways. The prosaic but important matter of book-keeping had been thrown into disarray by the loss of papers at Leuthen and afterwards. An officer noted that 'some regiments had lost everything, others only some, but all were affected to some degree. A captain of our regiment reckoned his loss at 8,000 florins.'[4] In March 1758 it came to Maria Theresa's notice that a Lieutenant d'Andrade had disappeared without trace at Leuthen, leaving a ten year-old daughter who was found wandering the streets in Troppau. Since nobody else would do so, the Empress took personal responsibility for the upbringing of the little soul.[5]

The continuing disorder in the Austrian army hit particularly hard in the winter of 1761/2, when the Chancellor Kaunitz initiated a number of cuts in the military establishment.

Lieutenant General Lacy knew that the reductions were dangerous enough in terms of numbers, but

> it does not end there, for I must emphasise another important point, namely, that after the unfortunate day of Leuthen, when we lost most of the officers of the army, we had to make up the deficiencies in great haste, and fill the gaps by all sorts of people. By now these men have acquired enough seniority to be spared from being cut, and the pity is that this sad fate affects just those officers who have been commissioned or promoted since that time in virtue of their proven courage, ability and merit. This is just a way of saying that the officers who are caught up in the reduction… are the ones we can least afford to lose.[6]

The efforts of Lacy, Loudon and the other officers of their new generation were doing much to make the army more responsive and on occasion aggressive, but the shock of Leuthen reverberated to the end of the war. 'No matter how desperate our affairs became [wrote a Prussian officer], neither the king nor his troops ever lost courage, always hoping that a second Leuthen would supply a remedy. Conversely our foes might be doing ever so well, but never dared to allow free rein to their good fortune. They too had another Leuthen at the back of their minds.'[7]

The Fate of the Commanders

It might be of interest to follow the later histories of a few of the principal actors. That of Soubise encapsulates much of what now seems reprehensible or admirable in a prince of the Ancien Régime. Secure in the protection of Louis XV and the Pompadour he lay low for several months after the battle of Rossbach, seemingly indifferent to the epigrams which were flying over his head. He emerged again in 1758, and in the later part of that year's campaigning he won Hesse-Cassel for his king, and the marshal's baton for himself. However Soubise could not escape the taint of favouritism, and the public began to compare him to his disadvantage with the Duc de Broglie, who beat a force of British-subsidised Germans at Bergen on 13 April 1759, and who on 16 December of the same year was made marshal of France at the age of forty-two. He was the second-youngest commander ever to reach that rank.

Everyone now seemed to fall out with everyone else. The French won another action at Corbach (20 July 1760), but Broglie and the acerbic Comte de Saint-Germain disputed the credit, and in the subsequent fracas Saint-Germain had to flee to foreign parts. Soubise and Broglie in turn became involved in a dispute as to who was to blame for the defeat at Vellinghausen (15/16 July 1761). Broglie lost the argument, as the less well connected of the two, and he was exiled to his estates, to the outrage of the army and the nation.

Saint-Germain sought his fortune in the Danish service, where he took command of the field army in 1762, and rose to the rank of field marshal. After further comings and goings he purchased a small estate in Alsace in 1773, where he lived happily until he went bankrupt and was faced once more with ruin. The German officers in the French service rescued him by raising a subscription on his behalf, and he spent a short (1776-7) but active spell as War Minister. Saint-German's religious sense of duty nevertheless led him to believe that he was failing in his task, and he died a disappointed man on 15 January 1778. There were curious parallels with the later years of Broglie, who was recalled to public life as War Minister on the eve of the Revolution. It was too late for reform of any kind, and in 1792 Broglie finally joined the forces of the Émigrés. He died in Münster in 1804 at the age of eighty-six.

Soubise abandoned his military career with the end of the Seven Years War, and slipped back into the role of courtier, in which capacity he advanced the rise of Madame du Barry. However his attachment to Louis XV went beyond promoting the king's pleasures, and he was the only one of the nobles to accompany the valets and pages to the king's burial at Saint-Denis in 1774 . The gesture did not go unnoticed by Louis XVI, who allowed Soubise to resume his place at the Conseil des Ministres. Soubise continued to maintain strings of opera girls at extravagant expense, and died on 4 July 1787, shortly before his world was extinguished.

The Prince of Sachsen-Hildburghausen had many enemies in Vienna, who included the rising Hofrat Borié (a favourite of Kaunitz) and the *Reichsvizecanzler* Count Colloredo, who was in charge of Austria's relations with the Reich, and who encouraged the heads of a number of German states to demand his resignation after the battle of Rossbach. Hildburghausen himself had no desire to stay, and wrote to Colloredo 'they wanted me to be beaten, and so I was, and very badly. At least my martyrdom is at an end. I would not hang on if the Emperor gave me a million a month... all I wish is to live quietly at home, that and no more.'[8]

Hildburghausen tendered his formal resignation to Emperor Francis Stephen on 26 January 1758. By that time Hildburghausen was probably aware that Soubise and his partisans, having denied his authority during the last campaign, now found it convenient to claim that he had been in sole control. He gathered his thoughts, and he sought to convey to Maria Theresa how he had 'never desired or sought that command, but took up purely from my attachment to Your Majesty. I lost honour and reputation in the process... and I only wish that I had also sacrificed my life. Why did not that damned hussar aim his cut one inch higher?'[9] Maria Theresa replied in her own hand to assure Hildburghausen that neither she nor the Emperor had ceased to hold him in high regard. Indeed 'the only accusation I have ever heard levelled against you is that you took too many risks with your person, which is confirmed by the blow you received.'[10] These words remained Hildburghausen's only comfort during his long and embittered retreat on his Thuringian estates, which terminated with his death on 14 January 1787.

Many sacrificial lambs were dragged to the altar before responsibility for the defeat at Leuthen was finally brought home to Prince Charles of Lorraine. The prince had set the tone for the official pronouncements when he wrote to Maria Theresa four days after the battle to lay the blame entirely at the door of the Württembergers and Bavarians, who had fled at the first shot and left the flank open.[11] Maria Theresa was eager to fall in with this version of events, as sparing the reputation of her brother-in-law, and she replied that she had no doubt that Prince Charles and Daun had done everything in their power, and that her army had done its duty to the full.[12]

On 10 December Prince Charles sent a draft for a public relation to Maria Theresa, and added a hint which further diverted attention from himself. 'I must draw yet another matter to Your Majesty's attention, namely that on the day before the battle we entered into an understanding with Count Nádasdy, whereby he was to form his troops into a flank, and take particular precautions with regard to the Bavarians and Württembergers. We relied completely on this agreement.'[13]

This target was never again given field command, 'and so the deserving Nádasdy, who had the same standing among the Austrian troops as Zieten with the Prussians, was driven from the army by spite, envy and cabals.'[14] Nádasdy took a post in the administration of Hungary, and laboured cheerfully over the following years to forward recruits to the army. Other scapegoats who were duly rounded up in the interests of the House of Habsburg-Lorraine included the shade of the headless Lucchesi, and Sprecher v. Berneck, who was accused (and later absolved) of the charge of surrendering Breslau before its term.

The force of public opinion was not to be underestimated, even in those times. Vienna was physically small but very crowded, and the talk at coffee houses, the theatre and in the great noble mansions increasingly spoke of Prince Charles as the true author of the defeat. He ignored hints from Maria Theresa and Francis Stephen that he should consider resigning from active command, and finally on 16 January 1758 Maria Theresa had to write in direct terms to tell him that he must go. Prince Charles took the news with such unconcern that she realised that she should have acted sooner. A new employment was found for him as Governor-General of the Austrian Netherlands. His easy-going ways and his love of high living appealed to the Belgians, and he lived there long and successfully until he died in 1780.

If Frederick was possibly the least pompous of the great captains, there were plenty of people to sing his praises for him, and the chorus never sounded more loudly than after his pair of great victories towards the close of 1757. Even in a neutral state like the Republic of Venice the populace had been riven by feuds between his supporters and enemies, and now the *Prussiani* gained added force in their battles against the *Teresiani*—combats which were fought out in the squares, in the coffee houses, and (with plates and mugs) in the refectory of the monastery of S.S. Giovanni e Paolo. In Britain, Prussomania reached its height, being expressed in pottery, tavern signs, broadsheets, and, in practical terms, the voting of a new subsidy, and the re-constitution of the army of Hanover and other sympathetic north German states, this time under the inspired command of a Prussian general, Prince Ferdinand of Brunswick.

Frederick was to know further critical passages in his war, but Russia and France in turn dropped out of the struggle, and Austria finally made peace, at Hubertusburg on 15 February 1763. He was confirmed in ownership of all his states, including stolen Silesia.

The Rival Nationalisms

There was something truly rotten in the elements of French society which termed the defeat of their own army at Rossbach as *la bataille amusante*. 'Over the whole course of history there has been no precedent for a battle like this, where friend and foe laughed at the generals of the combined army.'[15]

There was a striking and very significant shift in the perceptions of Rossbach as they registered with Voltaire. To begin with he expressed his astonishment at the turn of events, and his admiration for Frederick, and he went to the trouble of asking the king's favourite sister Wilhelmine, Margravine of Bayreuth, for an account of the battle.[16] The war was still far from over when we find Voltaire, quite unexpectedly, entering the lists as a champion of French martial prowess. He was provoked in the first place by the Italian man of letters Deodati da' Tovazzi, who maintained the superiority of the Italian language over the French *(Dissertation sur l'excellence de la langue italienne)*. Voltaire responded in a series of open letters in the course of 1761, and amongst other arguments pointed that whereas the Italian language had only three words for 'courage,' the French had nine or more. His choice of example was intended to establish the association between culture and military worth, and he cited a number of instances of heroic French leadership in the current war. Soubise is here represented as saving the army by his vigorous and valiant intervention at Rossbach, and Voltaire upheld the marshal's deed to further admiration in chapter 33 of his *Précis de la siècle de Louis XV*.[17]

Voltaire, the arch cynic, the cosmopolitan par excellence, now seemed to be acting out of character, for he was associating himself with a decidedly nationalistic turn in French public opinion. Outrage at the losses and defeats in the war was aimed in the one direction against the predatory British, who had gobbled up colonies and savaged the navy. The other target was the Austrians, who were conceived to be just as hostile to French interests, for having inveigled Louis XV through Madame de Pompadour into wasting precious resources on a land war deep in Europe. After the close of the French war (Treaty of Paris, 10 February 1763) the bitterness was unabated, and in such a context it was singularly unwise for the Bourbons to link themselves still more closely with the Habsburgs by the marriage of the Dauphin (the future Louis XVI) to Marie Antoinette. The Church, the Jesuits and Catholic internationalism in general were also seen as enemies of the French nation, and through such a progression 'much of the patriotic fervour associated with the Revolution was also present in the France of Louis XV. That the monarchy ultimately failed to associate itself with the new public mood says much about its problems both before and after 1789.'[18]

A counter-patriotism was meanwhile forming in the Germanic lands to the east, and the two forces were going to come into contact in little more than a generation. In November and December 1757 Frederick had unwittingly presided over the creation of a national myth as potent in its way as Blood River for the Boers, the Frontier for the United States, or Gallipoli for the Australians. Compared with the exhortations and Bulletins of Napoleon to his armies, the Parchwitz Address of 3 December 1757 was restrained and austere. It was not even original, for Frederick copied it from a recommendation in the works of the marques de Santa Cruz y Marcenado.[19] Its extraordinary effect derived from the fact that for the first and last time in his life this terrifying man was appealing to his army to support him. Among the king's officers, nobody was going to write more critically of his doings than Kaltenborn, but he tells us that as God was his witness, 'that no matter how many times I have heard this address repeated, the tears have sprung to my eyes. The men who spoke these words were mostly soldiers who had been rendered more than a little coarse and unfeeling by the trade of arms and the clamour of war, yet they would be weeping like children.'[20]

At Rossbach these men had taken their revenge on the nation which, in the imagination of Protestant Germans, had for generations launched its armies through their lands, and treated Germans as its cultural inferiors, to that the extent that their own rulers had aped the ways of Versailles. Frederick's aide de camp Gaudy testifies that among the motivating forces of the Prussians on that day was

> the natural hate which ordinary men in Germany, but especially those of Magdeburg, the Mark and Pomerania, feel in their heart for anybody who goes by the name of 'Frenchman.' It is a feeling which they imbibe with their mothers' milk. They do not know the reasons themselves, and when you press them for an explanation all that they can say is: 'French can't be Germans.' The sentiment is genuine enough, as was proved by that day's combat, when our troops were not content with doing their duty and advancing bravely against the enemy. If you had seen them at work you would have been convinced that they were fighting out of real hatred. This relates particularly to the behaviour of our cavalrymen when they were hacking their way into the enemy infantry, and our officers found it not at all easy to get the ordinary troopers to grant quarter.[21]

Frederick regarded educated Frenchmen as his intellectual brothers. He was probably incapable of putting together a paragraph in coherent and grammatical German, and it is a curious paradox that he never awakened to the revival of German thought and literature to which his two crowning battles of Rossbach and Leuthen gave the greatest single impetus. The schoolboy Goethe and his friends in Frankfurt-am-Main rejoiced unhesitatingly in those victories, even if their city was the place where the Emperors were crowned, and when the garrison of the occupying French behaved uncommonly well. Here and in the other towns of Germany the editions of cartoons, parodies and verses probably reached into the hundreds:

Hervor mit seiner Reiterei
Brach Seydlitz mörderlich
Welch' ein Gemtnetzel, welch' Geschrei:
'Wer kann, der rette sich!'

Forward with his cavalry
Murderous Seydlitz ran
Such shrieking and such butchery:
'Save yourself if you can!'

At the other end of the artistic scale Gleim penned a more than acceptable *Siegeslied nach der Schlacht bey Rossbach,* while the poet Klopstock adjusted a celebrated line of Caesar to read: *Sie kamen, sahn, flohn* (They came, they saw, they fled).

There was something arbitrary in the way people did, or did not qualify as patriots. The 'Fritzian' enthusiasts were at liberty to parody the Austrians for their accent, and to ridicule their fellow Germans of the *Reissausarmee* ('Dug-out Army') as being a version of the nation which had been corrupted by Romish superstitions, alien fashions and French and Austrian politics. Conversely the Jewish community of Berlin celebrated Rossbach on the first Sabbath (12 November) after the news of the victory reached their city. After the customary readings, and the singing of the prayer which began *He who renders help to the kings,* the cantor sang a hymn of thanks which had been specially composed for the occasion. 'And, when it came to an end, the whole community responded with a loud *Amen.*'[22] Here was one of the beginnings of the tradition of Jewish Prusso-German patriotism which reached its culmination in the distinguished efforts of Jewish soldiers and scientists in the First World War.

As so often happens, the defeated learnt more from the experience than the victors. After the Seven Years War, survivors of Rossbach like Broglie and Saint-Germain became significant figures in French military reform, spurred on by what had happened on 5 November 1757. It should not have come as a surprise. Seydlitz believed that the French at Rossbach had been good soldiers who were badly led, and he took to task people who passed disparaging comments on the nation as a whole. Twenty-five years before the birth of Napoleon Bonaparte, Frederick himself had written to Voltaire that the old glory of France had been tarnished of late by poor commanders, 'but that is something which may be restored by a king who is worthy to command that nation, who governs with wisdom, and gains the admiration of the whole of Europe... I would be prepared to express my humble admiration for what this great man might do. Nobody among the crowned heads of Europe would be less jealous of his achievements.'[23]

At the turn of the eighteenth and nineteenth centuries the French and Prussian military worlds collided once more, but a great deal had changed in the meantime. Frederick had died in 1786, and by that time the continuities and the lack of change in the Prussian army, which had been such an asset in the 1750s, were now a liability, whereas the patriotism and resurgent military prowess of the French gave unprecedented force to the armies of the Revolution, the Consulate and the Empire.

In the new wars large bodies of troops crossed the old battlefield of Rossbach on a number of occasions. The fiery Prince Louis Ferdinand of Prussia came that way in 1792, on his way to the intended conquest of France. The community of Reichardtswerben had set up a simple sandstone monument on the Janus Hill in 1766, and Louis Ferdinand noticed that it had become badly weathered. He had a new monument erected there on 28 May 1796 at his own cost. Early in the catastrophic campaign of 1806 Field Marshal Möllendorf (who, as a captain in the Garde, had stormed the gateway of the church at Leuthen), paused there to render due honours:

In this location, on a fine autumn day, Field Marshal Möllendorff gathered all the staff officers of his corps at the foot of the monument for a celebration. The guests, the field marshal at their head, took their places at the tables, which were set out in a wide circle around the monument. The atmosphere was cheerful in the extreme, and many were the toasts which were drunk in memory of the heroes who were buried thereabouts. Two large choirs were posted on the nearby hills, and gave voice in turn with military precision, whereupon the whole litany of favourite warlike songs was taken up by the entire assembly.[24]

Not long afterwards Prince Louis Ferdinand was killed at Saalfeld (10 October) and Möllendorf at Jena (14 October), and the next army to pass was that of Napoleon Bonaparte. He was riding over the Janus Hill when Berthier, his chief of staff, drew his attention to the monument. Napoleon, who was then consciously measuring himself against the memory of Old Fritz, dismounted, embraced the stone—and ordered it to be taken away to Paris. On the same day the French requisitioned fourteen men, four waggons and fifteen horses from Reichardtswerben, along with some local drivers, and had the stones dismantled and carted off. On reaching its destination the monument was re-erected near the Church of Saint-Roch.

For the Prussians, the manner in which Napoleon humbled their forces in 1806 and 1807, and re-ordered the German lands to his advantage, seemed to encapsulate in a brief span of years all the demeaning experience of Germany in the 'century of Louis XIV.' The vengeful Prussians were on the march westwards in 1813, and after the great allied victory at Leipzig a number of the officers of Yorck's corps were moved by the sight of the bare Janus Hill to commission a further monument, which was the third to stand on that site. The inscription read:

Napoleon's sappers topple the monument at Rossbach.

In Commemoration of the Battle of Rossbach.
5 November 1757.
Re-erected on the 23 October 1813
By the Prussian warriors of the Third Army Corps
On the March after the Battle of Leipzig,
the Liberation of Germany.

There was no sign of Prince Louis Ferdinand's monument when the allies reached Paris in 1814. There were reports that it had been thrown into the Seine, and perhaps its stones lie there still.

In 1858 Pastor Wiltsch, the Lutheran rector and antiquarian of Reichardtswerben, subsumed local tradition and his archival researches in a massive study of the battle of Rossbach. When he evaluated the reasons for Frederick's victory, the last and the most conclusive seemed to him to be the fact that the Prussian army was one which believed in God and respected His commandments: 'It went into battle along with God, and reposed all its trust in Him. And God was with it.'[25] Wiltsch drew parallels with the forces of the Protestant Henry IV of France and Gustavus Adolphus of Sweden, and by implication suggested that a Catholic army must be a godless one.

The invocation of a patriotic religion is highly significant, for it harked back to Luther's sense of the German people as a community 'with a common history and a way of life,'[26] and to the teachings of the eighteenth-century Pietists (p. 8), which helped to propagate the belief that 'to serve the state is to serve God' *(Staatsdienst ist Gottesdienst)*. Prussia was destined to follow its 'special path' *(Sonderweg)* to liberate humanity from materialism, and the new united German *Reich,* as founded in 1871, became the instrument of Prussia's mission to carry out its divinely-appointed task. Whereas in the Anglo-Saxon world the word 'intellectual' came to bear connotations of someone who was unfaithful to his wife (W.H. Auden), a number of German intellectuals convinced themselves that they had a special place in the scheme of things, that of reminding the German nation of its moral purpose.

Early in the twentieth century the myths of Rossbach-Leuthen and the War of Liberation were being pressed into service alongside the troops and the guns. The volume (VI, 1904) that the historians of the German Great General Staff devoted to the battle of Leuthen was strangely perfunctory, but there could be no mistaking the tone of the Introduction. It recalled how

> at the ordained hour of the morning of the 5th the Prussian army took up arms and, still enveloped by the shades of the night, addressed itself to its bloody and exacting task. It was not long before chorales sounded from the marching columns, testimony to the spirit of the little Prussian army in those moments. That spirit breathed in every one of those taciturn sons of the north German plain, and inspired every one of those simple and soldierly hearts. That was the spirit which impelled them to a victory whose mighty resonance even now awakens astonishment and admiration in their descendants, and which never ceases to urge on their posterity to match their deeds.[27]

After the First World War godlessness could be identified not just with the traditional enemies of Protestantism, but with the decadence and mismanagement of the Weimar regime, with Jews and capitalism, and with the Bolsheviks and the other elements which had helped to bring about the collapse of Germany in November 1918. It was the Protestant court chaplain Bruno Doering who on 3 February of that year had first given currency to what became known as the 'stab in the back' legend.

In the elections of 1932 and 1933 the Nazis found their firmest support among farmers, small traders, skilled workers, among Protestants generally, and especially those of Schleswig-Holstein, the old Prussian heartlands of East Prussia, Pomerania and Brandenburg, and in Franconia (which had been the source of the least reliable recruits of the *Reichsarmee* in 1757). For his part Hitler had prepared the ground in *Mein Kampf,* the statement of his political philosophy and life's purpose, in which he hailed the disciplined old Prussian state as the foundation of a new Germany. Victorious in 1933, Hitler chose to date the formation of the Third Reich from 21 March, when at a ceremony in the Garrison Church in Potsdam he bowed to Field Marshal v. Hindenburg as the embodiment of the Prussian tradition. 'Thus the living force of Frederick, the creator and leader of the army, reaches to the present day.'[28]

The state now gave its encouragement to the UFA film studio's series of feature films on episodes from the life of Frederick the Great. The battle scenes were disorganised and unauthentic, but in *The Anthem of Leuthen* and its companions the part of the king was taken by Otto Gebühr, who had an uncanny physical resemblance to Old Fritz, and played him with truly Frederician charisma and energy. In such a culture it was possible to proclaim that 'the spirit of Frederick the Great is living in the Third Reich, and it will continue to live as long as the swastika waves over Germany.'[29]

In 1939 the new Reich went to war, and its soldiers were told how in the Thirty Years War the romish Counter Reformation (as incorporated in Habsburg Austria and the old *Reich)* had extinguished the spirit and freedom of the old German peasantry in a sea of blood and ashes, opened Germany to foreign invasion, and allowed France to make off with entire provinces of the Fatherland:

> In Prussia alone, the first ground to be won by the German colonisation of the East, the heir of the Order of the Teutonic Knights, did the Lutheran protest against papal Rome take on the political form that would guarantee the future of German freedom. What made Prussia great? Its steely dedication to the fulfilment of its duty, the way its soldiers lived up to its concept of service, and the work of its philosophers, which combined to endow the *Reich* with a new form and a new order. But Prussia's deadly jesuitical enemies had an interest in perpetu-ating the disunity of Germany, and they built up Austria, the old *Ostmark* of the *Reich,* as the foundation of a new Counter-Reformation under the protection of a Imperialism that owed its allegiance to the Pope.[30]

Hitler recalled the example of Frederick to his generals on the occasion of the attack on Poland in 1939, and again concerning the offensive into the Low Counties and France in 1940. The name 'Seydlitz' could be seen painted on the probing German armoured cars. Indeed the outcome was worthy of Frederick himself, and the deposed Kaiser Wilhelm telegraphed to Hitler from his resi-dence in Holland that 'The Anthem of Leuthen is resounding in every German heart.'[31]

History is a wonderfully malleable substance for present purposes, and after 1945 it became convenient for Germans to recall the genuine differences between the Prussian military ethos and that of Nazi Germany, the part that old Prussian military families had played in the Bomb Plot of 20 July 1944, and (with less enthusiasm) that of the *General der Artillerie* v. Seydlitz-Kurtzbach, who had been captured at Stalingrad in 1943, and enlisted German *Seydlitz-Männer* to fight alongside the Soviets.

French statesmen nevertheless feared that there would be no end to the cycle of revenge which had originated in 1757, and was played out in 1806-7, 1814, 1870-1, 1918-19 and 1940. The solution which presented itself was to establish such close economic connections between the two nations and their neighbours as would render a new European war unthinkable. Effectively Marianne was embracing Attila in a hug which had little to do with affection, and by the beginning of the third millennium a new European super-state seemed to be in the making, even if it was unwise to enquire too closely into how it was being engineered.

The more recent history had also left its mark on the battlefields of 1757. After Soviet forces coursed through Silesia in their fulminating offensive of January 1945 the Communists turned their attention to the victory monument (1854) on Frederick's viewpoint on the Scholl-Berg at Leuthen, shattering the Angel of Victory and reducing the stonework to a shapeless stump. Much of the German population of Silesia was expelled, and its place filled in part by Poles who had been evicted in their turn from Galicia, which had been one of the most 'Austrianised' provinces of the old Habsburg Empire. This was an Austrian victory, though of the most indirect kind, and the new Polish possessors of 'Lutynia' were strangers in the landscape, whose history was totally unknown to them. In the days of the Warsaw Pact the highway running across the northern part of the field was strengthened, widened, and provided with turning places in order to serve as a supplementary military airstrip.

The country around Rossbach was used most brutally when Saxony was industrialised in the course of the nineteenth and twentieth centuries. Nearly all the original roads and paths were re-aligned or obliterated in 1852, while open-cast (strip) mining for the stinking, sulphur-laden brown coal (lignite) devastated much of the battlefield, and succeeded in reducing the Janus Hill to a hole in the ground. In the First World War the remoteness of the area from the battlefronts helped to determine nearby Leuna as the site for an oil refinery. In the next war, the synthetic oil produced at Leuna became of increasing importance to the Third Reich, and especially after the Soviets overran the oil fields in Romania and Hungary. By the same token the Leuna establishments offered a rewarding target for Allied air raids. The Germans now demolished the church steeples thereabouts, including the celebrated example at Branderoda, so that their anti-aircraft radars could enjoy an uncluttered sweep.

Germany was reunited on 3 October 1990, after the collapse of the Soviet hegemony in central and eastern Europe. In one sense the combined German population of 78,000,000 souls represented a new threat to France, though it soon became evident that the infrastructure of the former East Germany was in still more need of repair than anyone had suspected, and the refinery at Leuna had shared in the general rusty disintegration. Such was the background of a murky deal stuck in 1992 between the French President François Mitterrand and the German Chancellor Helmut Kohl, whereby the French Elf-Aquitaine Company (virtually a branch of the French government) bought the Leuna refinery and the Minol chain of service stations for a very handsome price, with a generous commission on top. Much of the cash was diverted to the coffers of Kohl's C.D.U. Party. All the same, the refinery at Leuna was given a new lease of life, and it remains even now the backdrop to the landscape of Rossbach, throbbing and steaming across the northern horizon. It is seldom that history describes so complete a circle.

Notes

Abbreviations used in the notes (see Bibliography for details)

KA = Kriegsarchiv, Vienna
CA = Cabinettsakten
FA = Feldakten
HKRA = Akten
HKR Protocolle = Protocols of the Hofkriegsrath
MMTO = Depositions of candidates for the Military Order of Maria Theresa

HHStA = Haus-Hof- und Staarchiv, Vienna

SHAT = Service Historique de l'Armée de Terre, Château de Vincennes
Al = Correspondance Générale
Série A1M 208 Campagne en Allemagne MDCLVII = Campagne en Allemagne MDCLVII. Mémoire ou Extrait de la Correspondance de la Cour et des Généraux Série A1M 208 Armée de Soubise = Correspondance ou Mémoire sur les opérations de l'Armée Commandée par M. le Prince de Soubise Lieutenant Général et combinée avec l'Armée de l'Empire pendant la Campagne de 1757 en Allemagne

WL, Colonel Nicolai, 'Betrachtungen' = Württembergisches Landesbibliothek, Cod Milit o 29, Colonel and Quarter-Master General Colonel Friedrich von Nicolai, 'Bemerkungen zurn Feldzug der herzogl. Württembergsch. Truppen bey der Kayserlichen Armee in Bömen und Schlesien im Jahr 1757'

Budapest, HL = Hadtörténeti Intézet és Múzeum, Hadik Lévéltar

Chapter 1 The Rossbach Armies

1. Richter, 1996, 9
2. Rohr, 1756, 1, xvii-xviii
3. Wiltsch, 1856, 290-1
4. Engelman and Dorn, 1988, 9
5. KA CA 1758 III 1, Lieutenant Colonel Rebain to 'Hoch Gebohrner Freiherr,' Neisse, 10 March 1758
6. Richelieu, 1793, IX, 139
7. SHAT A1 3433, Montazet, Lissa, 10 November 1757
8. KA CA 1758 III 1D, Rebain, Neisse, 10 March 1758
9. KA CA 1758 DI 1A, Rebain, Neisse, 10 March 1758
10. KA CA 1758 BI IC, Rebain, Neisse, 10 March 1758
11. For details of tactics see Brent Nosworthy's *The Art of Victory. Battle Tactics 1689-1760*, New York, 1992, and the present author's *The Army of Frederick the Great*, 2nd ed., Chicago, 1996
12. KA CA 1758 III 1A, Rebain, Neisse, 10 March 1758
13. Grosser Generalstab, 1901-1914, VI, 134
14. Catt, 1884, 83
15. Blankenburg, in Volz, 1926-7, II, 275
16. Richelieu, 1793, IX, 135, 155-6
17. KA FA Reichs- und Französische Armee 1757 XII 21, Hildburghausen to Maria Theresa, Vienna, 10 October 30. 1758; KA FA Reichs- und Französische Armee 1757 XI 5, Hildburghausen to Francis Stephen, Mücheln, 3 November 1757

18. Saint-Germain, 1789, I, 213
19. Wiltsch, 1858, 281-2
20. Quoted in Ibid., 280
21. HHStA Kriegsakten 410, Hildburghausen to Francis Stephen, Fürth, 9 July 1757
22. KA HKRA 1757 XI 55, Hildburghausen to the Reichsvizecanzler Colloredo, Lichtenfels, 15 November 1757
23. HHStA Kriegsakten 410, Franz Johann Brettlach to Colloredo, 27 November 1757
24. Quoted in Brodrück, 1858, 85
25. HHStA Kriegsakten 410, Hildburghausen to Francis Stephen, Fürth, 9 July 1757
26. HHStA Kriegsakten 388, 'Instruction und Anweisung' for Hildburghausen, 8 June 1757; see also KA HKR Protocolle 1757 July 799/3, Hofkriegsrath to Hildburghausen and Colloredo, 29 July 1757
27. Cogniazzo, 1788-91, III, 238
28. HHStA Kriegsakten 410, Maria Theresa to Hildburghausen, 26 November 1757
29. SHAT A1 3433, 'Mémoire raisonnée sur l'Armée de l'Empire'
30. KA HKRA 1757 XI 55, Hildburghausen to Colloredo, 15 November 1757
31. Quoted in Thüna, 1893, 2
32. Quoted in Brodrück, 1858, 175
33. HHStA Kriegsakten 410, Hildburghausen to Francis Stephen, Fürth, 9 July 1757
34. KA HKR Protocolle 1757 July 799/3, Hofkriegsrath to Hildburghausen and Colloredo, 29 July 1757
35. HHStA Kriegsakten 388, 'Instruction und Anweisung' for Hildburghausen, 8 June 1757
36. SHAT 1M 208, Campagne en Allemagne MDCCLVII
37. HHStA Kriegsakten 410, Franz Johann Brettlach to Colloredo, Fürth, 22 August 1757
38. See KA HKR Protocolle 1757 October 530, Colonel Wachenheim to the Hofkriegsrath, 19 October 1757; KA HKRA 1757 XI 55, Hildburghausen to Colloredo, Lichtenfels, 15 November 1757
39. Eicken, 1878, XLI, 1
40. Quoted in Wiltsch, 1858, 328
41. HHStA Kriegsakten 410. Franz Johann Brettlach to Colloredo, Fürth, 22 August 1757
42. SHAT A1 3433, Champeaux, 38 June 1757
43. Quoted in Wiltsch, 1858, 240
44. KA HKRA 1757 XI 55, Hildburghausen to Colloredo, Lichtenfels, 15 November 1757
45. HHStA Kriegsakten 412, Franz Johann Brettlach to Colloredo, Fürth, 4 December 1757; HHStA Kriegsakten 412, Franz Johann Brettlach to Colloredo, 25 November 1757
46. KA HKRA 1757 XI 55, Hildburghausen to Colloredo, Lichtenfels, 15 November 1757
47. KA HKRA XI 5, Hildburghausen to Francis Stephen, Mücheln, 3 November 1757

Chapter 2   The Gathering of Forces

1. SHAT 1M 208, 'Armée de Soubise,' 2
2. HHStA Kriegsakten 410, Hildburghausen to Francis Stephen, 6 August 1757
3. SHAT 1M 208, 'Armée de Soubise,' 8
4. Quoted in Wiltsch, 1858, 384
5. Quoted in Ibid., 18
6. Conference of 27 June 1757, Khevenhüller-Metsch, 1907-72, IV, 382
7. Mollinger, Fürth, 15 July 1757, in Brodrück, 1858, 80
8. HHStA Kriegsakten 410, Hildburghausen to Francis Stephen, Fürth, 9 July 1757
9. Quoted in Eicken, 1878, XLI, 2
10. Mollinger, Fürth, 15 July 1757, in Brodrück, 1858, 80
11. Frederick, 1879-1939, PC no. 9886, Frederick to Dohna, 2 April 1758, XVI, 346
12. Brabant, 1901-36, I, 222
13. SHAT 1M 208, 'Armée de Soubise,' 18
14. Bourcet, 1792, I, 23
15. Public Record Office, Kew, 30/8/89, Chatham Papers, 'Copie d'une lettre écrite de Gota le 17e Septembre 1757'
16. Quoted in Wiltsch, 1858, 15
17. Mollinger, Eisenach, 14 September 1757, in Brodrück, 1858, 92

18. SHAT 1M 208 'Armée de Soubise,' 35
19. Geheimes Staatsarchiv Preussischer Kulturbesitz, IV Hauptabteilung Rep I5A Geheimes Civilkabinett, Militaria, Pleissner's 'Tagebuch'
20. Ibid.
21. Ibid.
22. Tempelhoff, 1783-1801, 1, 264
23. SHAT 1M 108, 'Armée de Soubise.' 41-2
24. Quoted in Wiltsch, 1858, 209
25. Frederick, 1879-1928, PC no. 9,375, Frederick to Moritz of Anhalt-Dessau, Buttelstedt, 29 September 1757, XV, 388
26. Mollinger, Gotha, 4 and 5 October 1757, in Brodrück, 1858, 100-1
27. Mollinger, Langensalza, 15 October 1757, in Ibid., 104
28. KA HKRA 1757 X155, Hildburghausen to Colloredo, Lichtenfels, 15 November 1757
29. Mollinger, Erfurt, 18 October 1757, in Brodrück, 1858, 105
30. KA HKRA 1757 XI 55, Hildburghausen to Colloredo, Lichtenfels, 15 November 1757
31. Bourcet, 1792, I, 40-1
32. HHStA Kriegsakten 410, Loudon to Prince Charles, Gera, 7 November 1757
33. KA HKRA XI 5, Hildburghausen to Francis Stephen, Mücheln, 3 November 1757
34. Wiltsch, 1858, 56

Chapter 3 To Rossbach
1. Retzow, 1803, I, 201
2. Public Record Office, Kew, State Papers Foreign 90/70, Sir Andrew Mitchell, 27 October 1757
3. Mollinger, Teuchern, 29 October 1757, in Brodrück, 1858, 108
4. SHAT 1M 208, 'Armée de Soubise,' 111-12
5. KA HKRA 1757 XI ad 10, 'Copia Schreibens an die beede Ministres nach Wienn d.d. Freyburg den lten und 3ten November 1757 von mir Freyherrn von Widman'
6. SHAT 1M 208, 'Armée de Soubise,' 113
7. KA HKRA 1757 XI ad 10, Widmann, 'Copia Schreibens'
8. Ibid.
9. Ibid.
10. KA HKRA 1757 XI 5, Hildburghausen to Francis Stephen, Mücheln, 3 November 1757; HKRA 1757 XI 55, Hildburghausen to Colloredo, Lichtenfels, 15 November 1757
11. KA HKRA 1757 XI 5, Hildburghausen to Francis Stephen, Mücheln, 3 November 1757
12. Crillon, 1791, 66
13. HKRA 1757 XI 5, Hildburghausen to Francis Stephen, Mücheln, 3 November 1757; HKRA 1757 XI 55, Hildburghausen to Colloredo, Lichtenfels, 15 November 1757
14. HHStA Kriegsakten 412, Franz Johann Brettlach to Colloredo, 27 November 1757
15. KA HKRA 1757 XI 55, Hildburghausen to Colloredo, Lichtenfels, 15 November 1757
16. KA HKRA 1757 XI 1, Hildburghausen to Soubise, Storkau, 1 November 1757
17. KA Reichs- und Französische Armee 1757 XI 15, Journal of the Reichsarmee
18. KA HKRA 1757 XI 4, Hildburghausen to Soubise, 2 November 1757
19. Henckel v. Donnersmarck, 1858, I, 339
20. KA HKRA 1757 XI 55, Hildburghausen to Colloredo, Lichtenfels, 15 November 1757
21. KA HKRA 1757 XI 7, Széchenyi to Soubise, 3 November 1757
22. KA HKR Protocolle 1757 December 467, Széchenyi to the Hofkriegsrath, Gotha, 3 December 1757
23. SHAT 1M 208, 'Armée de Soubise,' 126
24. HHStA Kriegsakten 412, Franz Johann Brettlach to Colloredo, 27 November 1757
25. Pastor Schieritz, quoted in Wiltsch, 1858, 97
26. Pastor Schieritz, quoted in Ibid., 102
27. SHAT 1M 208, 'Campagne en Allemagne MDCLVII,' Soubise to Paulmy, 5 November 1757
28. Frederick, 1846-57, 'Oeuvres Historiques,' III, *Histaire de la Guerre de Sept Ans,* I, 213
29. Bourcet, 1792, I, 50

30. HHStA Kriegsakten 414, Loudon to Prince Charles, Gera, 7 November 1757
31. HHStA Kriegsakten 412, Franz Johann Brettlach to Colloredo, 27 November 1757
32. HHStA Kriegsakten 412, Fürstenberg to Colloredo, undated, early 1757
33. Mollinger, Teichel, 8 November 1757, in Brodrück, 1858, 114
34. The allied establishments and numbers are based on what seem to be the most realistic estimates, namely those in the 'État des Troupes' (SHAT 1M 208, 'Armée de Soubise) for the French, that of the German Great General Staff for the *Reichsarmee,* that of Franz Johann Brettlach for the Austrian cuirassiers, and that of Loudon for his Croats and hussars. On the evidence of the last two generals my assessment of the Austrian numbers is higher than will be found in other histories.
35. Northumberland Record Office, North Gosforth, Butler (Ewart) Ms. ZBU B2/1, Callenberg to Horace St. Paul, Brussels, 16 November 1757

Chapter 4 The Battle of Rossbach

1. Saint-Germain, 1789, I, 223-4; Bourcet, 1792, I, 51
2. KA HKR Protocolle 1757 December 221, Ludwig Carl Brettlach to the Hofkriegsrath, Erlangen, 27 November 1757
3. Bourcet, 1792, I, 51. Confirmed by Franz Johann Brettlach (who had been consigned to Freyburg by his surgeon) and by Mollinger
4. SHAT A1 3441, Hildburghausen to Soubise, 5 November 1757
5. HHStA Kriegsakten 410, Hildburghausen to Francis Stephen, 7 November 1757
6. KA HKR Protocolle 1757 December 467, Széchenyi to the Hofkriegsrath, Gotha, 3 December 1757
7. Bourcet, 1792, I, 52-3
8. Richelieu, 1793, I, 52
9. Bourcet, 1792, 1, 52-3
10. Ibid., I, 58
11. SHAT A1 3433, Manson's report
12. Custine's account, as recorded by Gaudi, in Wiltsch, 1858, 144
13. Kalckreuth, 1840, III, 184-5
14. Ibid., III, 185
15. KA HKR Protocolle 1757 December 467, Széchenyi to the Hofkriegsrath, Gotha, 3 December 1757
16. Mollinger, Teichel, 7 November 1757, in Brodrück, 1858, 115
17. KA HKR Protocolle 1757 December 467, Széchenyi to the Hofkriegsrath, Gotha, 3 December 1757. See also KA Reichs- und Französische Armee 1757 XI 22, Széchenyi to Daun, undated 1757
18. Pastor Schieritz, quoted in Wiltsch, 1858, 161
19. KA HKR Protocolle 1757 December 467, Széchenyi to the Hofkriegsrath, Gotha, 3 December 1757
20. SHAT 1M 208, 'Campagne en Attemagne MDCLVII,' no. 53, Castries to Paulmy, Sachsenburg, 9 November 1757
21. KA FA Reichs- und Französische Armee 1757 XI 19, Hildburghausen to Francis Stephen, 7 November 1757
22. KA FA Reichs-und Französische Armee 1757 XI 32, Hildburghausen to Maria Theresa, 10 October 1758
23. Ligne, 1883, 84-5
24. HHStA Kriegsakten 410, Hildburghausen to Francis Stephen, 7 November 1757
25. Tempelhoff, 1783-1801, I, 69
26. Du Val, quoted in Wiltsch, 1858, 168
27. KA HKR Protocolle 1757 December 221, Ludwig Carl Brettlach to Colloredo, Erlangen, 27 November 1757
28. Richelieu, 1793, IX, 225. The Marquis de Castries confirms that Mailly brought up only eight squadrons, those of the four regiments just mentioned. The regiments of Bourbonbusse and La Refine were out on the left flank, and not engaged directly
29. Richelieu, 1793, IX, 227.
30. KA FA Reichs- und Französische Armee 1757 XI 32, Hildburghausen to Maria Theresa, 10 October 1758
31. SHAT 1M 208, 'Campagne en Allemagne MDCLVII,' no. 59, Lugeac to Paulmy, Morthausen, 10 November 1757
32. KA FA Reichs- and Französische Armee 1757 XI 23, anon. Prussian relation
33. Bourcet, 1792, I, 56; Lieutenant v. Guardy (on the staff of the Bavarian general Holnstein), in Brodrück, 1858, 322

34. KA FA Reichs- und Französische Armee 1757 XI 32, Hildburghausen to Maria Theresa, 10 October 1758
35. SHAT A1 3433, Manson's relation
36. KA FA Reichs- und Französische Armee 1757 XI 28, Prince Georg of Hesse-Darmstadt to Hildburghausen, Lichtenfeld, 17 November 1757
37. Quoted in Brodrück, 1858, 322
38. KA FA Reichs- und Französische Armee 1757 XI 31, Ferntheil to Hildburghausen, Neussig, 17 November 1757
39. KA FA Reichs- und Französische Armee 1757 XI 29, Drachsdorff to Hildburghausen, Lichtenfels, 17 November 1757
40. Colonel v. Coll to the Prince Bishop of Trier, in Eicken, 1878, XLI, 6
41. KA HKRA Protocolle 1757 December 467, Széchenyi to the Hofkriegsrath, Gotha, 3 December 1757
42. Kalckreuth, 1840, III, 187-8
43. Mollinger, Teichel, 8 November 1757, in Brodrück, 1858, 115
44. KA FA Reichs- und Franzozische Armee 1757 XI 19, Hildburghausen to Francis Stephen, Weimar, 7 November 1757
45. 'Schreiben eines Freundes der Wahrheit,' quoted in Wiltsch, 1858, 183
46. KA FA Reichs- und Französische Armee 1757 35 1/2, Loudon to Major General Zechenter, in reply to Zechenter to Loudon, 6 February 1787
47. KA HKR Protocolle 1757 December 467, Széchenyi to the Hofkriegsrath, Gotha, 3 December 1757; SHAT 1m 208, 'Campagne en Allemagne MDCCLVII,' no. 53, Castries to Paulmy, Morthausen, 9 November 1757; Bourcet, 1792, I, 56-7
48. KA FA Reichs- und Französische Armee 1757 XI 23 114, anon. 'Relation'
49. Brabant, 1901-31, I, 336
50. Mollinger, Teichel, 7 November 1757, in Brodrück, 1858, 118
51. Frederick, 1879-1939, PC no. 9,849, Frederick to Wilhelmine, 5 November 1757, XVI, 8
52. 'Schreiben eines Freudes der Warheit,' quoted in Wiltsch, 1858, 183
53. Frederick, 1879-1939, PC no. 9,509, Eichel to Podewils, Leipzig, 12 November 1757, XVI, 23
54. KA FA Reichs- und Französische Armee 1757 XI 26, Keith to Hildburghausen, 1 14 November 1757
55. KA HKR Protocolle 1757 December 221, 'Extract,' 27 November 1757
56. SHAT 1M 208, 'Campagne en Allemagne MDCCLVII,' État de Mrs. les officiers de Cavalerie tués ou perdus ou blessés dans la journée du 5. 9bre 1757'
57. SHAT 1M 208, 'Campagne en Allemagne MDCCLVII, 'État des officiers et soldats tués, blessés ou qui manquent dans 27 Bataillons qui ont été à la bataille du 5. 9bre 1757'
58. Henckel v. Donnersmarck, 1858, I, 341
59. Mollinger, Teichel, 8 November 1757, in Brodrück, 1858, 117
60. SHAT 1M 208, 'Armée en Allemagne MDCCLVII,' no. 49, 'Mouvemens de l'Armée francoise et de celle du Roy de Prusse depuis le 27. 8bre, jusqu' au 5. 9bre 1757'
61. Quoted in Richter, 1996, 80
62. Retzow, 1892, I, 208
63. Gaudi, quoted in Wiltsch, 1858, 246
64. HHStA Kriegsakten 412, Fürstenberg to Colloredo, 20 December 1757
65. SHAT 1M 208, 'Armée en Allemagne MDCCLVII,' no. 54, Bourcet to Paulmy, Morthausen, 10 November 1757
66. KA FA Reichs- und Französische Armee 1757 XI 20, Hildburghausen to Colloredo, Weimar, 7 November 1757; HHStA Kriegsakten 410, Hildburghausen to Francis Stephen, Weimar, 7 November 1757
67. SHAT 1M 208, 'Armée en Allemagne MDCCLVII,' no. 53, Castries to Paulmy, Morthausen, 9 November 1757
68. Ibid, no. 61, Caulincourt to Paulmy, Morthausen, 10 November 1757
69. Ibid., no. 56, Bourcet to Paulmy, Morthausen, 10 November 1757
70. HHStA Kriegsakten 410, Hildburghausen to Francis Stephen, Weimar, 7 November 1757
71. SHAT 1M 208, 'Armée en Allemagne MDCCLVII,' no. 54, Soubise to Paulmy, Morthausen, 10 November 1757
72. Ibid., no. 56, Bourcet to Paulmy, Morthausen, 10 November 1757

73. Mollinger, Grafenthal, 11 November 1757, in Brodrück, 1858, 22

74. KA FA Reichs- und Französische Armee 1757 XI 32, Hildburghausen to Maria Theresa, 20 October 1758

75. SHAT 1M 208, Campagne en Allemagne MDCCLVII,' no. 54, Soubise to Paulmy, Morthausen, 10 November 1757

76. HHStA Kriegsakten 410, Hildburghausen to Francis Stephen, Weimar, 7 November 1757

77. KA FA Reichs- and Französische Armee 1757 XI ad 19, Soubise to Hildburghausen, Kelwing, 6 November 1757; SHAT IM 208, 'Armée en Allemagne MDCCLVII,' no. 51, Soubise to Paulmy, Sachsenburg, 9 November 1757; Ibid. no. 54, Soubise to Paulmy, Morthausen, 9 November 1757; Ibid., 'Mémoire ou Éxtrait,' 131

78. Local eyewitness, quoted in Wiltsch, 1858, 205-6

79. HHStA Kriegsakten 412, Franz Johann Brettlach to Colloredo, 28 November 1757

80. Mollinger, Teichel, 8 November 1757, in Brodrück, 1858, 118

81. KA FA Reichs- und Französische Armee 1757 XI 55, Hildburghausen to Colloredo, Lichtenfels, 15 November 1757

82. Mollinger, Erfurt, 7 November 1757, in Brodrück, 1858, 111

83. Mollinger, Teichel, 8 November 1757, in Ibid., 119

84. Frederick, 1846-57, 'Oeuvres Historiques,' *Histoire de la Guerre de Sept Ans,* I, 222

85. Quoted in Wiltsch, 1858, 257

Chapter 5 Austria Triumphant

1. Munich Kriegsarchiv, B 254, Baron A.H. v. Wittgenstein to Elector Max Joseph, Munich, 4 November 1756

2. WL, Colonel Nicolai, 'Betrachtungen'

3. Bratislava, Státny ústredeny Archív, Fond Rod Amade Üchtritz, 101-12-067, XVI, General Philipp Gottfried v. Wollwarth, 'Kurze Beschreibung meiner geleisteten Dienste'

4. Ligne, 1795-1911, XIV, Journal, I, 44; SHAT A1 3439, Champeaux, 7 September 1757

5. HHStA Kriegsakten 414, 'Relation von der Attaque… bey Moys'

6. KA MMTO, De Piza

7. Ligne, 1795-1811, XIV, Journal, I, 45-8

8. SHAT A1 3439, Champeaux, 8 September 1757

9. Kalckreuth, 1840, IV, 171; KA FA Hauptarmee 1757 XIII 467, 'Réflexions sur la Campagne de l'Annee 1757'

10. Ligne, 1795-1811, XIV, Journal, I, 53

11. Ibid, XIV, Journal, I, 55-6

12. SHAT A1 3440, Montazet, 27 September 1757

13. Northumberland County Record Office, North Gosforth, Butler (Ewart) Mss ZHU B2/1, Callenberg to Horace St. Paul, Brussels, 16 November 1757

14. HHStA Kriegsakten 417, note for Stainville, 3 October 1757

15. Budapest HL 1757 X 128, 'Befehle bevor man in des Feindes Land rücket'

16. Ibid.

17. Budapest HL 1757 X 127, Hadik to the Hofkriegsrath, Elsterwerda, 11 October 1757

18. Budapest HL 1757 X 132, Vecsey, 'Specification,' 14 October 1757

19. Budapest HL 1757 X 144, Hadik's summons, 16 October 1757

20. HHStA Kriegsakten 414, Hadik, 'Unterthänigste Relation über die Expedition in die Mark Brandenburg und die Einnahm der Königl. Preussischen Haubt- und Residentz-Stadt Berlin,' 19 October 1757

21. Archenholtz, 1840, I, 93

22. HHStA Kriegsakten 414, Hadik's 'Unterthänigste Relation'

23. St. Paul, 1914, 335

24. Retzow, 1892, I, 98

25. HHStA Kriegsakten 414, Hadik's 'Unterthänigste Relation'

26. Arneth, 1863-79, V, 343. There were eight florins to the ducat, and the taler was worth just under one florin

27. WL Colonel Nicolai, 'Betrachtungen'

28. St. Paul, 1914, 357

29. HHStA Kriegsakten 415, Maria Theresa to Prince Charles, 29 September 1757

30. HHStA Kriegsakten 414, Feuerstein to Prince Charles, 1 November 1757

31. KA MMTO, Rhédy

32. KA MMTO, De Vins

33. Ligne, 1795-1811, XIV, Journal, I, 63-4
34. KA MMTO, Zorn von Plobsheim
35. KA MMTO, Bärnkopp
36. Khevenhüller-Metsch, 1907-72, IV, 398
37. WL Colonel Nicolai, 'Betrachtungen'
38. HHStA Kriegsakten 415, Maria Theresa to Prince Charles, 1 October 1757
39. HHStA Kriegsakten 415, Maria Theresa to Prince Charles, 21 October 1757
40. HHStA Kriegsakten 415, Prince Charles to Maria Theresa, Lissa, 25 October 1757
41. HHStA Kriegsakten 415, Maria Theresa to Prince Charles, 11 November 1757
42. KA FA Hauptarmee 1757 XI 464, anon. 'Relation von der… den 22ten Novembris 1757 in der Gegend von Breslau vorgefallenen Bataille'
43. Ligne, 1795-1811, XIV, Journal, I, 73
44. KA MMTO, Nangle
45. Gorani, 1944, 72
46. Ligne, 1795-1811, XIV, Journal, I, 75
47. KA MMTO, Souhay
48. Cogniazzo, 1788-91, II, 42
49. KA FA Hauptarmee 1757 XI 67, Carl Hauss (?) to Prince Charles, Maria-Höfchen, 24 November 1757
50. WL Colonel Nicolai, 'Betrachtungen'
51. Northumberland Country Office, North Gosforth, Butler (Ewart) Mss. ZBU B2/1, Callenberg to St. Paul, Brussels, 11 February 1758; KA FA Hauptarmee 1757 XI 467, anon. relation, 24 November 1757
52. Khevenhüller-Metsch, 1907-72, IV, 143
53. Gorani, 1944, 72
54. Mitchell, 1850, II, 39. See also HHStA Kriegsakten 388, anon. letter, Königgrätz, 21 December 1757; Yorke, 1913, III, 227
55. Ligne, 1795-1811, XIV, Journal, I, 81-2
56. Arneth, 1863-79, 250
57. Sommers, R.J., foreword to James A. Kegel's *North with Lee and Jackson. The Lost Slory of Gettysburg,* Mechanisburg, Pa., 1996

Chapter 6 Leuthen

1. Grosser Generalstab, 1901-14, VI, 6
2. KA FA Hauptarmee 1757 XII 202, Prince Charles to Loudon, Breslau, 3 December 1757
3. Kutzen, 1851, 234
4. HHStA Letter Book of Prince Charles, Prince Charles to Maria Theresa, 18 November 1757
5. HHStA Nachlass Lacy, I, 1. See also SHAT A1 3442, Marainville, 17 December 1757; WL Colonel Nicolai, 'Betrachtungen'; Ligne, 1795-1811, XIV, Journal, I, 83-4
6. HHStA Letter Book of Prince Charles, Prince Charles to Maria Theresa, 26 November 1757
7. Kheverthüller-Metsch, 1907-72, IV, 142
8. HHStA Letter Book of Prince Charles, Prince Charles to Francis Stephen, Breslau, 28 November 1757
9. HHStA Letter Book of Prince Charles, Prince Charles to Francis Stephen, Breslau, 29 November 1757
10. Frederick to the Marquis d'Argens, Torgau, 15 November 1757, Frederick, 1846-57, XIX, 45
11. Frederick, 1879-1939, PC no. 9,558, Eichel to Finckenstein, 1 December 1757, XVI, 69
12. Frederick, 1879-1939, PC no. 9,559, *Disposition,* 28 November 1757, XVI, 70
13. Podgursky, 1843, II, 205-6
14. Tempelhoff, 1783-1801, II, 285
15. Retzow, 1802, I, 243
16. Herrmann, XXXI, 1918, 101-2
17. Retzow, 1802, I, 243
18. Cogniazzo, 178-91, II, 419
19. HHStA Kriegsakten 414, 'Relation von der- zwischen der Kayl. Königl. under der Königl. Preussischen Armee den 5ten December zwischen Neumark und Lissa, hauptsachlich in der Gegend von Leuthen vorgefallenen Bataille,' undated

20. Ibid., See also KA FA Hauptarmee 1757 XII 202, Prince Charles to Loudon, 3 December 1757; HHStA Letter Book of Prince Charles, Prince Charles to Francis Stephen, 3 December 1757 (two letters), and Prince Charles to Maria Theresa, 3 December 1757

21. HHStA Letter Book of Prince Charles, Prince Charles to Maria Theresa, 3 December 1757

22. KA FA Hauptarmee 1757 XII 65, 'Extract aus dem Rapport den lten Xbris 757 von der bey der Armee befindlichen Infanterie'; KA FA Hauptarmee 1757 XII 70, 'Extract aus dem Rapport den 3ten Decembris 1757 von der bey der Armee befindlichen Infanterie'

23. KA FA 1757 XII 3, 'Extract des dienstbaren Standes sammentlicher bey der Armee befindlichen Infanterie dd. lten Decembris 1757'

24. WL Colonel Nicolai, 'Betrachtungen'

25. Kalckreuth, 1840, IV, 118-19

26. Warnery, 1785-91, II, 302

27. 'Schreiben aus Neukirchen in Breslau,' in Kutzen, 1851, 219

28. KA FA Hauptarmee 1757 XII 218, 'Relation'

29. HHStA Letter Book of Prince Charles, Prince Charles to Francis Stephen, Lissa, 4 December 1757; HHStA Kriegsakten 414, Prince Charles to Maria Theresa and Francis Stephen, Lissa, 4 December 1757

30. WL Colonel Nicolai, 'Betrachtungen'

31. Ibid.

32. Rehtwisch, 1907, 280

33. Nicolai, 1788-92, V, 34

34. Hildebrandt, 1829-35, II, 39

35. Kalckreuth, 1840, IV, 126-7. We would ask readers, in their turn, to keep this information to themselves

36. Rehtwisch, 1907, 288

37. SHAT A1 3442, Marainville, 23 December 1757

38. Cogniazzo, 1779, 62-3

39. SHAT A1 3442, Marainville, 17 December 1757

40. HHStA Kriegsakten 414, Prince Charles to Maria Theresa, cover note to his 'Relation,' 10 December 1757

41. WL Colonel Nicolai, 'Betrachtungen'

42. Ibid.

43. KA FA Hauptarmee 1757 XII 218, Prince Charles, 'Relation'

44. WL Colonel Nicolai, 'Betrachtungen'

45. Podgursky, 1843, II, 213

46. Grosser Generalstab, 1901-14, VI, 146

47. KA FA Hauptarmee 1757 XII 218, Prince Charles, 'Relation'

48. KA FA Hauptarmee 1757 XII 223 1/2, 'Extract Schreiben eines Oesterreichischen Officier, Feldlager bey Freyberg in Schlesien,' 15 December 1757

49. Cogniazzo, 1788-91, II, 428-9

50. Podgursky, 1843, II, 213

51. WL Colonel Nicolai, 'Betrachtungen'

52. Archenholtz, 1974, 14

53. Barsewisch, 1863, 33

54. Ibid., 34

55. Ibid., 35

56. WL Colonel Nicolai, 'Betrachtungen'

57. Podgursky, 1843, II, 213

58. Cogniazzo, 1788-91, II, 431. The same point is made by the French attaché Marainville, SHAT A1 3442, 10 December 1757

59. SHAT A1 3442, Marainville, 17 December 1757

60. KA MMTO, Johann O'Donnell

61. Barsewisch, 1863, 35

62. SHAT A1 3442, Marainville, 23 December 1757

63. SHAT A1 3442, Marainville, 17 December 1757

64. Quoted in Kutzen, 1851, 118

65. According to the official Order of Battle the Batthyány Dragoons are shown as belonging to the corps of Nádasdy. Buccow nevertheless states clearly that the regiment was under his command, and his testimony is confirmed indirectly by the Prince de Ligne.
66. KA MMTO, Buccow
67. Ligne, 1795-1811, XIV, Journal, I, 86-7
68. KA FA Hauptarmee 1757 XII 223 1/2, 'Extract Schreiben'
69. WL Colonel Nicolai, 'Betrachtungen'
70. Berenhorst, 1798-9, II, 52
71. Cogniazzo, 1788-91, II, 433-4
72. Warnery, 1785-91, II, 272
73. Ligne, 1795-1811, X, 100
74. Podgursky, 1843, II, 139
75. Kalckreuth, 1840, IV, 128
76. Frederick, 1846-57, 'Oeuvres Historiques,' III, *Histoire de la Guerre de Sept Ans, I*, 242-3
77. KA MMTO, Caracciolo di S. Eramo
78. KA MMTO, joint attestation for Humbracht, 11 December 1757
79. KA MMTO, Amadei, Stampach
80. Quoted in Cogniazzo, 1788-91, II, 438
81. Nicolai, 1788-92, III, 320-1
82. Ibid., III, 236
83. Kutzen, 1851, 183
84. Grosser Generalstab, 1901-14, VI, 39
85. Kutzen, 1851, 116
86. Nicolai, 1788-92, III, 246; 'Briefe über die Begebenheiten des jetzigen Kriegs,' quoted in Kutzen, 1851, 239
87. Podgursky, 1843, II, 141-2, 143
88. Wraxall, 1806, I, 177-8
89. The most complete list is KA FA Hauptarmee 1757 XII 222, 'Aufsatz über bey der den 5ten Decembris nächst Lissa in Schlesien gewessene Action sich von der K.K. Armée ergebenen Todt, Blessirt und Verlohren gegangenen Staabs Ober Offrs. und Gemeinen,' undated. There are two omissions, those of the Hungarian infantry regiment of Haller and the Dessewffy Hussars. Their estimated combined loses of 393 have been reached by analogy with the average losses of the other Austrian infantry regiments of Nádasdy's corps (303), and the average losses of the Austrian dragoons (90).
90. Ligne, 1797-1811, XIV, Journal, I, 89
91. Cogniazzo, 1788-91, II, 437
92. Grosser Generalstab, 1901-14, VI. 149. A list in the Munich Kriegsarchiv (B 258, Anteil am Siebenjahrigen Krieg, Auxiliarcorps IV-XIII, 'Lista über die von denen Chur Bayr. auxiliar Trouppen bey den 5ten diesse vorgegangenen bataille,' 13 December 1757) specifies officer losses as known by 13 December at 47, namely 13 in the Leib-Regiment, 10 in the regiment of Minucci, another 10 in that of Morawitzky, and one in the artillery. The losses in the regiment of Kurprinz-Preysing were still unknown by that time.
93. WL Colonel Nicolai, 'Betrachtungen'
94. SHAT A1 3442, Marainville, 17 December 1757
95. Archives de la Ville de Bruxelles, Portfeuille no. 155, Correspondance du Capitaine Pesser. To Captain Pesser from his wife, Brussels, 26 December 1757
96. Ligne, 1928, II, 35
97. KA CA 1758 III 1, Rebain, Neisse, 10 March 1758
98. Cogniazzo, 1788-91, II, 426
99. HHStA Kriegsakten 414, Maria Theresa to Prince Charles, 14 December 1757
100. Munich Kriegsarchiv B 258, Anteil am Siebenjährigen Krieg. Auxiliarkorps IV-XIII, Elector Max Joseph to Count Seyssel, 16 December 1757
101. Warnery, 1788, 251
102. Frederick, 1879-1939, PC no. 9,702, Frederick to the Queen of Sweden, undated, January 1758, XVI, 184. See also no. 9,571, Eichel to Finckenstein, 9 December 1757, XVI, 79
103. HHStA Kriegsakten 414, Maria Theresa to Prince Charles, 14 December 1757

104. KA CA 1758 III 1, Rebain, Neisse, 10 March 1758. Oddly enough the French believed that the Prussian cartridges at Rossbach were also under-powered. Perhaps the Prussians at Leuthen were using another batch from the magazines at Glogau.

105. Frederick, 1846-57, 'Oeuvres Militaires, 'Disposition pour les colonels d' artillerie Dieskau et Moller,' Praussnitz, 30 June 1758, I, 148

106. Wamery, 1788, 242/ See also Hertzberg, 1787, 201-2

107. Public Record Office, Kew, State Papers Foreign 90/ 71, Mitchell, 11 January 1758

Chapter 7 Reaping the Harvest

1.   Gorani, 1944, 77
2.   Ligne, 1795-1811, XIV, Journal, I, 90-1
3.   Belach, 1758, 127
4.   Podgursky, 1843, II, 222
5.   KA FA Hauptarmee 1757 XII 210, Serbelloni, 'Unterthänigste Rapport,' Oels, 9 December 1757
6.   WL Colonel Nicolai, 'Betrachtungen'
7.   Frederick, 1879-1939, PC no. 9,573, Frederick to Zieten, XVI, 83
8.   HHStA Letter Book of Prince Charles, Prince Charles to Francis Stephen, 9 December 1757
9.   HHStA Letter Book of Prince Charles, Prince Charles to Francis Stephen, 10 December 1757
10. WL Colonel Nicolai, 'Betrachtungen'
11. Munich Kriegsarchiv B 258, Anteil am Siebenjahrigen Krieg 1757 Auxiliarcorps IV-XIII, Feld-Kriegs-Commissarius M. Mayer to Elector Max Joseph, Plassendorf, 13 December 1757
12. WL Colonel Nicolai, 'Betrachtungen.' See also Ligne, 1795-1811, XIV, Journal, I, 93-4
13. Ligne, 1795-1811, XIV, Journal, I, 95-6
14. KA FA Hauptarmee 1757 XII 223 1/2, 'Extract Schreiben,' 19 December 1757
15. HHStA Letter Book of Prince Charles, Prince Charles to Maria Theresa, I 1 December 1757
16. HHStA Kriegsakten 415, Prince Charles to Maria Theresa, 14 December 1757
17. Hildebrandt, 1829-35, II, 39
18. Ibid., V, 127
19. Gorani, 1944, 78
20. KA MMTO, Bülow
21. SHAT A1 3442, Marainville, 3 January 1758
22. Frederick, 1846-57, 'Oeuvres Historiques,' *Histoire de la Guerre de Sept Ans,* I, 267-8
23. WL Colonel Nicolai, 'Betrachtungen'
24. Khevenhüller-Metsch, 1907-72, IV, 143; Cogniazzo, 1788-91, II, 445
25. HHStA Kriegsakten 403, 'État des Exigences extraordinaires qu'on a fait après la Catastrophe du 5. Décembre 1757. Pour remettre les Armées de Sa Majesté l'Impératrice Reine en État d'opérer l'Année 1758'

Chapter 8 Prussia's Glory

1.   Khevenhüller-Metsch, 1907-72, IV, 137
2.   E.g. HHStA Kriegsakten 415, Cabinet-Schreiben, signed by Francis Stephen, 12 December 1757
3.   Gorani, 1944, 93
4.   KA FA KA Hauptarmee 1757 XII 223 1/2, 'Extract Schreiben' 19 December 1747
5.   KA HKR Protocolle 1758 March 690, Hofkriegsrath to Maria Theresa, 17 March 1758
6.   HHStA Nachlass Lacy, 1, 4, Lacy to Baron Koch, 3 December 1757
7.   Warnery, 1788, 252
8.   KA FA Reichs- und Französische Armee 1757 XI 20, Hildburghausen to Colloredo, 7 November 1757
9.   KA FA 1757 Reichs- und Französische Armee 1757 XII 32, Hildburghausen to Maria Theresa, 20 October 1758
10. Maria Theresa's note on the above
11. HHStA Kriegsakten 414, Prince Charles to Maria Theresa, 9 December 1757
12. HHStA Kriegsakten 415, Maria Theresa to Prince Charles, 14 December 1757
13. HHStA Kriegsakten 414, Prince Charles to Maria Theresa, 10 December 1757
14. Cogniazzo, 1788-91, II, 445
15. Tempelhoff, 1783-1801, I, 271

16. Meyer, CXLIV, 1976, 38-9
17. Everson, XII, no. 2, 2001, passim
18. Swann, 2000, 114. See also O'Brien, LXII, no. 5, passim
19. Santa Cruz, 1735-40, V, 252
20. Kaltenborn, 1790-1, I, 530
21. Quoted in Wiltsch, 1858, 256
22. Ibid., 225
23. Frederick, 1846-57, Frederick to Voltaire, 15 September 1743, XII, 140
24. Quoted in Wiltsch, 1858, 260
25. Ibid., 260
26. Steigmann-Gall, 2000, 281
27. Grosser Generalstab, 1901-14, VI, 20
28. Franke, 1936, vii-viii
29. Wolfslast, 1941, 171
30. Ziegler, 1939, 30-1
31. Augstein, 1968, 8

Select Bibliography

Manuscript Sources (in approximate order of degree of usage)

Vienna, Kriegsarchiv
Cabinettsakten
Feldakten
Hofkriegsratlich Akten
Protocols of the Hofkriegsrath
Archiv des Militär-Maria Theresien-Ordens

Vienna, Haus-Hof- und Staatsarchiv

Kriegsakten
Letter Book of Prince Charles
Nachlass Lacy

Vincennes, Service Historique de l'Armée de Terre
Series A1, Correspondance Générale, reports of Champeaux and Marainville
Series 1M 208, 'Campagne en Allemagne MDCCLVII, Mémoire ou Éxtrait de la Correspondance de la Cour et des Généraux,' and 'Armée de Soubise. Éxtrait de la Correspondance ou Mémoire sur les opérations de l'Armée Commandée par M. le Prince de Soubise Lieutenant Général et combinée avec l'Armée de l'Empire pendant la Campagne de 1757 en Allemagne'

Stuttgart, Württembergisches Landesbibliothek
Cod Milit o 29, Colonel and General-Quartmaster Friedrich von Nicolai, ,Bemerkungen zum Feldzug der herzogl. Würtembersch. Truppen bey der Kayserlichen Armee in Bömen und Schlesien im Jahr 1757.'

Munich, Kriegsarchiv
B 200, 204, military correspondence of Elector Max Joseph
B 258, Anteil am Siebenjährigen Krieg. Auxiliarcorps IV-XIII

Budapest, Hadtötenéti Intézet és Múseum
Hadik Levéltár

Berlin, Geheimes Staatsarchiv Preussischer Kulturbesitz
1V Hauptabteilung, Rep 15A, Geheimes Civilkabinett, Militaria, for Pleissner's 'Tagebuch,' and the two General Staff Studies 'Ergebnisse der Erkundigung des Schlachtfeldes von Rossbach am 18ten März 1898,' and 'Zur Schlacht bei Leuthen'

North Gosforth, Northumberland County Record Office
Butler (Ewart) Mss. ZBU B series, for the unpublished papers of Horace St. Paul

Kew, Public Record Office

State Papers Foreign 90 series, for the unpublished papers of Sir Andrew Mitchell 30/18/89, Chatham Papers

Bratislava, Státny Ústredeny Archív

Fond Amade Üchtritz, 101-12-067, XVI, General Philipp Gottfried Wöllwarth, 'Kurze Beschreibung meiner geleisteten Dienste'

Brussels, Archives de la Ville de Bruxelles

Portefeuille no. 225, Correspondance du Capitaine Pesser

Documentary Collections: Memoirs, Letters and Commentaries of Contemporaries and Near-Contemporaries

Archenholtz, J.W., *Geschichte des Siebenjährigen Krieges in Deutschland*, 5th ed., 2 vols, Berlin 1840
—— *Gemälde der preussischen Armee vor und in dem Siebenjährigen Kriege*, reprint, Osnabruck, 1974
Barsewisch, C.F.R., *Meine Kriegs-Erlebnisse während des Siebenjährigen Krieges 1757-1763*, Berlin 1983
Belach, A., *Der Christ im Kriege und in der Belagerung*, Leipzig 1758
Berenhorst, G.H., *Betrachtungen über die Kriegskunst*, 3 vols, Leipzig, 1798-9
Bourcet, P.-J., *Mémoires Historiques, sur la Guerre que les françois ont soutenue en Allemeigne depuis 1757 jusqu'en 1762*, 3 vols, Paris 1792
Catt, H., *Unterhaltungen mit Friedrich dem Grossen*, Leipzig 1884
Cogniazzo, J., *Freymüthige Beytrag zur Geschichte des östreichischen Militärdienstes*, Frankfurt and Leipzig 1779
—— *Geständnisse eines östreichischen Veterans*, 4 vols, Leipzig 1788-91
Crillon, Duc de, *Mémoires Militaires de Louis de Berton des Balbes de Quiers; duc de Crillon*, Paris 1791
Frederick II, King of Prussia, *Oeuvres de Frederic le Grand*, 31 vols, Berlin 1846-57, includes the *Oeuvres Militaires de Frederic le Grand*, 3 vols, Berlin 1856
—— *Politische Correspondenz Friedrichs des Grossen*, 46 vols, Berlin 1879-1939
—— *Die Politische Testamente Friedrichs des Grossen*, Berlin 1920
de la Cour de Gardiolle, P., *Guerre de Sept Ans*, Nîmes 1883
Gorani, G., *Mémoires de Gorani*, Paris 1944
Henckel von Donnersmarek, V.A., *Militärische Nachlass des Königlichen Preussischen Generallieutenants... Victor Amadeus Grafen Henckel von Donnersmarck*, 2 vols, Leipzig 1848
Hertzberg, Comte de, *Huit Dissertations... lues dans les Années 1780-1787*, Berlin 1787
Kalckreuth, F.A., 'Kalckreuth zu seinem Leben u zu seiner Zeit... Erinnerungen des General-Feldmarschalls Grafen von Kalckreuth,' *Minerva*, 1839, IV; 1840, II-IV, Dresden
Kaltenborn, R.W., *Briefe eines Alten preussischen Officiers verschiedene Characterzüge Friedrichs des Grossen betreffend*, 2 vols, Hohenzollern, 1790-1
Khevenhüller-Metsch, J.J., *Aus der Zeit Maria Theresias. Tagebuch des Fürsten Johann Josef Khevenhüller-Metsch, Kaiserlichen Obersthofmeisters, 1742-1776*, 11 vols, Vienna 1907-72
Ligne, C.J., *Mélanges Militaires, Littéraires et Sentimentaires*, 34 vols, Dresden 1795-1811
—— *Oeuvres Choisies du Prince de Ligne*, Paris 1883
—— *Fragments de l'Histoire de ma Vie*, 2 vols, Paris 1928
Mitchell, A., *Memoirs and Papers of Sir Andrew Mitchell*, 2 vols, London 1850
Podgursky, K., *Selbstbiographie des Husaren-Obersten von ...ky*, 2 vols, Leipzig 1843
Retzow, F.A., *Charakteristik der wichtigsten Ereignisse des siebenjährigen Krieges*, 2 vols, Berlin 1802
Memoires du Duc de Richelieu, 9 vols, Paris 1793

Rohr, F.M., *Des Herrn Grafen Turpin von Crissé ...Versuche über die Kriegskunst*, 2 vols, Potsdam 1756

Saint-German, C.-L., *Correspondance particulière du comte de Saint-Germain avec M. Paris Duverney*, 2 vols, London 1789

Santa Cruz y Marcenado, marquès, *Réflexions Militaires et Politiques*, 12 vols, The Hague 1735-40 St. Paul, H., *A Journal of the First Two Campaigns of the Seven Years War*, Cambridge 1914

—— *The Journal of Horace St. Paul* (ed. Cogswell, N.), 4 vols, Guisborough, 1997-8

Tempelhoff, G.F., *Geschichte des siebenjährigen Krieges in Deutschland*, 6 vols, Berlin 1783-1801 Volz, G., *Friedrich der Grosse im Spiegel seiner Zeit*, 2 vols, Berlin 1926-7

Warnery, C.E., *Herrn Generalmajor von Warnery sämtliche Schriften*, 9 vols, Hanover 1785-91

—— *Campagnes de Frederic II, Roi de Prusse, de 1756 à 1762*, Amsterdam 1788

Wraxall, N.W., *Memoirs of the Courts of Berlin, Dresden, Warsaw, Vienna 1777-9*, 2 vols, London 1806

Yorke, P.C., *The Life and Correspondence of Philip Yorke Earl of Hardwicke*, 3 vols, Cambridge 1913

Secondary Works

Aretin, K.O., *Das Reich: Friedensgarantie und europäisches Gleichgewicht, 1648-1806*, Stuttgart 1986

Arneth, A., *Geschichte Maria Theresias*, 10 vols, Vienna 1863-79

Augstein, R., *Preussens Friedrich und die Deutschen*, Frankfurt-am-Main, 1981

Bernhardi, T., *Friedrich der Grosse als Feldherr*, Berlin 1881

Brabant, A., *Das Heilige Römischer Reich teutscher Nation im Kampf mit Friedrich dem Grossen*, Berlin and Dresden, 3 vols, 1901-31, reprinted Bad Honnef, 1984

—— Extracts translated and edited by Sharman, A., and Cogswell, N., *The Campaign for the Liberation of Saxony*, 2 vols, Buchholz 1998

Brodrück, K., *Quellenstücke und Studien über den Feldzug der Reichsarmee von 1757. Ein Beitrag zur deutschen Geschichte im 18. Jahrhundert*, Leipzig 1858

Buddruss, E., *Die Französische Deutschland Politik, 1756-1789*, Mainz, 1995

Duffy, C., *Frederick the Great. A Military Life*, London 1985

—— *The Army of Frederick the Great*, 2nd ed., Chicago 1996

—— *Instrument of War*, vol I of *The Austrian Army in the Seven Years War*, Chicago 2000, reprinted Warwick 2020

Eicken, H., 'Die Reichsarmee im siebenjährigen Krieg. Dargestellt am kurtrierischen Regiment,' *Preussische Jahrbücher*, XLI, Berlin 1878

Engelmann, J., and Dorn, G., *Friedrich der Grosse und seine Generale*, Friedberg 1988

—— *Die Schlachten Friedrichs des Grossen... Führung, Verlauf, Gefechts-Szenen, Gliederung*, Friedberg 1991

Franke, W., *Die Instruktion Friedrichs des Grossen für seine Generäle von 1747*, Berlin, 1936 Gawthrop, R.L., *Pietism and the Making of Eighteenth-Century Prussia*, Cambridge 1993

Gerber, P., 'Die Schlacht bei Leuthen,' in *Historische Studien veröffentlicht von E. Eberling*, XXVIII, Berlin 1901

Grosser Generalstab, *Der Siebenjährigen Krieg 1756-1763*, 13 vols, Berlin 1901-14

Hagen, E., 'Die Fürstlich Würzburgische Hausinfanterie von ihren Anfängen bis zum Beginne des Siebenjährigen Krieges 1636-1756,' *Darstellungen aus der Bayerischen Kriegs- und Heeresgeschichte*, XIX, Munich 1910

—— 'Die Fürstlich Würzburgische Hausinfanterie vom Jahre 1757 bis zur Einverleibung des Fürstbistums in Bayern 1803,' in Ibid., XX, Munich 1911

Helmes, H., 'Kurze Geschichte der fränkischen Kreistruppen 1714-1756 und ihre Teilnahme am Feldzuge von Rossbach 1757,' *Darstellungen aus der Bayerischen Kriegs- und Heeresgeschichte*, XVI, Munich 1907

Herrmann, O., 'Prinz Ferdinand von Preussen über den Feldzug vom Jahre 1757,' *Forschungen zum brandenburgischen und preussischen Geschichte*, XXXI, Berlin 1918

Iverson, J.R., 'Voltaire's Militant Defense of the French Language,' *Seven Years War Association Journal*, ed. Mitchell, J., no. 2, Crown Point (Indiana) 2001

Kennett, L., *The French Armies in the Seven Years' War. A Study in Military Organization and Administration*, Durham (North Carolina) 1967

Kutzen, J., *Friedrich der Grosse und sein Heer in den Tagen der Schlacht bei Leuthen*, Breslau 1851 Meyer, H., 'Voltaire in War and Peace,' *Studies on Voltaire and the Eighteenth Century*, ed. Besterman, T., CXLIV, Banbury 1976

Montholon, comte de, *Mémoires pour servir à l'Histoire de France sous Napoleon*, 2 vols, London 1823

Neuhaus, H., 'Das Reich im Kampf gegen Friedrich dem Grossen. Reichsarmee und Reichskriegführung im Siebenjährigen Krieg,' in Kroener, B.R. (ed.), *Europa im Zeitalter Friedrichs des Grossen. Wirtschaft, Gesellschaft, Kriege*, Munich 1989

Nicolai, F., *Anekdoten von Konig Friedrich II. von Preussen*, 6 vols, Berlin 1788-92

Nosworthy, B., *The Anatomy of Victory. Battle Tactics 1689-1763*, New York 1992

O'Brien, C.C., 'The Wrath of Ages. Nationalism's Primordial Roots,' *Foreign Affairs*, LXII, no. 5, New York 1993

Pengel, R.D., and Hurt, G.R., *The Reichsarmee: Organisation, Flags and Uniform Supplement 1756-1762*, Knighton 1992

Quimby, R.S, *The Background of Napoleonic Warfare. The Theory of Military Tactics in Eighteenth-Century France*, New York 1957

Rehtwisch, T., *Leuthen*, Leipzig 1907

Richter, K.C., *Friedrich Wilhelm von Seydlitz. Ein preussischer Reitergeneral und seine Zeit*, Osnabrück, 1996

Rohdich, W., *Leuthen 5. Dezember 1757. Ein Wintertag in Schlesien*, Wofersheim-Berstadt 1996 Roussset, C., *Le Comte de Gisors 1732-1759*, Paris 1887

Steigmann-Gall, 'Apostasy or Religiosity? The Cultural Meanings of the Protestant Vote for Hitler,' *Social History*, XXV, no. 3, Hull 2000

Swann, J., review of Edward Dziembowski's *Un nouveau Patriotisme français. La France face à la Puissance anglaise* a *l'Époque de la Guerre de Sept Ans* [1999], *in British Journal for Eighteenth-Century Studies*, XIII, no. 1, Oxford 2000

Thüna, L., *Die Würzburger Hilfstruppen im Dienste Osterreichs 1756-1763*, Winzburg 1893; reprinted Buchholz 1996

Wilson, P.H., 'War in German Thought from the Peace of Westphalia to Napoleon,' *European History Quarterly*, XVIII, no. 1, London 1998

—— *German Armies. War and German Politics 1648-1806*, London 1998

Wiltsch, J.E., *Die Schlacht von nicht bei Rossbach oder die Schlacht auf den Feldern von und bei Reichardtswerben den 5 November 1757*, Halle 1858

Wolfslast, W., *Die Kriege Friedrichs des Grossen*, Stuttgart 1941

Ziegler, M., *Soldatenglaube, Soldatenehre. Ein deutsches Brevier für Hitler-Soldaten*, Berlin 1939

Index